I NEVER WANTED TO BE A PRINCESS—GOOD THING!

or

How I Lost Three Hundred Eighty Pounds without Diet or Exercise

C.R. Rae

ISBN 978-1-64003-629-1 (Paperback)
ISBN 978-1-64003-630-7 (Digital)

Covenant Books, Inc.
11661 Hwy 707
Murrells Inlet, SC 29576
www.covenantbooks.com

DEDICATION

To Vicki and Kimberly,
I hope you find strength among these pages.
I am proud of the women you have become. I love you!
Emmie,
thank you for more support than my underwire
gave me during this life journey.
And to family and friends, those present and lost,
thank you for giving me the best gift a person
could give to another—your time.
It has been greatly appreciated. Money would have
been awesome—but time was nice. Love to all.

CONTENTS

PROLOGUE

or
The Part Everyone Reads Before Buying the Book

The events in this book are real, true life experiences, including the issues with the chocolate syrup cans.

It is a love story in a sense, sometimes sad, sometimes angry, more times humorous, with a little sarcasm and some inspiration thrown in for good measure. That is my intent—to inspire others to keep up the good fight, and punching a forty-pound-long bag helps one to keep fighting.

We all have storms in our lives, and many have had more "him-a-canes" and "her-a-canes" than I have had. But it is my intention to show others that we, as humans, can persevere and make a new chapter of our lives when things go ... not so much as planned.

My situation is not uncommon, but it is one of the hardest things I have ever had to deal with, and I hope I never have to deal with it again.

Writing this book has given me the insight and desire to go on and want a better life and find myself, as they say. I have, and it is a healthier, happier, and more successful life.

I never take myself too seriously. A sense of humor helps to get through day-to-day life. I somehow managed to get through life's trials and tribulations, even when I ran out of chocolate chips.

I am not the princess type to sit around and let my nails dry while others are playing soccer or doing a project around the house— not saying that is wrong, just not me. Actually, I might have been better off being a princess ... or maybe, not so much!

I prefer my soccer shorts and T-shirt over formal attire, but I can clean up pretty good when I want too. Personally, I think tomboys have more fun, or as my kids call me, "tom moms" have more fun, but I can't really judge that because I have never been a princess. An Elsa or Anna I am not, and it looks like I never will get the chance.

Just so you know, I am the type person that continually begins a diet on Monday but usually quits by Monday night or early Tuesday.

I rather laugh than cry, and that is proven in this book as we laugh our way through the pages together, discovering this new chapter in my life. I have a deep faith and am not going to second-guess that there is a man or woman above that helps us through life and has our best interests at heart.

I did suffer a weight loss, but it was not a healthy diet and not without its share of pain. Tipping the scales broke my heart. Don't get the idea that this is a diet book; if you saw me, you would know I don't know much about dieting and exercise!

But it is a book that will encourage you, make you shed a tear, give you a laugh, and make you gain a deeper understanding of what it is like to sit on the cold, hard toilet seat of life.

YOU CAN'T TELL THE PLAYERS
WITHOUT A PROGRAM

This section is dedicated to giving you the who's who in this story. Some names have been changed to protect the guilty.

C. R.
That is me—a mom, wife, friend, and non-princess.

Husband
Otherwise known as the Apprentice, the Tin Man, the Scarecrow, the Lion, Admiral, and any titles related to Prince Charming, including but not limited to—Prince of Charm, Charm, the Man of Charm, and P. C.—one of the main characters. He is so logical that he can't think with his heart. Everything in his world is black or white—never gray.

Vicki and Mike
Our oldest daughter and her husband, Mike. They are a great couple. At the time of the story, they had just been married and moved to Florida. They moved back to Ohio and then back to Florida where they now raise my two awesome grandsons, Ryan and Tyler.

Kimberly and AJ
Our youngest daughter and her husband, AJ. Kimberly was in college at the time this book began. (Note: They have two children—

Lucy, my granddaughter, and Anthony, my grandson, who insists his name is Bubba.)

Precious (deceased)
My dog, a black cocker spaniel with a mind of her own.

Soccer Buddy, Chief Petty Officer, Prin-cess NotSo Charming, NotSo, NotSo Buddy
Together, we could conquer "almost" anything.

Mark and Karen
My brother, Mark, and sister-in-law, Karen, and my nephews, David and Stephen. Karen and Mark now resided in Georgia—everyone moved south and left me!

My father (deceased) and my mother and my husband's mother and father (both deceased)

The Groupies—Stan (deceased), Shelly, Betty, Jim, Cindy, and Mo.

Emmie
She is a kindred spirit as you will learn throughout the chapters. A friend is a friend, a forever kind of friend.

Emmie's family
Her sister Sylvia, brother-in-law John, sister Eileen, brother-in-law John, her brother John (deceased), and her mother Martha (deceased). There are so many Johns in her family you can't keep them straight.

Friends
My friend Kay—her real name is Karen but, we already have one so she is Kay.
Dee (deceased and missed so very much): a longtime friend and neighbor.
Debbie: also a longtime friend and is missed because she decided to move south and leave me!

Kathie: my friend and college roommate.

Bill, Estelle, and Linda: friends of Emmie that have become my friends.

You will also see some familiar names and some that are self-explanatory.

God

His name has not been changed because he is not guilty of anything. You probably have heard of him.

CHAPTER I

The Schoolgirl and the Apprentice
or
Tomboys Have More Fun

I grew up in a pint-sized town in Ohio. We had our local football hero, the farmer who welcomed all the school children in to watch him make maple syrup, and a small restaurant where you could get an ice cream cone that was taller than your little brother.

My first years were spent in a craftsman-style home with a big front porch with pillars and a railing, making for great climbing and a grassy large side yard for playing with the neighborhood kids. I attribute my growing up as a tomboy to living in that neighborhood. Four other girls lived on my street. We were various age levels, and that left me right in the age group with the boys on the block. Because of that, there were more boys in that extra lot, playing football, baseball, hide-and-go-seek, and tag.

I spent nine years in that home with my mother, dad, and my brother, who was three years younger than me. It was in that light green craftsman that I remember one particularly disappointing Christmas morning. Even though, I was five years old at the time. I remember the holiday vividly even today at a much older age. TV cowboys were popular, and I wanted a cowboy outfit. I was thrilled when I pulled back the Santa wrapping paper on the first gift, and there was a gun and holster set. I couldn't wait to open the next gift, all the time knowing that good Old St. Nick was going to come through. It was on our annual trip to visit the red-suited man that I whispered my secret wishes in his ear. I think it was his ear, under that white beard and long white hair; no one could be sure.

The next bright-colored wrapped package contained a red fringed vest with silver decorations—another piece of the must-have outfit. My anticipation of waiting until it was my turn to open the next package was killing me. And then there was the package right in front of me; it was my turn. I tore off the red bow and ribbon, right through the snowman wrapping paper, and there, there they were—brown cowboy boots! Now all I needed were the chaps and my ensemble would be complete! There was no stopping me to get to that next package; I couldn't wait for my turn. I ripped it open and pulled the garment from the box, and much to my dismay, I was holding a red fringed skirt! Where were my chaps? I didn't whisper *skirt* in Santa's ear; it was *chaps*! Did the man not speak English? Did he ever see cowboys on TV? They didn't wear skirts; they wore chaps. Dale Evans wore a skirt, but she didn't do a lot of cattle rustling, roping, and shooting. She just sang with Roy Rogers.

There are disappointments throughout life. Without disappointments, like red fringed skirts, we would not know how to enjoy those moments when we are pleasantly surprised with life's goodness. I was young. I tried to make the best of the skirt, but mostly, I just did not wear it.

A few years later, just after I had turned nine, we moved to a different neighborhood—same town. The neighborhood was a mixture of different-type houses. Some were smaller cottages on the lake, and some were average-sized homes. My house was one of the larger homes—not because we were rich but because the lady that built the house embezzled money from the bank where she had been employed. She put all the high-end fixtures in the home, and when she was arrested, the bank sold the house cheap. For years, we checked all the dark corners where there might be money tucked away, but we never did find even a bill with Washington's picture on it.

In our new house, we no longer had that nice big porch, but we did still have a large yard where we continued to play sports with the neighborhood kids, and we did spend a lot of time playing hide-and-go-seek. In the summer months, running through the neighborhood with the kids gathering a jar full of lightning bugs was always fun.

School friends lived up the street, and now that I was older, I could travel greater distances to play with those friends. Because there was a lake just a block away, many hours during the crisp winter months were spent sled riding down the hill to the lake and ice skating.

Looking back on those days that were filled with fun, I realize that playing sports, sledding, ice skating, and spending as many hours outside as possible led to my being a tomboy. It helped to shape me for my future.

As a fun-loving child, I don't remember a lot of disappointing moments, except that red fringed cowgirl skirt. It was my high school years that were a disappointment. I was not very outgoing; I had friends, but just like every other girl, I wanted to date the quarterback of the football team and be liked by everyone. I was just average in looks, academics, and personality; but I excelled in intramural sports, like softball and basketball. Unfortunately, I was stuck in the wrong decade. For you younger readers, I am not ancient as it may sound, but I am "mature." There were not varsity sports for girls.

I did have success in the band. I was first chair trumpet, but that only made things worse. Boys did not like girls who were better than them at something. I was born to lose in the popularity column of life.

I was not sure what I wanted to do when I graduated from high school. According to my mother, you had to be married by the time you were twenty-one, or you were an old maid. Maybe I would have been better off, but I digress.

Graduation came and went, and I just decided to go to work for a while and think about what I would do from there. I got a job as a secretary in an office of a heating and cooling company. I was a one-woman office—hear me roar! The company consisted of the owner, myself, and the guys that came in to get their job assignments for the day and go on to work. The owner was in and out and did not even have an office there. My desk was the office.

I was really cool at seventeen—so cool that my dad drove me to and from work every day! I dreamed of earning enough money to buy a shiny bright-red Pontiac Firebird. At one dollar and sixty cents an hour, working forty hours a week, that equaled sixty-four dollars a week before taxes. The Firebird was a pretty big dream.

A stripped-down Firebird back then was three thousand five hundred dollars. The sporty dream car is no longer made; however, rumors are swirling around that it might make a comeback. When I last was able to find the price of a new Firebird, the cost was thirty-nine thousand dollars!

Still living at home with my parents, I paid a little rent and just got by. I could not afford that shiny red Bird. Actually, I could not afford anything on four wheels. I could have possibly paid for some bird seed.

I was so naive at this point in my life I had what I would now call a very embarrassing experience. I was going through a drawer in my desk and found a bunch of these rubber things. I was afraid of what they might be. They were not the rubber bootlike things men wear on their shoes when it rains. They were, well, what we now refer to as condoms.

Eventually, after the fact, I realized that those "little" items were really rubber fingertips. You know, the things you put on your fingers for turning pages. Well, what did I know? I did think they were awfully short to be used for my original thought of what they were. I guess I just thought they had a lot of stretch to them. Again, what did I know?

I had no real passion in my heart to do anything in particular. But one day, something happened that gave me the desire to continue my education. It was the day my sixty-five-year-old boss came in to the office, knelt down on one knee beside my chair, put his hand on my leg—slightly raised up—and kissed me! That was a shock to my naïve-ridden little life. It not only took me by surprise but stunned me to the point I didn't know what to do. I didn't tell anyone right away as it was the most traumatic moment of my young life. It was upsetting, and I knew I had to tell my parents, especially since my dad would plan on driving me to work on Monday, and I was not so sure I could go back into that situation. At this point, I wish I had taken karate!

A sixty-five-year-old man that can still do yard work may look good to me now, but not when I was seventeen. I never went back to that office. My "former" sixty-five-year-old boss called me and basically begged me to come back to the office. He said he was in the hospital with a brain tumor. Not sure that was for real. I am normally not an uncaring person, but no amount of begging was getting me back into that office! Now I was an even a more scared teen, but it seems I suddenly became more popular, at least with the grandpa crowd.

I had a job offer from a man that had been in the office one day to meet with my boss. He owned a heating and air-conditioning company and said if I ever needed a job to come see him. So after my refusal to go back to the kissing grandpa, I called the man with a job offer and soon began working at his company. But I was still so cool as I was leaving the driving to my dad.

The company was an upgrade. I was no longer the only secretary. There were several offices and many more people working, including a young apprentice. I guess I turned his head a couple of times because he asked me out, and we did have a couple of dates. We went to Cedar Point for a day and to a movie one night.

While working at this company, I was struggling to figure out what it was I wanted in life and as a career. It wasn't like I didn't have interests. I just did not know what to pursue and how to go about pursuing whatever it was that I wanted to do. I did not see a great future still making sixty-four dollars a week before taxes, and I continued to have that twinkle in my eye for that Firebird.

I was good at music; in fact, I was known as one of the best trumpet players in my county, but girl trumpet players in college? I figured I wouldn't have a chance to get in to a school, let alone excel in my music. I had really thought it would be great to be the first girl in the navy band, but my parents wouldn't let me join the navy. So how about a flight attendant? My parents did not like that idea either. I think, basically, their goal for me was to become a wife and mother; however, I called it off with the young apprentice for a couple of reasons.

I applied at a new college in Ohio, Mount Vernon Nazarene College (now known as Mount Vernon Nazarene University). I auditioned for a music scholarship and got it. The city of Mount Vernon was hometown to a previous boyfriend—someone I thought I really loved, but for some reason, I told him that I needed to move on. He was a high school boyfriend, and we had fun together. I am not sure why I broke it off. Here I was: a girl trumpet player, with a scholarship to a college in the hometown of my "previous" boyfriend. Eventually, I rekindled my relationship with him. I told the young apprentice that I was leaving town to go to school and that my boyfriend and I were back together.

Eventually, that previous boyfriend and I split again. I believe I was heavily influenced by my parents. They said if I married him, my last name would begin with a Y, and that would make my initials C. R. Y. My parents said if I stayed with him, that would be what I would do—cry.

CHAPTER 2

The College Years
or
Take Some NoDoz, Here Comes the History

Speaking of history, I have a history of getting homesick. You know that feeling that settles in the pit of your stomach when you are away from what you know as home? That historic homesickness was largely due to a lack of self-confidence—I believe. I had always been afraid of doing the wrong thing with a fear that someone might make fun of me, or think I was dumb or stupid, you get the point.

I was never comfortable being away from home. In my senior year of high school, the marching band went to camp, and I had a difficult time with being homesick. No one ever knew how terribly homesick I was. I sucked it up and went out and had fun during the day, practicing with my fellow band's men and women. While we were very busy, I could hide it, but I would quietly cry myself to sleep at night.

Once settled in my dorm at college, I had that homesickness thing going on once again. However, unlike the teary band camp, I found that I quickly became comfortable. When my parents and I arrived on campus, we received the directions for where I was going to be living and met my roommate, Kathie. We opened the trunk of the Pontiac (not that shiny read Firebird) and began unloading all the things that came from my home and moved into my future home—a small but nice dorm room. It consisted of two twin beds, two nightstands, two dressers, and two closets. There were also two study desks in it. It was reminiscent of Noah's ark—two of everything, identical. I began to experience feelings of sadness, but on the other hand, I was feeling excitement of starting something new.

Within a few days, my new friends surprised me for my birthday with cupcakes from the vending machine—candles and all. It was a great celebration.

I warmed up fast to my situation. I got along great with my roommate and made new friends quickly. It was fun, and I liked my newly found independence.

One day while walking back to the dorm from a class, I found an injured wild baby bunny. I picked it up, hid it under my coat, and took it in to my room. Kathie supported me in the effort to save the campus wildlife. The bunny—FruFru as we named him or her—had a large cut on its "foot leg," as I called it. (You know how a bunny's foot is long and flat but kind of part of its leg?)

I was so concerned; I just had to find a way to stitch up his cut foot. Not being much of a seamstress myself, I thought I should find someone that had more than a "seventh grade make a beach towel in home economics class" experience.

Kathie and I called the local veterinarian at his house and got him to open up his office. Then we had to find someone with a car. With the help of a couple of dorm mates, we took little FruFru to the vet. The kind bunny doctor stitched up the "foot leg." Not having much money, I was worried about the cost. By pulling our change and dollars together, we were able to pay the vet's fee of fifteen dollars.

We kept the little brown bunny in a big box in our room and managed to keep it hidden from our dorm mom. Even that one day she walked in our room, she did not ask what was in the big box sitting in the middle of our room. We brought food from the cafeteria to feed little FruFru. We figured if he or she could survive that, he or she was ready for the wild. Eventually, it was time to return our furry little roommate back to his or her natural habitat. We took him or her back to the well bush-covered area where I first found FruFru and released him or her, hoping he or she would live a very hopping life.

It was different back when I went to college than for today's students. The only male gender person that was allowed in the dorm was the maintenance man. There were no coed dorms, and we—are you ready for this—had a curfew (a time that was considered reasonable to be locked in the dorm with the door alarms on). That is what it was like in the "olden" days.

One thing that was difficult for me was writing papers. I was absolutely terrible at reports and term papers. I could draw the diagrams, maps, and that kind of stuff. But writing, I stunk. Fortunately, for me, Kathie was on the staff of the newspaper and eventually became editor. She could write. I gathered the info and set it down on paper to the best of my ability, and she typed it and made it sound good. I drew her maps, tracing the steps of Jesus for the required religion classes as well as her biology diagrams, and it worked for both of us.

I loved college. I was on my own and was studying music, my favorite thing. Gym class, or PE as the younger generation calls it, was great. It was not like high school where you had to try everything the teacher threw at you.

I liked gym in high school, but it was when we had to do gymnastics that threw me for a loop. The pummel horse scared the heck out of me. I got around it though. All through high school and to this day, I have never tried that horse. That's the only good thing about having a menstrual period; I just told the teacher I had bad cramps on those days.

That is where college was different. I could choose a sport: tennis, badminton, basketball, etc. I was in heaven with my two best subjects, music and gym. I played on intramural sports teams and had fun. Once again, I was born too early to play organized women's sports even in college.

Some of my best memories of those higher education years were not in the classroom but of crazy things my friends and I did, such as the time Kathie and I were planning a surprise party for a friend. When she ran to the shower, we went to her room to talk with her roommate to plan the party. Well, the party girl came back unannounced—seems she forgot her shampoo. When we heard her coming back, we tried to hide. I jumped in the closet, and when she said she had forgotten the shampoo, I reached down on the floor, picked it up, and handed it to her. She never noticed and headed back to the shower room while the three of us had a great laugh!

There were some strange things that happened to me. People in the community would stop me on the street because they recognized me as the person that played the trumpet solo in the community and college performance of Handel's *Messiah*. It was a difficult part to play, but the worst part was I am afraid of heights, and I had to stand at the edge of the organ loft way up at the tippy top of the very large church in a very cramped space looking right over the edge. It was so cramped I could not move my feet once I was set up and standing in my position.

I would also be recognized for another reason. Kids would turn around in church and stare at me, telling their parents Carol Burnett was there. I had a resemblance to the popular comedian when I was younger and, uh, thinner. I even dressed as Ms. Burnett for Halloween. She was what I wanted to be. I loved doing skits and making people laugh.

The girl, Vicky, that I handed the shampoo to, was a piano major and an excellent performer. She and I were always entertaining our roommates by doing musicals, dancing, singing (I could not sing, but she certainly could), and telling our story in song. My impression of the lion from the *Wizard of Oz* singing "If I Were King of the Forest" was famous.

The best performance of all time took place in our dorm room. Vicky and I were doing our thing—singing and acting. When I threw my leg up in the air doing my ballet leap, I fell and hit the ground hard, hitting my head on the heater and kicking Vicky in the leg. They were all so concerned about me hitting my head. It was fine, but I broke two toes when I kicked her. As I lay on the floor laughing, I pointed to the toe that now looked like the letter L. Eventually, we all went to the hospital to get the not-so-straight phalanges taped back to the direction they belonged.

Ahh ... the college years. I also had my fairy tale handsome prince moment back then. It was during an intramural basketball game. While going up for a layup, I came down wrong on my ankle and could not walk. I looked up, and there was the handsome star of the boys' basketball team looking down at me. He scooped me up in his strong arms and drove me to the hospital.

The hunk of a sports hero wheeled me around from the emergency room to X-ray and back in the hospital wheelchair, racing the halls as fast as he could run pushing me. I thought my prince had arrived, but once again, I was too late; he had a girlfriend. So ended the fairy tale.

Just sayin'—Kathie and I followed the rules at the college, but we could stretch them once in a while. One rule we sort of broke was cooking in our room. When Kathie came to college, she brought with her a popcorn popper. It was a stainless-steel beauty. The bowl was perched on an enclosed heating element, and it had a glass lid so you could see the corn popping. The popping of corn was not where we broke the rules. The rule was we were not allowed to cook in the room, like on a hot plate. It was not stated anywhere that we could not cook other things in the popcorn popper other than popcorn. So we made the most of it.

One of our favorite things to cook were fried potatoes with onions. As the spuds cooked in that stainless bowl, the aromas permeated throughout the first floor and drew attention to our room. We ran interference so as to distract the girls from knowing where the luscious odor was coming from. While one of us was guarding the potatoes, the other one was out in the hall asking, "Who is cooking? It smells like onions out here." Fried potatoes and onions never tasted better—almost like home.

I often thought it would be great to write a popcorn popper cookbook for students, but too many years passed; and microwave ovens, refrigerators, and TV's were no longer "ruled out" in dorm rooms. Once again, I was born too early. I might be older now, but I can still tell you how to make SpaghettiOs and caramel apples in a popcorn popper. Yep, caramel apples! We were very creative in many ways. It was fall, and we had a hunger for the sweet taste of the apples covered in sugary caramel. We figured out how to slowly melt the caramel and not burn it in the silver cooking wonder. Once melted, we would roll the apples around in the caramel to cover them. We did have one problem: getting the caramel to harden. Using our creativity, I found myself hanging out of the one window in our room holding the apples in the snowy, cold weather to harden. After having my boobs resting on the cold marble windowsill and my pajamas stuck to the frozen metal window frame, we were eating those sweet apples in no time.

CHAPTER 3

The Arrival of Prince Charming
or
The "Historic" Honeymoon Was Over

I did have another prince charming moment. It happened in the form of a letter. Before Christmas break, I received a letter (before e-mail) from the secretary at the heating company where I had worked. She asked if I would consider going to the company Christmas party with that young apprentice that I had dated a couple of times. I wrote back and said, "Yes." He called and asked; I accepted.

I had a good time at the party, and we saw each other while I was home on Christmas break. As time went on, he sent letters and started to visit me at school.

We would do things like go to movies, take a day and go to Columbus, see the sites, eat dinner. He even was known to pack a picnic or two, and we would go for a drive and have a picnic.

Prince Charming started to visit me every weekend or, on occasion, would come pick me up and take me back home for the weekend. I would get to visit with my parents and brother as well.

We became an item, and eventually, one night while he was visiting, we took a walk to the river that ran through campus, and we talked about marriage. Soon after, on a visit home, we went out to dinner, and he proposed; I said yes. After the event, we went back to my house where my mom, dad, brother, and Charming's family and some friends were waiting to surprise us with a party.

In that proposal, the young apprentice, my prince charming, promised to take care of me for the rest of his life. He did not want his wife to work; he would earn the money. Let's all sing, "Macho, macho man." It sounded like a deal to me. Unlike today's world, he would bring home the bacon, and *I w*ould fry it up in a pan, and well, he was paying for the pan.

We had the usual church wedding. Kathie was maid of honor. A college friend sang "We've Only Just Begun" and "Shampoo." Vicky played the organ.

We went on the honeymoon of *his* dreams: Washington DC and Williamsburg. No offense to either city; they are both great places. I like the history of our country and the sacrifices our forefathers and foremothers made—it just was not the getaway I had in mind for a romantic honeymoon. (Note: I have been back to both places more than once and enjoyed the trips, but as a newlywed, I just didn't want to spend my time looking at old things.)

Once we were back from the excitement of the "historic" honeymoon, reality hit me. When my husband, Prince Charming (we will call him P. C. for short), went off to work, I realized my life was made up of several aspects. There were no more college classes, acting out our musicals, playing in the band, or making fried potatoes in a popcorn popper at midnight. My life now included cleaning, laundry, grocery shopping, and other chores.

We had a one-bedroom apartment, and cleaning it was not very difficult, but the massive amount of laundry took a lot of time to wash, dry, fluff, and fold. Not to mention putting it all away. Well, the Prince of Charm wore a set of work clothes each day that, during the winter months, included long underwear (top and bottom), work pants, a couple of pairs of socks, an undershirt, underwear, two sweatshirts, a jacket that was washed each day, gloves, stocking cap, and sometimes a one-piece insulated suit. In the summer, it was not much better, as he often changed socks and shirts while at work.

But that was not the worst of it. He also insisted on having a clean set of towels each day. Some of us reuse the drying towel for a couple of days. After all, we are clean when we dry off. He used one washcloth, a hand towel, and two large bath towels each shower plus another hand towel in the morning.

I had heaps of laundry and not enough self-confidence to go to the laundry room in the apartment building by myself. I did most of my laundry at my parents' house. I was not good about doing these things alone or feeling that I could do things correctly. Someone in the laundry room might laugh at me. All kidding aside, it was terrifying to me.

This life change did not afford me an identity of my own. All my friends continued their education and got jobs, and here I was with my new best friend, the vacuum cleaner, and the vacuum had more confidence than I did.

I did not realize it at the time, but I did everything Charm's way—and willingly. I did what I thought was the right thing for a wife to do. Eat when he said to eat, go to the store when he said to go, watch what he wanted to watch on TV, cook what he wanted to eat, and make it the way he wanted it prepared—no casseroles, no mixing of anything together, and no new recipes. Everything was to be meat, potatoes, and corn.

Probably one of the things I would have done, at the time, had I known differently was refuse to get up and pack his lunch at five o'clock in the morning. He had me frying hamburgers for his lunch before the sun came up. I certainly did not have a problem frying the hamburgers, packing the lunch, and filling the thermos. I just did not understand why I had to get up and do it in the morning when he just put them in the refrigerator at work and ate them cold at lunchtime. Why couldn't I make them the night before? I could pack everything and put it in the fridge for him to get in the morning when he left. Frying hamburgers did not set well with me early in the morn. The smell ... ugh! I just never understood the reasoning behind it. When I asked him why I couldn't cook them the night before, he would just respond with something like he wanted them fresh that morning. Too bad, he didn't have that silver wonder popper at work; he could have cooked his own cheeseburgers. We did not have microwaves at work back then.

There are hazards to asking a nonmorning person to do things like cooking before sunrise. There were a couple of incidents, but one that stands out is the time he bit into his hamburger at lunch, which had the required two slices of cheese on it. The cheese slices were still wrapped in their little wrappers ... oops! I swear, I did not do it on purpose. Wish I would have thought of it though. Subconsciously, maybe I did leave the wrappers on because I hated getting up in the morning and smelling those hamburgers. Maybe the devil made me do it. However, I am thankful it was an accident because his reaction was not a pleasant one or quiet one. I was accused of doing it on purpose.

Don't get me wrong, I am not saying that there is anything wrong with being a domestic engineer, but I had been in school and was the lead trumpet player in the college band. I wanted to do something with the passion I loved so much: music. It meant so much to me. I was identified by my music. It was something I was good at and I loved, and I wanted more than just practicing my trumpet in the apartment with a mute stuffed in the bell silencing my notes. I needed to be heard!

CHAPTER 4

Packin' on the Pounds
or
Cake and Cookies Didn't Cause the Growth in My Girth

Life went on at the one-bedroom apartment. We made our own entertainment. One of our big purchases was a ping-pong set. Not the table, just the paddles, ball, and net. We set it up on the kitchen-dining room table and challenged each other for a few games most evenings. We also played cards, and life was good. It was nice doing these things as a couple. We did not go to many places; we just hung out at home and with family for the most part.

After a year, we moved out of the one-bedroom and into a townhouse apartment. This gave us a little more space, including a patio where I could plant a few flowers, and a common area where people gathered to play badminton and volleyball.

The prince really did not want to socialize. We were invited to join in, but we did not. I would sit in the apartment listening to the others laughing on their patios. I wanted to socialize; I always have enjoyed being around people and having fun.

At this time, we began talking about having children; after all, in our "new place," we had another bedroom. However, a couple of things took place during this year.

We took a trip to Florida for our first-year anniversary. We flew and stayed at Miami Beach. Ahh, the good life. How I loved lying in bed at night, listening to the waves of the ocean while the breeze blew in through the opened sliding glass doors. It was like a "romantic" honeymoon, not a "historic" one. We visited Cypress Gardens and Disney World, which was fairly new. It was fantastic, except I still can't get the song, "It's a Small World" out of my head. Some of you that are a little older will enjoy this tidbit. We flew economy class, and they served filet mignon on china! That was not the end of it. We ate with real silverware, drank out of glass glasses, and the sky marshal hooked us up with champagne—the good old days when the skies were friendlier.

It was shortly after this cool trip that I began to gain weight. It was a sudden gain of fifty pounds. I did not understand what was happening. In college, I weighed one hundred ten and was too thin, but now, I tipped the scales at a much higher number.

I was having a difficult time swallowing, and Charming, my knight in shining armor, made fun of me. He said I made too much noise when I swallowed. I tried not to, but I couldn't help it. I found what I thought was a small lump in my throat. I eventually had it checked out by my doctor, and he sent me to a surgeon, who said (keep in mind I was a twenty-two-year-old timid girl), "It is just a small cyst. I will just cut your throat here and pop that right out."

That was a little bit scary, but you gotta do what you gotta do. So off to surgery I went. Waking up in the recovery room was, as they say, quite a rude awakening. I woke up with the nurse changing the sheets underneath me. She stated she had to change them because there was blood around my legs. What? Did I misunderstand something about this surgery thing? I thought this was a little incision in my throat. I know the neck bone is connected to the backbone, and the backbone is connected to the hip bone, and so on. But what kind of a connection was the neck to below the waist?

I eventually got it. My monthly visitor, my period—Ramona as Kathie referred to "it"—had great timing and decided to join in the fun of the surgical event. There I was—my throat cut at one end and Ramona's visit to the other. All I wanted to do was sleep, but I couldn't. There was a lot of loud snoring going on in this recovery room. I can't say that I never snore, but this? This was like being in the center of a sawmill. Even with all the anesthetic in my system, I could not go back to sleep. Waking up in a strange place after being put to sleep for hours is scary enough, but then, hearing the sounds of snoring resembling a freight train rumbling along the tracks from a fellow passenger in the recovery room only added to the stress. After a half hour or so of the train noises, I realized I was never going to see the caboose, so I begged to go back to my room so I could sleep—well, as much as a shy person would beg. It was more like "Can I please go back to my room so I can get some sleep?" Okay, so I asked once and very politely. That is when they told me I could not go back to the silence of my room until I quit throwing up. Apparently, the medical staff does not like you to throw up when you have your neck cut open.

With the endless freight train traveling on the tracks next to me, Ramona visiting, and the numbness wearing off, I have to say that it just added to my day when the nurse came over and said, "Oh my god, I have to change this bloody bandage." What happened? Did they hit my jugular vein? The expression on her face was almost enough to stop my heart, but the rumble of the train started it back up.

She took the bandage off and laid the next one on with her hand pushing down on the wound. I felt pain all the way across my throat when she did that. Why would it hurt across the entire neck when it was a little half to one-inch incision? The doctor said, "I just need a little incision to pop that little cyst out."

I asked, "How long is the incision?" She responded quickly with "It is all the way across your throat," tracing it with her finger. What was wrong with me? Did they do the wrong surgery? Will I be able to sing? Probably not; I couldn't sing before the surgery. Not to keep you in suspense any longer, I had a goiter. A goiter is an abnormal growth of the thyroid gland. Normally, goiters grow forward in the neck, showing outwardly. Mine had grown back into my throat instead of forward. It wrapped around my windpipe. The doctor said in two weeks I probably would have choked to death! Hence, the reason I swallowed hard. I did have a scar from one side clear across to the other side. They had removed almost my entire thyroid, just leaving a tiny little piece in the center of my throat. I am thankful that it was caught in time. (Note: The goiter was inherited, so to speak, from my grandmother on my dad's side. Goiters are found in women and skip a generation. I was the one out of four female cousins that received the inheritance.)

Once I healed from the surgery, I had to deal with the weight gain. I battled the problem month after month, and I continually asked the doctor if the lack of having a whole thyroid gland was keeping me from losing the weight. He did not think so, which was a letdown. I wanted an excuse for not being able to lose the weight that had attached itself to me. I finally took the attitude to do it for myself and no one else. I just got the bug about losing weight and worked hard at it by riding a bike and walking every day. Also, I ate veggies and tried to eat light. I lost the fifty pounds I had gained.

I was feeling good, and after three and a half years of marriage and moving into a house, I found out I was pregnant. In the wee hours of the morning on October 2, which was one day after my due date and the morning of my twenty-fourth birthday, I was standing in the nursery watching it snow. I couldn't sleep, and I was all set for the new little bundle. In those days, we did not know if we were having a boy or a girl, so there was a surprise at the end of the nine months.

After my checkup at the gynecologist on October 18, seventeen days after my due date, it was decided that the next day, 19, I would go to the hospital for labor to be induced. At five o'clock in the morning, Charming and I traveled through the snow, and many, many hours later, we had a baby girl.

I loved her. It is true what they say … you do not understand what that kind of love is until you have it. I now added washing diapers, baby bottles, making formula, and walking the floor with a colicky baby to my things to do.

I loved her and loved the time I spent with her in the middle of the night. I am being serious; I knew those moments would not last forever and that the next years would go by very fast. P. C. was still bringing home the bacon. I was frying it up in a pan, and we were living happily ever after. At this point, I was still getting up and packing fresh cooked hamburgers each morning after being up with the baby throughout the night. With this lack of sleep, I know I can continue to cut the cheese but can't be sure I will remember to unwrap it.

As our daughter—Vicki Lynn— grew, life became more fun. All the interesting things she learned and did. Eventually, Charm and I decided it was time to think about another child. Soon, I was pregnant.

I remember one day that Vicki and her charming father were outside shoveling and playing in the snow—we had a blizzard. I wanted to go out and play in the snow with them. I can't help it; I am just one of those people that never lost the "kid" in me. That day, I just wanted to go outside with my little girl and have fun. I stepped out the side door, and as my foot hit the step, my feet went out from under me, and I slid right under the car.

My whale of a tummy stopped me from going totally under the car. I yelled for P. C. to help me up, and as clear as if it were this morning, I can remember him standing above me, yelling at me while I was lying in the snow under the car. The tears began to form in my eyes and freeze to my eyelashes all while he stood over me, looking down yelling and telling me that this was why he told me to stay in the house. So there I was, lying there with no hand extended to help me up. Maybe I should have just changed the oil while I was down there, making good use of my time. All I heard was "What do you think you are doing? You were not to come out of the house." He continued barking at me, and eventually, I pulled myself out from under the car and got up. I went in the house and warmed my frozen tears with fresh ones. That event has stuck with me all these years. I did not need a princess moment, just a gallant moment on his part. Helping me up and making sure I was all right would have been nice.

It was not too many days after the incident that I began making trips to the hospital. "Trips?" you might ask. Yes, we made three middle-of-the-night and early-morning trips to the hospital before another beautiful daughter, Kimberly Marie, was born.

CHAPTER 5

Dropping the Pounds Is Hard Work
or
Tipping the Scales Broke My Heart
(Not Really a Diet Story)

This was not my first rodeo when it came to dieting. Here I was once again... I found myself needing to lose many pounds. I would be happy with fifty pounds or maybe even forty. If you remember, I lost that original fifty-pound weight gain... Then somehow, like a lost prized possession, I turned around one day, and there it was: those lost pounds were following right behind me. Actually, at this point, forget the forty or fifty pounds, even a pound would be encouraging. Once you are of a certain age, you are not expected to be pencil thin—I hope!

As we age, we tend to gain a little padding. It is designed that way—in case we fall, it might save a hip. For your information, here is a little mature knowledge for you if you don't know: it is only natural that people who live in the north tend to head south for the winter. Well, so do parts of your body as you age.

Women especially tend to gain a little weight as they age. After all, if God wanted us to be skinny, he would have never grown cacao trees (cocoa trees) and give someone the gift to make chocolate from their beans.

Here is the truth. I am not a doctor or even work in the field of medicine, but I am pretty sure that losing weight is supposed to be good for your heart, not break it.

This is a story that began one day when I was so down on myself that I could do nothing but cry. I had wanted to lose weight again and tried, but no matter what I did, it just did not happen. It was tough having another weight gain. I had always been one of those people that could eat anything and be thin, especially as a child. I could out eat anyone and eat all day long. I could eat noodles, macaroni and cheese, sweets—you name it, and I ate it. Now even when I throw pasta against the wall to see if it is done, I gain a pound!

My story begins one day when I was entertaining the bloat. You know how that works—clothes do not fit or look the same as they would on a nonbloated day. In fact, I have found that it is easiest to arrange my closet in two categories: the bloat clothes on one side and the nonbloat clothes on the other.

Diets are really tough and frustrating, aren't they? You count calories, read diet books, study the calorie counters and carb counters. There are low-fat, high-protein diets, the cabbage soup diet, grapefruit diet, exercise, and all that brings me to telling you about that one particular day in my diet-ridden life.

I had tried to wish the fat off, and I had tried to pray it off. Nothing worked until ... well, all I can say is, be careful what you wish for. I don't remember why I was so down about it on this particular day. Probably, I had tried on bathing suits for an upcoming family spring break vacation. I was actually crying and sitting on the floor in the hallway of my three-bedroom ranch. I needed to go on a diet quickly. At this point in my life, I had managed to outgrow everything, including my wedding gown. I was literally begging for a little help from the man or woman upstairs, but there were no sudden bolts of lightning or any other noticeable signs.

After a while of wallowing in self-pity, I picked myself up, wiped my tears on my sleeve, and went into the bathroom to find a tissue. The box was empty, so I used the last bit of toilet paper, blew my nose, and then began drowning my sorrows with Coke.

That was regular, not diet—two liters, not one of those little cans. Then I ate a bag of chips. It was not a little lunch-sized bag; it was one of those big bags with the five extra ounces for free, and that is where the diet began—I was out of dip. A chip without dip is a diet in my book.

It was time to cook dinner. I got out the hamburger and potatoes, thinking all the time that homemade french fries were probably not the best thing on a diet, but one last meal would not hurt me since I was going on a diet. I had not started it yet.

I always make it a rule to rid the house of everything that I should not eat while dieting. I would guess I am fairly normal in the fact that I cannot start a diet until I eat all the chocolate in the house. It didn't bother me to rid the house of chocolate. I was very brave about it. I knew there was always a backup.

That is the great thing about being a mom: you always have chocolate chips on hand for the children in case they want cookies. Of course, my kids never saw chips in their cookies when I was dieting. I always ate them before I could make the cookies.

If the tiny chocolate morsels ran out, there was always a shot of chocolate syrup. They make it so much easier nowadays to get a shot of the luscious syrup. The plastic bottle with that pull-up squirt top is much easier to grab from the fridge and to tip up and squirt in the mouth quickly before the kids see you do it. Back in the "day," we had cans of chocolate syrup. We had to open the can with one of those triangular metal can openers. The holes were not always perfectly even, and they got crusted over with dried chocolate. When flying by the fridge for a shot of chocolate in the process of tipping it up, it often went off to one side and missed the mouth. That's usually when my kids caught me with that dark chocolate syrup drooling down my face. There have been times when I was so desperate for chocolate that I would eat spoonfuls of Nestlé's Quick and even Ovaltine.

As this evening went on, I really had the best of intentions to begin the diet but decided I would eat the hamburger and fries to get them off my mind. At least, the potato chips were gone—well, that bag was.

Most of us seem to feel we need to start a new diet on a Monday. I wonder how many Mondays I have started a diet, only to crash and burn before the end of the week and plan to start again on the following Monday.

This was a Monday, so this time I was going to try starting the diet on Tuesday. I was thinking I had better have dinner early so I could eat as much junk food as possible before I went to bed—after all, there was another one of those jumbo bags of chips in the freezer, and I better eat it.

I was looking forward to my husband coming home; I wanted to have dinner ready. He would be a distraction from the focus on the overweight thing. He was not someone I could talk to about my feelings. He never listened to my thoughts, dreams, or problems. I realized, at some point throughout our courtship and marriage, that he was not my best friend as he should have been. However, there had been a change in hubby, and I was enjoying the new him. Over the years, I had competed with TV cops, baseball, football, and Farah Fawcett. We were becoming empty nesters, and he was actually putting down the remote that had been attached to his hand for many years. He got out of his recliner, with the permanent butt imprint embedded in the tan material, and began spending some time with me. I was thrilled. I figured this empty nest thing was kind of nice. I saw a sparkle in his eye. We really were starting to regain some fun, in what had become our very dull lives. I digress to give you a little more history.

Just sayin'—Although I am talking about my diet, this is not really a diet book, tips on dieting, or even a health talk!

I am not an expert in the above areas; however, I am an expert at getting chocolate out of my clothes after missing my mouth with the chocolate syrup. I have dieted for years, with and without results, as many of you have done as well. I am sharing my story to support and encourage those going through a not-so-happy time as well as to give you a few laughs!

CHAPTER 6

Music to My Ears
or
Bringin' Home the Bacon

Some historical facts. One night, some years ago, and shortly after having children, P. C. came home from work and said there was a recession that would affect his work. "You better get a job. You can go down to the Red Barn"—a popular local fast food restaurant—"and work there" is what he said to me or more or less demanded of me.

There is nothing wrong with working at a fast food restaurant, but I had studied music, and it was my passion. I would much rather find something to do in my field of somewhat expertise. I decided to see what I might be able to do in that field first. Thus began my "career," so to speak. I began giving music lessons at a local music store. I worked some evenings from about four o'clock in the afternoon to nine o'clock in the evening, and that left P. C. home with the children. He was good with the kids; he made sure they were fed, gave them a bath, put them to bed.

Eventually, I began to get more and more students and was working every night and Saturdays. Then I got a job as a church choir director. That was something I loved to do. Oh, not the singing part, as I do not have a good voice (as we discussed earlier). I loved the people, the worshiping, and doing something for God. I had a purpose—and one that mattered.

Was I the best choir director ever? No. But I knew music, and I loved music. Having studied music in college, I was required to take voice and required to be in the choir, but that was their problem! I knew how to warm up their voices and all the basics I needed. Most importantly, I did have that passion for church choir. I liked that my family could be there with me, even though, as time went on, it was just the kids and I making the pilgrimage every Sunday to church. Charming did not usually join us.

The years continued, and I was doing my music thing, and we were making it through financially. The kids were great and at very cute ages. I enjoyed them, but once they were in school, I missed the evening time with them. I was off teaching music, and they were home with the Prince of Charm.

I was at home when the kids got home from school, and then a babysitter would cover after I left until Charm would get home. During that time, my good night kisses came after they were asleep.

Throughout the kids' elementary school years, I began to gain back weight, and then my jaw locked up, and I could not chew or put anything in my mouth that did not come through a straw. That got the weight back down better than Slim Fast.

It was determined that all those years of playing trumpet had just destroyed the meniscus disk in the joint of my jaw. I went through a lot of torture before it was determined that I needed surgery. I went to a dentist that made a dental procedure an experience. Basically, the man in the white coat and his assistants hung me upside down in the dental chair to put trays of goo in my mouth to make a mold of my teeth. That goo ran down my throat and caused me to gag and, in turn, throw up. I showed them not to mess with me. Then they made bite plates for me to wear. Now my jaw is basically locked, and I can hardly open my mouth, and they expect me to put these bite plates in. And, even worse, I could not get them out!

Then came the best of all. The dentist's thought was since my jaw was now locked and I could not wear those expensive bite plates, he would hook me up to a machine to loosen the muscles in my face.

It was some sort of an ultrasound-type thing. This literally happened; he instructed me to hold on to the countertop next to me and not let go or I would get a good shock. I was scared to death. My hands were shaking and sweating, and my fingers were within inches of the metal sink... duh! What if I would sneeze or cough and my hand would jerk away from the counter? Who does something like this?

Lastly, he sent me for a test that I was told (and have confirmed) is one of the most painful things a person could go through—right up there with childbirth, but there was no little bundle of joy when the pain subsided, just pain in the jaw.

The test began with an injection of Demerol. Then they shot dye into both jaw joints. It was extremely painful, but it was the reaction after the test that shook me up.

I had been lying on a hard cold stainless-steel table. I sat up, per instructions, and everything shook. It was like the whole room was shaking, but no one else seemed to notice. I was nervous that it was the medication. I asked if anyone else felt the room shake; of course, the answer was no. They were all busy doing their jobs—never felt a thing. I felt better later when I was told that there had been an earthquake—the largest ever in the area.

The test showed that both disks in my jaw had fallen out of place and was keeping my jaw from opening, which meant I needed surgery. The disks they were going to put in my jaw joint were made of Teflon, which eventually became a hazard to my health. The slippery Teflon-coated surface allowed for me to open and chew faster, which meant weight gain.

Back to the business at hand, I now had a purpose in life outside of the home. I loved using my music background that had gone by the wayside to get married. I was living the American dream of a house, two cars, and two-point-five children. We had the house, the cars, but only two children, although we had a dog.

The dream continued, but sometimes the dream turned to nightmares, as Michael Jackson said, "Thriller, thriller!"

CHAPTER 7

I Never Wanted to be a Princess—Good Thing!
or
Burying the Sweaty Towel

As the years went by, I continued teaching music and having fun attending the kids' events. Between work, swimming, soccer, band, orchestra, church obligations, etc., I kept pretty busy. After all, I was still helping to bring home the bacon, shopping for the bacon, frying it up in a pan, shuttling the kids, working, doing the laundry and yard work, cleaning, doing the dishes, cooking—whew, need I go on? But... I am not bitter! When we reached the milestone of our twenty-fifth anniversary, we celebrated with friends and family. At the same time, we were becoming empty nesters. Vicki was getting married, and Kimberly was going off to college.

I have to say I was worried about what we were going to do now that everyone but the dog was out of the house. That left the two of us home alone. We had always been wrapped up in the kids and their activities. Now we no longer needed to be involved and had no real "things that we did together."

To my surprise, sometimes it actually turned out to be fun. Like I said earlier, my charming husband put down the remote and got out of his recliner. We went hiking, to movies, and golfing. We actually were doing some things together as long as important games (which were all of them)—football, basketball, or baseball—were not on TV.

He still did not help around the house. After all, that was a "woman's work," but once in a great while, he decided to throw a load of laundry in. You have to understand this is the way it had been for twenty-five years. I did the "woman's" work, and he did the "man's" work, which had whittled down from yard work, washing and waxing the cars, taking out the trash, etc. to watching TV from his recliner and hanging on to the remote so it did not get lost. I did the "woman's" work and the majority of the "man's" work, but I am not bitter!

The prince spent more time in his recliner, and I spent more time working outside of the home—both at my job and in the yard. I was to take care of my own car, which included washing, waxing, and repairs. He did take care of washing and waxing his truck, but as far as the repairs, it was up to me. I would either fix the problem or be inconvenienced while he took my car to work, and I had to find someone to fix the truck. Whether it was my day to work, volunteer at school, or whatever I might have planned, it did not matter.

A little insight into me, I am the type that needs a buddy. I like to have someone to go to the store with; I don't like to go alone. I am a "nonloner." My husband really was not my friend. It was great that he began to do things with me. It reminded me slightly of our dating days, but he really was not my friend.

Growing up in that neighborhood of boys, I liked playing ball, building things with my dad rather than sitting in the house doing my nails. It is a good thing I had paid attention working with my dad because I was the "Mrs. Fix It" of the family.

My husband felt we should call someone every time something went wrong, and I thought I could fix it. My theory was if the dishwasher was already broken, then why not try to fix it? I couldn't break it; it was already broken. We really did not have a lot of money to hire people to do things.

Most of the time, you would find me in my jeans or shorts and a T-shirt or sweatshirt. It was not that I did not like to dress up or could not clean up pretty good, but the laid-back casual was my comfort zone. I have told my children that when I leave this earth, I do not want to be buried in one of those chiffon-y pastel gowns; I want to be buried in my jeans or Umbro's (soccer shorts for those of you that do not know) and a T-shirt or sweatshirt, depending on where I would be buried and if it was a warm or cold climate. Ohio, please dress me warm; if it is Florida, go for the casual cool look with flip-flops and shades.

It was also not unusual to find me at the other end of a shovel or screwdriver, under the hood of a car, or with a paintbrush in my hand. I really did most of the fix-it, spruce-it, and redo-it projects in the house. I loved to build and create. When everyone went to bed at night, I went to the basement. I would spend hours down there constructing furniture, refinishing furniture, building shelves, or fixing something for friends. If someone wanted something done, they came to me to see if I could do it.

My husband did not wait on me hand and foot or cater to me. In fact, some days, I wondered if he knew I existed. His face was always in a newspaper or staring at the TV, and his butt was always in the recliner. Everything was scheduled around his schedule. When there were no sports on TV, he would mow the lawn. That was okay as long as it got done, but that was basically what he did: he mowed the lawn, did the weed whacking, and would blow the grass off the sidewalk. I dug the flower beds, planted the flowers, and much more. I never wanted to be a princess, but it would be nice to be treated like one once in a while.

You might be thinking it was nice that he went out and mowed the lawn, and that is true, but it was when he came back in that was not so nice. "Oh, why?" you ask. Because he would come into the kitchen, get something to drink, after complaining that I did not bring him a drink while he was mowing, and then he would proceed to use my dish towel to wipe the sweat from his forehead *and* from under his arms. I explained to him several times why this was not a good thing to do, but he could not understand why it mattered. You get the idea of what I was feeling and the fact that, if I ever had a thought of being a princess on the arm of a prince charming, it was just a fairy tale—and the sweaty dish towel is evidence.

There were times I thought about drying his dishes with the unwashed towel, but I kept that urge to myself. Remember, this comes from the man who needs two clean bath towels, a hand towel, and a washcloth every time he takes a shower.

I am not trying to paint that it was a miserable life; there were good times, and the kids really made each day worthwhile. As I made my way through the years, I wondered if everyone had the same kind of relationship we had. Was this just the way marriage was, or was something just not quite right?

It seemed that my friends' husbands were more attentive and helpful around the house—teamwork! But who knows what went on behind closed doors.

CHAPTER 8

Life Is Like a Rock in the River
or
Woman Overboard

I have always been fortunate to have many friends. It is easy for me to make friends. I am one of those people that dogs love. You know, they say animals can pick out the person in the room that is an animal lover and has that soft spot in their heart ... or the dog treat in their pocket.

It seems to work for me with cats too. I always had cats growing up and when I was first married. The cat I had when Vicki was born was a little on the wild side. I was afraid this wild feline would hurt Vicki, so I took the cat to my aunt and uncle's farm where she could roam free and be as wild as she wanted across the border in Pennsylvania.

Within a year or so, after the cat bought the farm—well, moved to the farm—I found that I was allergic to cats. When visiting someone that has a cat or dog, for some strange reason, the pet always sits beside me. I love animals, but boy do I suffer from the cats. Every time I am near a feline of any kind, it is sneeze city. My eyes swell. I lose my voice, and I am just miserable. In fact, when I was tested for allergies, I passed out from the cat test. I have the distinction of being the only one to do so at the doctor's office.

I guess it seems to be the same thing with people. I tend to attract those with the sad puppy dog eyes, and eventually, the dander gets up my nose, causing violent sneezing and "tears" to run down my legs—if you get my point.

That animal sad-eye attraction is how I met one friend in particular. I played on a senior league soccer team (that is, "senior" as in over thirty, not "senior" citizen). I finally got that chance to play sports, and I was well over thirty. Actually, most of the team members were closer (just a little closer) to "senior" citizen than thirty. We were not the kind of team that was on our way to the World Cup but rather the kind of team that could not lift the World Cup. In fact, we had one lady on our team that was so worried about our memory problems that when it came time to pick the numbers for her jersey, she picked 911 so we would remember who to call if she got hurt. I just hoped if she did get injured, she would land facedown, so I did not have to remember to roll her over to get the number.

While playing on the team, I became acquainted and soon friends with the newest team member. She had those sad puppy dog eyes. She and her husband had been coaching one of the "younger" girls' soccer teams—younger as in elementary school.

I kind of envied them because they had something that they did together. I never had that with Charming. There was nothing I liked to do that he liked to do. When we did do something together, it was about him and what he wanted to do.

I did have opportunities to go do things but only by myself. All my friends' husbands would come to our soccer games, but not my man of charm. I could count how many times he came to my games on one foot even without using the broken toes I acquired from playing the game.

Actually, I broke more toes than I could count, but I can count how many times he supported me at my game. It hurt that other husbands and families were there for my teammates, but my husband was seldom there for me. He thought my playing soccer was a stupid thing to do.

I began sharing rides to the game with that newest team member, and we eventually became friends. I enjoyed her company, and we had a lot of the same interests. We both did things around the house, other than cleaning and laundry. We fixed appliances, cars, did yard work, etc.

She was a dental hygienist and worked four days a week, and I was working giving music lessons in the evening. On her day off, we would go work out, run errands, have lunch—you get the point. We became buddies.

Often, couples from the soccer team would get together for an evening, and the Prince of Charm actually participated in these events, to some extent. We would go out to eat, play Pictionary, go to a movie, things like that. That is how I met our newest team-mate's husband, and as time went on, I realized he certainly was not a prince. He had quite a temper and was not afraid to show it.

As time went on, I learned more about her sad life. I felt bad for her and wanted to do everything I could to cheer her up and make life better. She was very unhappy in her married life. After a period of time, she decided to divorce him due to his violent temper and controlling personality.

In one instance, her husband was mad and drove his van multiple times through the garage door while their kids were standing beside the van and close to the door. On more than one occasion, I thought he was going to hit me when I would stand up for her.

Eventually, my friend and her two children were afraid to be home, so they stayed with us until they felt safe to return home. I also spent nights at their house when they were afraid. I left my family, my house, my husband to help her. I feel I did all I could for her and did not realize just how much I gave. Actually, I almost gave my life!

My life almost ended because she needed another adult to go on a church youth group white water rafting trip. She asked Kimberly and I to go along. I always wanted to go white water rafting, but P. C. wouldn't go. It always seemed like the boat (or raft, in this case) always left without me in life. Now the opportunity was right in front of me. I was not going to miss out.

The rafting trip began with our arrival at the river and the guides providing detailed instructions of the how-to of white water rafting. If signing the release of "if you die, you won't sue" isn't enough to keep you from going in the river, then the dos and don'ts of rafting might.

Once we had the instructions, we were told to pick up the rafts and get them in the water. I approached this like I do many things—by jumping in with both feet and the rest of my body. I had no idea how heavy a runner raft could be. We were with a small group of about four younger kids and had to lift this thing and get it in the water. After a struggle, we got the raft in the water, and we loaded into the floating device and played "row, row, row your boat." Having the younger kids seemed to make things harder. It was hard to get some of them to do the correct paddling instruction, especially with the P. K. For those of you that never went to a Nazarene college filled with P. K.'s, I will explain—preacher's kid. That is the one that usually does not listen to what you tell him to do. They are usually found crawling under the pews during church—you know, the one that is ornery as hell.

As captain of the boat, I could not get the P. K. to follow directions. I am usually a very patient person with kids, but I was starting to lose my patience. When you are taking on the responsibility of another person's child, you can get a little testy when they don't listen in an intense moment of terror and fear. I really did not want to be responsible for drowning one of my crew. When I said, "Back paddle left," I meant him too, not just the rest of the paddlers.

Somehow, we managed to get down the river through a variety of rapids. Until we got to the final and worst rapid. God put a very, very large rock right in the middle of the rapidly flowing river rapid. I was hoping that I had all the paddle procedures down pat. I bellowed out the instructions, paddle left, back paddle, etc. We had been warned about this rock. We were instructed to paddle toward the rock and then quickly paddle to go right so as not to hit the huge boulder. The instructor said if we collided with that rock, we would most likely find boatmates in the water.

I really have no fear of the water, which was probably why God chose me to swim with the fishes. Why not? There is a reason I took those Red Cross lifesaving courses as a teenager. I just did not realize the life I would be saving would be my own.

You probably have the picture by now. Yes, we were doing fine until we came upon Suicide Rock or whatever it was called. We paddled and paddled, and I gave the signal to paddle to the right so we would turn before hitting that rock. We fiercely did so, and in only seconds, my team became the poster children for "don't do this while rafting."

The instructors had said if we hit the rock, the raft would flip over, and we would all fall out. We hit that rock; we did not flip over, and only one of us fell out. Actually, I was literally catapulted through the air and landed in front of a raft filled with other rafters. They quickly went floating over me, and I was drug under and into a whirlpool that whisked me underwater. I bounced off rocks on the river bottom and on my bottom too. I thought I was never going to see the sky again.

I did not panic, even though my foot became caught between some rocks and I was being held underwater. I relaxed and was able to pull it out. I followed all the instructions of pulling my feet up and allowing the current of the river to take me downstream. Once again, the boat had left without me, but I still had both contacts in my eyes and could clearly see the other rafts passing me by. I waved as I floated down the river. When the last guide came through, he helped me into his raft, which was quite a feat in itself, and we met up a little while later with my crew.

From there on out, it was a leisurely ride down the river. Although I was exhausted, the rest of the trip was very enjoyable and relaxing. I dried out in the warm sun as we gently rowed along.

It was the following year and another youth group rafting trip that brought my white-water career to an end. It was a beautiful day for a river cruise—sunny, warm—and I had a happy crew aboard the *USS Swim with the Fishes*. It was Suicide Rock—the sequel. Can I stay in the raft? Will everyone fall out? Will we make it through safely? Stay tuned.

This time, my soccer teammate was not in my raft, and I was the only adult. I was to captain the floating death trap with a rookie crew.

51

I thought about it all year and became mentally prepared to face the big rock once again. I was not going to let it stand in my way of having a good time. I was determined to stay dry this time around.

Once my boatmates and I reached the treacherous rock off our port side, I was going to get it right and not lose any passengers or I was not going to fly out of the raft. We paddled hard left and got ourselves in the correct current...so we thought. That raging current swept us right into the side of that darn rock. Once again, I, the captain of the raft, went flying through the air and into the water. This time around, someone standing on the rock was able to extend a paddle out for me to grab before I was past the area of no return.

I grabbed on and was pulled to the rock. This rock was probably close to twenty feet high and forty feet in length. I crawled up to safety where the guides or instructors barked out instructions to keep other rafters from making the same mistake I made—whatever that was. I am not exaggerating when I tell you that one of the instructors yelled for me to come up to the top of the rock. I was thinking I was going to get yelled at for not proceeding through the rapids in the proper and correct way. Actually, yelling at me would have been much better than what did happen. I climbed to the top of the rock and the guide said, "Get ready to jump." Was he making me jump back in the river as punishment for messing up? "Come on, buddy, it is a long way down" is what was going through my mind. I guess you can say it was not a punishment, but when the next raft bounced its way through the rapids and came close to the rock, the instructor pushed me to the edge and barked, "Jump!" I remember thinking, "Say what?" and I jumped. As my body was falling rapidly toward the fast-running water, I thought about what my mother always said in reference to following what other people did. "If they jumped off a bridge"—or in this case, a huge boulder—"would you?" Well, I guess I answered that question. I had jumped on command without thinking of the consequences.

Much to my surprise, I landed in a moving raft from what seemed like the top of the Empire State Building. It was quite an experience. What if I would have missed? I would have landed in the raging rapid that would have slammed me into the side of Suicide Rock, probably knocking me out, as in unconscious.

My new raft buddies were more than surprised—they were shocked that this not-so-small lady dropped from the sky and plunged into their raft without any warning. I should have had the presence of mind to yell, "Special delivery—air female," on my way down. All I could think of was what would happen if I went right through the bottom of the raft. On my descent from the rock, I am pretty sure I heard the words "holy crap" coming from the minister. With his eyes turned to the sky, they looked like large collection plates. He dropped to his knees in the raft and had what I am sure was a Jesus moment.

Once I landed safely in the bottom of the raft—not through it and not on one of the unsuspecting crew members—I heard a faint whisper, "Thank you, God." I sat up, and I was looking at the minister right in the eye. God was looking out for me; what better boat to land in than the minister's. I said, "Surprise, I am your new crew member."

The shocked crew got us safely around the rock, and I arrived back to my raft and crew down the river, right there in the same spot I met them last year after my previous river incident. I gave up white water rafting. At least, I did not end up as "a piece of the rock," but I did call my insurance agent when I got back to dry land.

My soccer buddy was the friend that no matter what we did, it was fun. We had a great time together. I trusted her with my kids, my thoughts, my money, and as you just read, I guess my life.

CHAPTER 9

The Meat and Potatoes
or
Dessert Was Served

Now that we have spent some time going through the history that brought me to where I am today, let's move on. Back to the dinner I was cooking. My last meal before my diet was going to begin.

During dinner that night, while stuffing my face after crying all day that I needed to lose weight, I learned that you should always be careful what you wish for. Let me tell you God has quite a sense of humor.

I had a rapid weight loss—a loss of about three hundred eighty pounds, and that was without diet and exercise. I know it sounds like it was easy, but it was not without its share of pain. I did not lose it all at once, mind you. I lost the first two hundred thirty pounds that evening when my loving husband announced he was moving out.

That announcement stopped me midbite of a french fry. My life was in the dumpster, and that is where I had put my dinner. I no longer was hungry. Dessert was served; my husband was moving out. It was not a sweet dessert.

He informed me he needed time to think, and I quote, "While standing, looking at the Pacific Ocean"—we had just come back from San Francisco—"I realized that I have been unhappy for the last thirteen years." Excuse me? What was he telling me? After twenty-five years of marriage, I now hear that my spouse, my partner, my prince charming, the one I vowed to love till death do us part has been unhappy for over half of our blissful marriage?

I am sure that my mouth was hanging open, probably all the way to the floor, even with my bad jaw. Where did he get off deciding he needs to walk out and have time to think? If you need to think, go out in the garage and think, and while you're out there, sweep the floor.

I think he needed to rethink his thinking. His announcement included the fact he was going to his mother's to think and take charge of his life. I had no idea or understanding as to what was happening.

He stayed in the house that night, but not in my bed. I laid there wondering what went wrong, and my thoughts began reflecting back to our recent trip to San Francisco.

CHAPTER 10

I Left My Heart in San Francisco
or
I Should Have Stayed There with It

Things were not seeming to add up about this situation. As I was lying in bed thinking about Charm's announcement; it felt like there were pieces of a puzzle flying around in my head every waking moment. The "awake" moments of my nighttime and daytime hours were more plentiful than the sleeping hours.

Every once in a while, a piece of that puzzle fit into place, and one of the biggest pieces was our trip to San Francisco. As the days continued to pass by, I would see more clearly what had been going on "undercover." Or maybe we should say, "under the covers," so to speak. I could do nothing but shake my head in disbelief of every-thing that happened to me on the San Fran trip.

It had always been a dream of mine to take Prince Charm to San Francisco. I went there on a family vacation to visit my uncle and aunt when I was sixteen and never forgot that city by the bay. I remembered it like it was yesterday. I had told P. C. for years that I wanted to take him there. Now was my chance. I told Charm it was up to him to decide if he wanted to go, but I knew he would not regret taking the time to visit the city. Turned out that the only one that regretted the trip was me. In the city I had remembered since I was a teen, I lost my heart and soul.

I should have told you about the San Francisco story earlier, but it took me some time before I drug it back up to the front of my mind from where it had been buried. The San Francisco fog has lifted at this point, and I now can write about this important corner piece of the puzzle.

It all began when Charm came home one night from work and said he had to go to Reno for business. My soccer buddy was there at the time, and we both said, "Not without us." After a few days of discussion and seeing if it were possible, we made reservations on a big silver bird.

I had always wanted to go to Reno. I had an aunt that lived there. Actually, she was the one that I had visited in San Fran on my very first trip to the Rice A Roni city. I had not seen her for a long time. I had dreamed of seeing Lake Taco—I mean, Tahoe. I also was excited to see the sign across the road that states Reno is "The Biggest Little City in the World." My excitement was sometimes dampened by a feeling. Have you ever had one of those feelings that something was going to go wrong? Maybe the plane was going to crash or there would be a car accident, something just gnawing at you. Well, that was how I was feeling—apprehensive—which is very unusual for me.

I could not understand those feelings as the trip sounded like so much fun. My husband would be in meetings most of the days, and I had a buddy to travel around the area with instead of being alone. After his meetings, we could continue exploring the things he wanted to see. He had one free day, so that was when we planned the trip to San Fran.

We got up at the crack of dawn so we could tour some of the city and be at Fisherman's Wharf for lunch. We made it, but it was not pleasant. About two hours into the trip, we stopped at a rest area. Charm said something that really hurt my feelings, and of course, at this time, it is so overshadowed by other happenings. I can't even remember what was said that hurt so deeply. I just remember that while at the rest stop, he said he was sorry that "I took what he said wrong." That's the way it always was; he would turn and twist things until it was my fault. I was so hurt that when I got back in the car, I got in the back seat (which, for me, was not so smart because I have a severe case of motion sickness). This left my soccer buddy to ride in the front seat.

I have never, in my whole life or ever will again, seen such a demonstration of cruelty as I did from the back seat of that rented car that day. I sat back there hiding my tears behind my mirrored sunglasses. I was resting my head against the back of the seat. I was quiet, but after witnessing Charm's not-so-nice behavior, I became speechless.

As I sat there, I witnessed Charm's inappropriate behavior. That picture will forever be burned in my mind. It was like he was a teenage boy lusting after a girl. He would watch me, his wife of twenty-five years, in the rearview mirror, and then look at my soccer buddy and reach over and touch her. This continued constantly for about thirty minutes. I just sat and watched and listened as they talked about nothing important. Then I saw Charming mouth the words "I love you" to what I thought was one of my best friends. This man was really cocky and full of himself. I thought I was going to leap from the seat and choke him on the spot, but no, not me. I continued to torture myself. Shortly, he again mouthed, "I love you." I was furious.

These unkind acts continued a few more minutes with him watching me, looking at her, and then reaching over and touching her hand and leg, and then the biggest move of all (and there is no doubt in my mind), he was touching her chest! I jumped at that point. My only mistake: I did not lunge for the jugular!

They had a million and one excuses. First of all, when I jumped, I kicked the console holding the soda cans, and it made a lot of noise. They both asked, "What is wrong?" I said," I went to sit up and kicked the cans." I should have kicked the bucket, both of theirs, out of the car! Who did they think they were? Of course, at this point, they kept asking me what was wrong, like they were too stupid to know. I finally said, "I was watching you acting like a teenager infatuated with a girl."

"I did not do anything" came spilling forth from Charm's mouth.

I think I will put my picture on this book so you can judge if I look as dumb as they thought I was that day. I finally started yelling, and of course, my NotSo Soccer Buddy began to cry.

The prince of a man pulled over, and he said, "What is wrong?" I said, "You mouthed the words 'I love you' to her."

Do you know what he said? "No, I didn't."

My mirrored sunglasses must distort words. I said, "You liar, you did so, and you did it twice. You just lie more and more all the time."

"I am not lying," he said. It just went on and on; I was so frustrated. The charming prince of a man kept saying, "I did not do that." Give me strength.

My poor soccer buddy was just hysterical, poor baby (sarcasm). I am the one that just lost everything! What the heck?

She got out of the car and got into the back seat and told me to get up front, and I said, "I will." I got out, and I started walking. I did not care if I saw either one of them again. Actually, there was a gas station, and I thought I would get something to drink, hopefully more than a bubbly soft drink, and maybe call my aunt to come get me.

I guess when I left the car, my buddy started yelling, "Go get her, don't let her walk away!" I guess Charm could not worry about me walking away in California because he was so concerned about the other "her." He finally came after me and simply said for me to come back. Wow, that statement took a lot of thought. I said, "No way, I am tired of lies and this situation. I am not doing it anymore."

Eventually, I did get back in the car, and I confronted them with what I had witnessed. His response was "Are you ready for this? I said, 'I love this,' not 'I love you.'" Like that one?

I responded by telling him I knew that was not what he said. What did it matter? After all, they were both saying it with their hands. Charm's paws were leaving prints all over her as he clawed his way over her body. If I were to be honest, it probably took a lot of pawing around to find the fruit he was looking for—tiny shrunken prunes. Not much larger than what she had been searching for in the nut department.

He was sneaky, and I told him I would not tolerate these kinds of actions. I added that when I was sitting up front, he did not even talk to me and that he did all these actions on the assumption that I was sleeping. He, of course, denied that and said he knew I was not sleeping, and I could have been included in on all of this. What! Give me a break; they were so absorbed in each other that they could have very easily driven away without me at the rest stop. They would have never noticed I was not in the car.

Charm decided that we should just go on and try to have a good time. He asked both of us if we could do that, and we both said yes. I said it, but I knew I could not forget what just happened. But a good time did not happen. It was a quiet ride, and there were no laughs in that car or even the rest of the day—rightfully so. I was assured that this cruel act of theirs was just a one-time thing.

At Fisherman's Wharf, I left them alone while I went to find out about tours of Alcatraz. I did so because I thought they wanted to go, although I had other thoughts running rampant in my mind of it being a great place to leave them hopefully chained up somewhere.

I was taking care of everything, finding out about tickets and all because I have to take care of everyone. It just seems to be part of who I am. It is my assumption that while I was checking on tickets, Charm told my soccer buddy that he was going to leave me for her. She was not right the rest of the day. On the outside, she was sad, dejected, and sometimes had tears in her eyes, but I just bet on the inside she was jumping for joy!

We all had a big fight at the Golden Gate Bridge, and I was just miserable. I was trying to make it a good day for them. Why? What was wrong with me that after what had happened on the way there, I was busting my buns to try to make their day better? I think God wrote "sucker" on my forehead in some kind of ink that everyone could see but me. Neither one of them deserved the kind of love I have for people. Someday someone will appreciate it, I am sure.

When we came back across the Golden Gate Bridge to go back to Reno, Soccer Bud said she felt bad with a headache, and her stomach was bothering her. No kidding! Standing at that bridge, she and I talked. It was very sad. I had that sick feeling buried deep in my gut.

She was sick all the way back to Reno with a headache. I was sick all the way back with a broken heart. And Charming—well, he was just sickening. Even though I am more of a Hershey's syrup person, maybe just this once, a little "Southern Comfort" might work better.

We continued the trip for the next two days. All the time, I was wondering where my life was going. On the plane coming home, Charm sat with another employee of his company. I sat with the person I will now call Prin-cess NotSo Much. I tried to talk to her and ask what was wrong and what was going on. She said she really just needed a little time alone—away from Charm and me. We were to just leave her alone.

Once we arrived home, she went her way, and the prince and I went quietly on our way. Now that you know all the dirty little lies, this brings us back to the next evening's dinner when Prince Charming told me he was going to his mother's to think.

CHAPTER 11

When Scorned, I Can Roar
or
Caught in the Act of Thievery

Coming back to reality, after the shock of Charming's announcement that he was going to move to his mother's house to think, I began to talk. I tried asking what was wrong, what was going on, and what I could do to make it right. Charming just kept saying he needed to leave and think. Personally, I think he wasn't thinking! I really wondered what he was thinking. He led me to believe that he would be back, and he just needed this time.

On that Monday evening, I continued to talk to him. Not only did I talk, I begged him to reconsider. I told him we could go to counseling or whatever it would take to make things right. I talked all night, and all he said was that he would leave on the weekend.

At that point, I decided to take control of my life. If he was taking control of his, I could do the same. I told him if he was leaving, he should leave immediately. I was not allowing him to stay all week and leave at his convenience. I was woman, and he heard me roar.

That night, he told me to tell our daughters that he would be at Grandma's house because he needed to think and take control of his life. "Tell them I love them," he said. I was still roaring, I simply told him that if he was going to leave, he needed to call and tell them himself. He called them, and they were very hurt and upset, crying and asking, "Why?"

The next night, he came "home" from work and took some clothes and left. On Wednesday, he came back for dinner, and we paid bills; he had me sign the tax refund checks…that was a big mistake! I continued trying to talk with him, but there was no changing his mind. He left and said he would be back on Friday to get a few more clothes.

He actually came back the next night and loaded a dresser in his truck, saying he needed a place to put his clothes. That broke up the bedroom suit we had since our wedding. But he would be back, and the suit would be whole again, and so would our lives.

You might wonder where my "friend" NotSo was during this time. I called her as soon as it was possible after Charming left. She did not answer. I left messages, but still no call back. It took a while, but eventually, I spoke with her. I told her that he left. This is where it got weird. In my friendships, if someone had called and said that to me, I would have been on their doorstep to support them. Instead, this buddy of mine said she needed some time to herself and that maybe it would be best if I found someone else to help me through this difficult time.

What? I had been there through her entire divorce, helping her and her children through it. Now what is with her? I did not understand this reaction. The next day, I went to her house, but get this, her door locks were changed. I really believed she was home, but she did not answer the door.

As the week continued, I went to work as normal, all the time trying to hide that my life at home was falling apart. On Friday as I sat at my desk, I got instantly sick to my stomach. I really didn't think I had the flu, and I was sure I wasn't pregnant, but I could not control the sickness and the huge lump that was swelling in my throat.

I still had not said anything at work about my husband leaving as I was hopeful that he would change his mind and he really was coming back. I just could not shake the horrible feeling I had.

I got up out of my chair, picked up my purse, and walked out the door without saying a word. I just went home. Upon pulling into the driveway of my safe haven, I found my husband loading his truck with everything he owned and some of what I owned.

When I walked through the door, I said, "I thought you were just going to your mom's to think." He replied that he needed his stuff. "You need your bowling ball and pictures from the walls to think?" I asked.

Let me tell you, I saved a lot of things from going out of that house. My coming home unexpected chased him out of there quickly. He was gone, and I went in the house, locked the door, looked around, and sat and cried.

There was a lot of pain, but I think there was even more frustration as I just did not understand what the issue was with him.

I skipped dinner and went to bed. What else could I do? I laid there thinking about how I was good about making repairs around the house and sometimes even to the car. I could always fix something that was broken. But when it came to my broken heart, it was beyond repair.

I felt like life was floating all around me and that I was sitting back watching it on TV. It certainly was not a sitcom. "Like sand through the hourglass ... so are the days of our lives." Where would I be when I tuned in next week?

As the days continued, I found myself sitting cross-legged on the living room floor, typing on a Word Processor that I had no idea how to use. I thought about what a mistake this was. Not writing but sitting on the floor. Do you know how hard it is to get up and walk after spending hours sitting like that?

I would type late into the night. I was obsessed with writing my thoughts, feelings, emotions, and everything that was happening in my life on this processor and printing it out. I was totally unamused at this situation. However, I could usually find something funny in the day's situations to put on the paper.

Before Charming's disappearance, I was beginning to settle in with what I thought was going to be a new way of life. For the first time in our twenty-five plus years of wedded bliss, he finally decided he was going to help out around the house and take over the duties as the male version of the head laundress. I have to admit I was a little worried about him doing the laundry because I really do not look good in pink, and I am not sure he knew the "no reds with the whites" rule. The idea that he was going to help me was exciting and gave me hope at the time. I had never had this feeling before in my life. It was like he cared and understood how much work I did, like he appreciated it. It was amazing and made me feel special in some small way.

Now here I sit, not sure what was going to happen to me. I don't feel special now. I feel like I have been set out on the curb for garbage day. What was going on with him? Was it that he really was thinking? Maybe pondering life, or was it that he was not thinking? Just what was he thinking? I continued to call him and try to get him to talk to me and find out just what was going on in the head of Charm. I got nowhere.

There was a twist to this story that swirled me around more than a piece of broccoli in a tornado. But that is another story in itself. Hang in there; you just need to know a little more history.

CHAPTER 12

A Trip Away from Reality
or
The Phantom's Opera Was a Little Off-key

A few days passed, and I was still in a quandary as to what was happening, and I was stuck with three very expensive tickets for *Phantom of the Opera* in Toronto. I had saved my money and bought the tickets for the three of us to go see the play. Charming and I had seen it in a smaller theater but never the original in Toronto.

It was something Prin-cess and I talked about doing with a group of girls, and "Charming honey" wanted to go too. I thought it would be a fun surprise as a Christmas present. The plan was to attend this function with my husband and friend. Now the phantom husband was out thinking and sorting out his life, and the phantom friend was locked in her castle surrounded by a moat. I was in a proverbial daze, standing still as the rest of the world moved around me.

In my time of shock, I thought I would try something to see if I could get some idea of what was going on in their phantom brains. I sent sheet music from the *Phantom* and a letter saying, "Hey, we can still go to the play and maybe figure out what is wrong here," but it created only more silence. What was going on with them? What have I done?

I finally did receive a response from the prince, and he said he did not feel it was a good idea to go to the play. I told him maybe he and I could go and work on whatever was wrong. He yelled no and slammed the phone down. I was devastated. At this point, I had not told anyone what was going on. He had told the children and was cruel about it, giving no reasons for his disappearing act, and he did not seem to care about their feelings. Charm did not ask if he could come over and talk on Monday; he just showed up. I will never forget St. Patrick's Day. Not because my great, great, great, etc. grandfather was the first king of Ireland but because that was the day when my prince told me he wanted a divorce. I asked over and over what I had done, but all he could come up with was that I liked my friends better than him. He tried to chocolate coat it as he admitted it was his fault because he never paid attention to me. He really did not want to listen to me whether it was talking about my day, the kids, or work. He did not support me in anything I did. It was always a sore spot with him that I would spend so much time with my friends, but that was the reason why … I did not have a friend at home.

He told me that he had seen a lawyer, and we could just divorce through the same attorney, and it would save money. Yeah, right! I will be talking to my own attorney. Now it is time to clue in the rest of my family. I am sure my children have already told them. I also had to tell my friends what was happening. I truly had a problem now, and the friend I could really confide in was not speaking to me. I knew I could always count on my faith. I know God has a plan for me, but what?

I was rejected by two people I thought I would always be able to count on. Since my husband and my friend were being phantoms, I decided I was not going to let the tickets go to waste.

I asked my daughters to go with me. Vicki was unable to go, so Kimberly and I took off for the big city in Canada along with a friend from my work. This friend had recently gone through a similar situation, so I knew she could understand and relate to my dazed and confused state. We had fun—well, they probably did. I can only remember the fact that I was numb, and the rest is a blur.

I drove, I think, and we went straight to the hotel and got dressed to go to the famed production. Having dinner downtown near the theater was nice, but my heart was crushed. I had never been to Toronto. Charm had visited there on a work trip, so I was told, and promised he would take me someday. The someday was here … where was he?

I had been so excited about this play and getting a chance to see the city, but on this trip, it basically was to use the tickets; I just could not be excited. Throughout the performance, my mind continually wandered, and that wandering led me to "Where were they? What is she so mad about? What am I going to do?"

I remember thinking that maybe someday, in the future, when I had thawed out from this life-freezing pain, I would return to the Phantom City. Maybe then I could see what the city is really like when I am not seeing it through a fog.

The entire time I was gone to the play, I could think of nothing but getting home. I felt I was unprotected; my house was unprotected, and my heart had taken up residence in my throat. I guess you could say I was anxious.

Normally, I am a very calm person, so I am not sure what being anxious felt like. But my heart was beating in my ears, and I was not so sure that it wasn't going to jump right out of my chest.

I just remember I wanted to go home as quickly as possible. I needed to make sure everything was all right. Maybe Charming had come home, or NotSo had called, and I was not there. We did not own cell phones at this time.

I do remember some of the drive home, which is good, considering I was driving. We hit a blizzard near Erie, Pennsylvania. It was a total whiteout, and inches of the white stuff fell faster than you could count them. It was a tense ride, and I did not want to stop for anything. I was headed for the barn, as they say, and there was no stopping me. However, being women, there is always a request for a bathroom break. It was requested, and I obliged, but it better be quick!

The snow lessened as we entered Ohio, but my heart was only pounding faster, and my fear became fiercer. Finally, after what seemed to be the longest drive ever, I arrived home and could not wait to get in the house.

I parked the car, grabbed my suitcase, and flew straight to the answering machine, even before the bathroom. That was a first! Much to my disappointment, there were no messages from either of the perpetrators.

CHAPTER 13

Here I Sit; Where are They?
or
Victimized by a Rescue

I don't know what life has in store for me. My faith in God keeps me going on an hourly and daily basis. Surely, God has something in mind for me.

My only hope is that I will work hard enough and be able to trust enough to follow his lead. I know there will be a happy ending. Some days I think I have things figured out. I become a little comfortable with the situation, and then I suddenly receive a wake-up call to reality.

Reality has certainly set in today. I've had every human emotion possible. I've been on my knees on the floor, crying harder than ever. I am ready to tell Charm and NotSo to eat a big hairy bug. I do not have a clue to what feelings I should be having. Where are the guidelines written down for these situations and an explanation of emotions that should be coordinated with them? Who makes them up? You need guidelines to make sure you are all right. Kind of like the right shoes or purse to go with your outfit. I am being held hostage by two people I cared about. I do not see that I have done anything to them. All my life, I have been quick to take the blame for everything that goes wrong with anyone close to me. I never, in Prince

Charming's or Prin-cess NotSo Much's minds, do anything right. I do not believe in myself and continually apologize for anything and everything. Even when I'm not at fault, I work until I can find fault.

My whole life has tumbled down around me, and for the first time, I am not at fault—at least, that I can find. It is truly the first time I have felt guilt free. If there is anything that I am guilty of, it is loving people far too much and forgetting to love myself.

Here I sit at eleven thirty-eight on a Saturday night. I am at the computer to write down my running wild emotions. Those emotions have been running at high speed on high test, and I just do not know what to think.

Two weeks ago, the man of charm told me that he had spoken to the NotSo Prin-cess. He said that he had called her "just to see where she was at." According to my facts, she is still at the same address! What does he mean to see where she is at? Do I believe this nonsense? He continued to explain to me that she said she was enjoying her time at home and that she just needed to be away from us, meaning Charm and me. Keep in mind that this is his side of the story, and I'm not sure of her feelings. So this leaves me sitting, wondering, and suspecting, "Do they talk? Do they see each other? Is NotSo treating us equally? Or am I being left out of the loop and they are talking? She said she didn't want *us* to bother her."

So here I am; where are they? I am left alone with my mind racing to different scenarios. The mind is a very funny instrument, and I am wondering if there is another mind out there that thinks like me.

What I can't believe is that I still feel compassion for the two people that have torn my heart to shreds. My heart is in a turmoil and is racked with pain, and I am wondering what Prin-cess's parents are thinking and what they've been told.

Why can they not contact me? If Ms. NotSo Prin-cess told them Charming was leaving me, would they not want to see if I were all right or at least say that they were sorry? Just what is going on?

Remember, her parents are people I choose to take into my heart and share my life with. They were included as family at my daughter's wedding, sitting in the appropriate family pews. Christmas Eve, over the last years, they have been included in our family evening.

Thanks for all the love and support, everyone! Yes, that was a little sarcastic, but I am happy that I am the type person that was there to give my total love and support to the family. That is the real me, and I hope I do not lose sight of myself out of fear of loving and trusting again. I've been kicked a lot, but I do thank God for making me a caring and loving person.

My friend says when I am rescuing people, I become the victim. "Victimized by Love" could be a new title. Seriously, you cannot even be a nice guy and care about people without getting your heart handed to you on a silver platter—a very tarnished silver platter.

I truly have become a victim by loving so much. Mr. Charm makes a drastic decision that he is unhappy with his life, and he takes a happy hike whistling along a new path and out of my life. The NotSo Prin-cess decides she is unsure of her feelings. She said she never made a life for herself after her divorce and wants to hide in her castle, draw bridge up. Is the man of charm with her?

Then they both laid down the rules. She said she does not want to be bothered. She changes her door locks, so I no longer can get into her castle. She will not come here to my lonely hearts' club-house. Charming says that I can only call him at work or page him. I am not to call him at his mother's. Where is that written? The hurters get to make the rules and punish the "hurt-ee"? Actually, I really am punishing myself because I choose to care. I need not to care. Let them create rules for each other. Wallow in your self-created mud. I am taking a shower and cleaning this mess up.

I care so very much, and I'm not sure that the others care about anything but themselves. I thought Charming and Prin-cess were very caring human beings, but I found out otherwise. I'm certain, at this point, I have been living with blinders on. They are running out of time as I am getting closer to not being so patient.

Actually, the patience ran out yesterday with Mr. Charm. My attorney received his so-called offer to me for separation. He must be joking! He has me below poverty level. He suggests cutting the phone bill down. I was to ask my boss for more hours, and I should get another job teaching in the evenings.

Let's get this straight, Charm. You leave me, and we are not sure of the exact reason why, and you still feel the need to run my life? He says he needs to get control of his own life? I told him he has always had control of his own life and mine too.

On the other side of the court, we still have NotSo Prin-cess. She won't talk to me, and Charm is choking me. Maybe I should just drop the anchor and let them both sink.

Today the minister gave a sermon just for me. He said when we have rough situations, they are storms in life. A storm? This is a full-blown disaster! He continued with the fact that we all have storms in our lives. At this rate, I will be spending all my time in the storm shelter. When you're in a house and the weather is stormy, you wonder if there will be any damage to the house and property.

Think about that and relate it to people. Even when an earthquake happens, it is not over; there are aftershocks. I think that relates to life as well. I worry that the damage that is being done to me will be permanent. Will I be myself again? Will I be able to function in the real world and love and trust again? It is like being caught in the eye of the storm and everything is swirling around me, and the answers keep changing, and I can't catch the right one.

The minister continued to say when you have a storm in your life, like a broken relationship, you might want to turn to your closest friend or spouse. Where does that put me? I seem to have lost both of those—at least for the time being.

I just need someone to throw me a life preserver in this storm, and then and only then can I get on with this turmoil that my life has become.

CHAPTER 14

I am Not Related to Mr. Clean
or
Taking a Dump

The day after the *Phantom* trip, after not hearing from Charm or my phantom friend, I decided to adopt a new attitude.

I have junk piling up all around me. I have a choice. I can let this junk sit and do nothing, or I can clean up the mess that the man of charm has made for me and take it to the dump.

I have chosen to clean up the mess. I feel something better must be waiting for me. It is time to clean it up and go on. This is not an unusual position for me to be in—cleaning up the mess my husband made, that is. Charm picked up what he wanted and left everything else lying around. Example, it was common for him to go to the kitchen, make a sandwich, and leave the bread and most likely the mustard or catsup out on the counter, as well as the dirty knife and crumbs. He had a habit of leaving the silverware drawer open while making the sandwich. That single move turned into crumbs mounting up in the drawer, and the worst part, he would leave the cheese slice wrappers lying on the counter. The whole mess would sit there until I picked it up. Sometimes I would leave it there just for a while to see if he would clean it up—never happened.

Now I am cleaning up another mess he left me—my life. This mess is not going to sit on the counter waiting to see if it will be cleaned up by Charm. I may not be related to Mr. Clean, but I could not stand it any longer. I had to clean this mess up.

Where do I start? First of all, I cleaned up the junk left—literally. He left his things lying around, and I'm going to clean them up and start with a blank canvas to paint my life. I started by packing up the personal items he left. He told my daughter he did not want anything in the house; however, a letter from his attorney stated differently. There were a few things listed that he wanted.

I began cleaning. I was moving furniture and sweeping away the dust and dirt I was left with (metaphorically). I was setting up the house for my new life, no matter what "life" throws at me. I decided not to wait on the prin-cess to be my sounding board and help me through this, so I am considering going to counseling and to a divorce recovery group.

I'm not going to fight with anyone or say a harsh word. However, I will continue to let the prin-cess know I am here and that I care about her. I will not give up on our friendship until she spits in my face. It just is not fair to drop a friendship like we have without some in-person dialogue. I feel Charm does not want to hear a thing I have to say. He made it very clear that my cards and thoughts were meaningless. He will have to figure out on his own the love the kids and I have for him; he will not listen to what we say.

Someday I will share with the prin-cess what I have learned from this whole experience. Nothing is forever. I was so secure with these relationships and enjoyed life, and then the dam burst.

I spoke with a friend last night. She had a very interesting outlook on life. She told me that she always told her husband if he had to move on to make his life work, fine; however, she wanted the relationship to be as it started—as best friends. He is the person that she runs to for everything. That is something I never had with Charm. He never really cared about what I was feeling or dealing with emotionally. Any problems I had could never be as important as the problems he had—in his mind. Any emotions I would have toward our children, family, friends, or life, he would make fun of, laugh, and say it was dumb for me to feel the way I was feeling. He was my husband and not my friend.

Whenever he would say something to hurt me and I confronted him with it, he would tell me it was not meant that way, and I "took" it wrong. Isn't it funny how I can always be at fault? According to Charm, I just take things wrong. Trust me, I will never allow that to happen again in my life. So far, I have shown little emotion even going through this painful ordeal because I have always seen my feelings as being dumb or too insignificant to be bothered with. I do not show my emotions easily because I do my crying in private. Sooner or later, I'm sure it will all come out.

Loving each other is very important. You never know when you might lose someone. You can survive anything if you have people around you. God says, "Love one another." I think Charm has been listening to the Youngbloods a little too much, like their song "Get Together," "You got to love one another right now." He took it literally!

CHAPTER 15

Prisoner in My Own Life
or
Phantom Friend

After my "off-key" trip, even though I had changed the locks to the house, I still felt insecure. I don't know why I didn't want to be away from my house.

I received a call from Charming. Finally, something positive. I was filled with excitement. I was thinking, "Finally, he is thinking about coming back." He was thinking about me and the kids. I was quickly brought back to reality when he spoke. His call was all about giving me more instructions.

Those instructions were not to call Prin-cess. He said he tried to talk to her again and that she wanted to be left alone. That was an interesting turn of events.

Now the "man of charm" was calling me, telling me what to do, giving me orders in that demanding way I knew so well. He wanted me to pay certain bills and wanted to control my every move, much like our many years of marriage. However, my thoughts were circling around in my head. What right does he have to do that now that he has gone astray?

He left to take charge of his life, but instead, he is trying, like always, to be in charge of my life. Charge he did; he cancelled all the credit cards and told them to send me the bills, changed the utilities to my name, and cancelled the checking accounts after cleaning them out!

How many bills did he expect me to pay on my little income? How was I supposed to pay the college bills and support our daughter? So I sat back and did my own thinking, trying to figure out the orders I was given to leave NotSo alone. He did all that within the first couple of weeks of his thinking period. Seems to me that he was on his "period."

I knew in my heart that I had tried to do everything I could to hold this relationship together. I really tried to understand the reactions of Charming and NotSo Charming. Everyone reacts in different ways, and maybe she was just reacting in the way that best fit her. I just don't know. I don't know if I will ever know.

CHAPTER 16

Easter Day
or
All the Bunny Left Was Little
Round Brown Droppings

Easter was a cloudy, dreary day, not to mention very cold. Kimberly and I went to church, and it was very crowded, which made it difficult to find seats. We chose an aisle and headed down it until we came across some seats.

Partway down the aisle, I saw NotSo and her family. That is when I wanted to turn tail and run. However, right along with a stunned feeling, was a sickness in my stomach and just a twinge of anger coming out. Yes, anger, enough to make me continue down the aisle and sit right in front of her family, including her mother, father, brother, sister-in-law, and all the kids. I was afraid that they would all think I was causing trouble, but I have to be honest; I never thought she would show up at church. Charming and I and Prin-cess and her parents had been attending this church for a few months. If she wanted a break from me, why would she show?

I had been here a couple of Sundays since this whole thing began, and none of them had shown their faces, so I thought I was safe on this special day. After all, there were three services, all packed to the rafters, and just my luck, I end up at the same place, same time. What is that old saying, "Same church, different pew"?

I turned and spoke to everyone, and her brother's children wanted to talk to me, so I talked to them since the adults would not speak to me. What was up with that?

After the service, I walked out right behind the NotSo Charming Prin-cess and tried to talk with her. I had sent her an Easter card. She thanked me for it as we were walking out the door of the sanctuary. I asked her how she was doing, and she returned the question. I said that I was not doing well, but I was trying hard or something similar to that.

I asked if I could call her, and she paused. I just added that I was not going to talk about what was happening. She answered that maybe I could. We continued the usual small talk that you make when you see someone that is an acquaintance or maybe even a stranger, and she walked out the door.

I went down to the nursery where her brother had the youngest children, and I talked with him and his wife. They seemed on edge, and I felt very left out. Kimberly and I continued to the car, and she cried all the way home.

Vicki and her husband, Mike, came over for dinner, and I managed to hold everything together through the meal and watching a movie; however, I was wondering all the time what was going to happen to me and my life. In a way, I was angry; in another, I was hopeful that I would get my friend back, and it would help a lot to have a friend to help me cut through this pain.

When Vicki and Mike left, I bawled like a baby, and Kimberly and I had a long talk. I began to feel better, and tears turned to hurt, and the hurt had a little twinge of anger right in the middle.

Then Charming called because he wanted to tell Kimberly goodbye as she was going back to school; spring break was over. She said they chatted a little while, and then she asked him if he was going to tell her "Happy Easter." He said it was not a very happy Easter, so he did not want to make it worse. That is when I was encouraged. She shared with me that when she told him that her day had been sad, he said, "We will all have better days." I thought that was encouraging, and my hope and wish was, by this time next year, things would be back to the way they were.

The strange thing was that the man of charm had e-mailed Vicki earlier in the day and told her happy Easter. But he did not want to wish Kimberly a happy Easter? I did not get it.

Besides dealing with my emotions and confusion, I found my daughters were confused as well. I don't know if he realized what he was doing. Did he have any idea what he might be giving up? All I can say is that I do have a strong faith, and I was certainly using it. I continued to pray and hope that the next Easter would be filled with more than rabbit "droppings"!

CHAPTER 17

The Bunny Hopped On
or
Bunny Droppings Hit the Fan

Once the bunny had hopped on, I decided to call the NotSo Charming Prin-cess and see if she had calmed down from whatever had been bothering her over the last weeks.

One of our favorite things to do was play golf; I simply asked her if she wanted to play golf with me on Wednesday, her day off. Her response was "I don't think so." I came back with "How about if we have dinner one night?" Her response, "No, I don't think I want to." I paused for a moment and said, "May I ask why?"

That simple word *why* began a thirty-minute conversation that was stressful. I now knew for sure where she stood—right beside *my* husband! As they say, the body was not even cold yet. They had been seeing each other for some time.

When this conversation took place, it was about seven weeks since Charming had fled. You might recall that he said he was leaving to "think." Obviously, he had done his thinking and was acting upon his thoughts.

I had found out that NotSo was checking the balances on my checking and savings accounts by using Charm's card the very first week of his "thinking" process. Now that the fog had lifted from the

San Francisco trip and his leaving, I began to see things for what they really were. I had tried desperately to give them the benefit of the doubt, but now any reasonable doubt went out the window.

After asking her why she would not go to dinner with me, she—with a very stern, determined voice—said, "I think you know why." She thinks I know why? Do I have bad breath? I took a shower. What was the reason? I did not know why, or at least I was trying very hard not to know why. I did suspect that they were together, but I lacked that real proof. However, after the conversation with Un-Charming, what I felt in my heart and the pit of my stomach rang loudly in my ears. I think everyone else knew or was suspicious, but I didn't want it to be that way. Things just do not always go the way you want them too.

Our conversation continued, and she wanted to know why my parents had been in her parking lot. I had no idea what she was talking about, but she would not believe me. I told her all I wanted to do was to see her and talk to her. "I have done everything you asked. I have left you alone. I have not come to your house or called. I feel we need to talk," I said. She responded with "About what?"

That was when I said that I thought we needed to talk about the situation, and I needed to know where she stood. I did not want to hear it, but there it was right out in the open. From NotSo's lips to my, what I wished to have been, deaf ears. "I think you know where I stand," she said.

I told her I really didn't know what she was thinking. I then told her the least she could do is sit down with me face-to-face and tell me where she was coming from. I felt she owed me that. She said, "Everyone seems to know, and I thought you did. Just go on with your life." That is what she had to say to me. "Just go on with your life!"

I decided to ask her how she would feel if I would have just "dumped" her, so to speak. Her thought on that was she would have just gotten on with her life. Well, the conversation still did not come to an end at that point. This is where she said, "You made me make the choice between the two of you." Excuse me? I made her choose between me and my allusive husband? It was shortly after that I asked her if she was with the "prince of charm," and she emphatically said, "Yes, that is exactly what I am telling you."

I simply said, "Thank you. Goodbye."

As I was getting ready the next morning for work, the phone rang. You won't believe it—it was Un-Charming. She said, "Hi." I repeated that simple word. She said she just called to say she was sorry. "If I had seen this coming, I would have stopped it. I did not mean to hurt you. I just do not know what else to say," she added to her "sorry" apology.

I told her that she could have stopped it. "Friends do not do this to each other," I replied back. She was silent. She broke the silence with "I realize if I make this decision, I would cause a lot hurt, and I will have to endure a lot." I was thinking, *Yeah, you got that right, so why would you make that kind of decision?*

It was at this point that I told her the story behind my parents being in her neighborhood. I had asked them about it. They were coming from the store and saw Charm outside of her house. I had previously told my parents, which is what I believed to be true, that the female perpetrator in this ongoing saga of boy meets girl was not having anything to do with either Charm or me.

After my parents went to dinner, they drove back by to see if he was still at the perp's house, and he was.

Once I told her that story, I asked why she had checked my bank accounts, to which she replied, "I only did it twice." I confronted her with the fact that according to the printed bank statement, it was four times. She said Charm had asked her to do it because he was paying the bills. The truth was I was paying the bills. I had the checkbook. So basically, I said to her that they have both been lying to me. She said, "Take care of yourself," and hung up.

That conversation took care of twenty-five and a half years of marriage and seven years of what I thought was a great friendship. I still have no idea as to how I made her make a choice. Makes no sense. I guess she had to blame someone for her issues.

I hope, for those of you that are reading this, that you will never allow yourself to be treated in this manner. It was very hurtful. I just did not know where to go or what to do. I knew God had a plan for me, but the impatience was getting to me.

I found that Kimberly had been lied to as well. She had asked her dad, at one point, if he was with NotSo. He quickly and matter-of-factly told her, "No!"

We can't always control what happens to us, but we can control what we do after it happens. Our response to situations is what matters. Throw yourself into something that is a passion. We all have our own story and need to use it to benefit others and improve our lives. Let go and move forward. Choose to live your life the way you want it to be.

Just sayin'—That I have found some pluses to living alone—you live differently. I am really into manners, but there is no one I have to say "excuse me" to. I don't have to say, "Please pass me the salt." I can just say "salt," then get up, and get it for myself.

I have told Precious that I am sorry a few times when I forgot her treat or when I tripped over her in the dark hallway.

Have you ever run into a store manikin, a door, or wall and instantly said, "Excuse me"? That is inborn politeness. You kind of lose that when you live alone. You can run to the washer and dryer with no garments adorning your body. You don't even have to run; you can just meander to get the underwear you have drying. No one will ever see you. Just don't scare yourself if you pass a mirror.

I don't recommend this if you are going out, but staying at home, you can just turn your underwear inside out to rewear every other day—saves on the laundry bill—*just sayin'*.

There is no one there to see the holes in your socks or undies.

Sometimes living alone is problematic. If you forget your soap when you are in the shower, you have to get out soaking wet, walk across the room, getting everything in your path wet, retrieve the soap, and get back in. However, if you live alone, who is there to know that you didn't use the soap? You get back to the shower . . . and the phone rings!

What's really cool is that you don't have to share the remote with anyone. Channel surfing is in your control!

Why not have a ring in the tub? You don't have one on your finger. It is your ring, not someone else's.

Scramble an egg in the morning and throw the pan in the sink or leave it on the stove, and that night you can fry your hamburger, fish, potatoes, or whatever in the pan. Saves on water, dish soap, time, and effort.

Leave your nonperishable items in the bags after grocery shopping and just get out what you need when you need it.

A downside is scratching your back, but a doorway or hairbrush can solve that problem.

You can eat celery at midnight, in bed. Get the cream cheese out of the fridge, grab a stalk of celery, and dip. Double-dipping is legal if it is just you.

No need to hold back on eating the beans. Well, no one is around to hear the echo—*just sayin'*.

CHAPTER 18

The Truth Be Known
or
Trimming the Ugly Fat

Now you know where I lost the other one hundred fifty pounds. Seems the prince was really not moving in with his mother; he had moved in with what I thought was one of my best friends, my soccer buddy. I might have exaggerated those pounds a little, but she is not here, and it makes me feel better.

The thing is I did not know—or let's say I could not confirm—this living situation for almost seven weeks. Sounds strange and impossible, but it is the truth. The girls or I would call Charm at his mom's house, and whoever answered would just say he was not there and that they would give him a message.

Then mysteriously, within a few minutes, he usually called back. It was strange. He had his family lie for him. He was at NotSo's house, and they would call him and let him know that one of the members of his "first family" had called. Then he would call back.

So you are thinking, "But what about caller ID?" It was out there, but not something we all had at the time, nor did everyone have cell phones. It did enter my mind that he was with her, but there was always an explanation as to why he was not at his mom's to answer the phone.

I know you are sitting there reading this, thinking, *What is wrong with this lady that she could not see this?* I guess I just had more faith in the prince of charm and prin-cess than to believe that they would lie to me and do something underhanded. I learned, didn't I?

Although Charm did call me back once in a while (not that I called him often), he would not talk about "us." What was I to do now? I really had no one to talk to about this situation. After all, NotSo Much (NSM) had been my sounding board. The one I could tell my true feelings to. I could tell her what drove me nuts about the man in my life, his bad habits, the fact he hid money from me. You know how it works: that someone that you can complain to but is trustworthy. It is a code among us "girls," but she broke the code. I know it is difficult to believe that it took me so long to know for sure what the situation was, but it did. I think in my heart, I knew. But without proof, I did not want to accuse and be wrong. Things had happened along the way, making me suspicious.

At one point, I even asked him what was going on. Did he have feelings for her? He assured me that if anything ever happened like that, he would come to me. He would be honest about it. Honest? Ha! He always had a logical explanation for those "suspicious moments" that continued to throw me offtrack.

My husband left for greener pastures, or what was grazing in them, and there I was—stunned, confused, and totally *unamused.*

I sat wondering what I should do next. After all, I had lost these three hundred eighty pounds of ugly fat, and my body had not changed; my appearance had not changed. But my heart sure did. I was numb, had a headache, couldn't sleep, and did not know what to do.

I learned something about myself. Although I was generally a quiet, laid-back, and peace-loving person, when scorned, I found I could spring into action like a lioness ready to pounce on a predator going after her cub. I now know why they refer to it as a catfight. I think I started growing claws.

I decided I was not going to allow their fleeing to get me down. I would find a different road to travel. It hurt—it hurt a lot. But I would find a better path. I did not know where my life was headed, and neither one of the perpetrators, as I like to refer to them, would speak to me.

I felt I needed more support than my underwire was giving me, so I went looking for help. I did not know if there was such a thing as a support group for what I was going through, but I went looking and found a divorce recovery group at one of the local churches. I was really not sure that I was going through a divorce, but I suspected this marriage would end.

It took a lot of courage on my part to walk into the first recovery group—alone. I sat in the parking lot for some time before entering the building. Upon going in, I was kindly greeted and paid my fee. I found a seat and began to scan the room to see if there was anyone I knew. No dice. I sat there quietly, hoping a familiar face would walk in, but there was none.

I had been handed a notebook with the papers of the things I was going to learn in this, my new "learning experience." Also in the notebook was a list of members of the group. Among the names was one I recognized, but the person to go along with that name was not in the room. Eventually, as I got the nerve to speak, I asked about the familiar name. The person I asked said she was on vacation and would be back next week. Vacation. I could not even think of going on vacation in the state of mind I was currently experiencing.

The name I saw in the notebook was that of Emmie, someone I had known for many years. I actually knew her before my kids went to kindergarten as we had mutual friends, but we became more acquainted when Kimberly was in Emmie's kindergarten class. I volunteered in her classroom for years.

I made it through that first meeting. Even though I had no idea where my life was really headed, it was good to hear that others were making it through their devastating times. I looked forward to the next week and hoped Emmie would be at the meeting—just a familiar face.

The next week, Emmie was there, and we reunited. Emmie was friends with several others from the support group, and they spent time together—going to movies, plays, concerts, out to eat, and other activities. I was very fortunate that Emmie asked the other groupies to include me, and they agreed.

I continued to sit on the living room floor typing my feelings. I was suffering a pain far worse than just physical from sitting on the floor. My heart was breaking, and I did not know what to do to fix it. I had finally hit the point where I could kick back a little with my husband, relax, and get into a life "after children." Little did I know that this life was going to be alone.

I was really perplexed as to what was going on. I just tried to avoid the issues at hand. Even though I was pretty certain they were together, I still couldn't help wondering where they were and what they were doing. After all, Charm had never mentioned that he was with Un-Charming.

Basically, I felt that my life was going down the toilet, and the little man in the rowboat floating around in the tank was not even offering me a life preserver. For those of you that are of the younger generation, check out the old Tidy Bowl commercials.

I needed to face the facts and save myself. It was time to get the attitude that this day was the first day of the rest of my life. I was going to have to deal with the hand that had been dealt. The only thing was I needed to check the rule book for how to play this game. I felt like I could deal with anything if I just knew exactly what I was dealing with.

I began reflecting back on things that had happened. Little things that I really did not think about at the time now began to make sense to me. Prin-cess NotSo Charming insisted on helping to throw the prince of charming and me a twenty-fifth anniversary party. She worked with our children and my mother to do so. The party was a surprise, and we had a great evening with many friends and relatives. Although the evening was very special, I felt that there was something strange in the air.

It seemed a little strange to me that my husband and I were to go through the buffet line first, and somehow NotSo was in between us, and the charm man was talking to her and not me. I remember thinking how nice it was to include her as she had just gone through a divorce and would not experience a milestone like this. I was happy about that, but I also remember thinking that Charming should have been talking to me and act like he was at the party with me—very interesting! Even though Charm and I said the normal "I dos," he was no longer "doing" what those vows stated.

CHAPTER 19

Just What Is It About People and Their Thought Processes
or
The "Do It If It Feels Good" Generation

This seems to be the slogan anymore. If it feels good, do it! No wonder, people seem to be so selfish. Is this what we are teaching our children? Any more you hear people say they have to think of themselves. What happened to thinking of others and their feelings? What about giving the generation a foot up on life and teach them a little caring? It must feel good for Charm and NotSo because they are doing it—right in front of God and everyone. My mother told me there would be days like this.

I listen to a lot of Michael W. Smith music, and I don't think he had this idea in mind with his song "Love One Another." It seems like every Tuesday is to be the day for new plateaus. Kimberly decided to brave it and call her father. She has not talked to him for about a month. He has not contacted her either. My explanation for this lack of conversation is his guilt feelings.

Kimberly called him for a couple of things. His sister had surgery last night, and Kimberly wanted to know how her aunt was doing. She had not heard from him, and she told me she missed his hugs. Also, she was going to ask him for some money to buy shorts.

He had told her that if she needed anything, call him. During the conversation, she asked him if he was at Grandma's. Although I was pretty sure he was not living at his mother's, I had not told my girls about my previous suspicions of their dad and NotSo. I also had not told them about my conversation with NotSo when she admitted they were together. Charm answered Kimberly by saying he was not at Grandma's but at NotSo's. She did not know what to say. She said all she could do was cry.

Okay, that was quite a blow to her. I had not told my kids anything that I found out. I just wanted to get Kimberly through this quarter of school, which was just about six more weeks. Not the man of charm. He is cocky as all get out (take that any way you want); he could not wait to let his daughter know they are sleeping together.

Just tell me a couple of things. First of all, here is a man that has tried to teach his daughters right from wrong. What do you see wrong with this picture? Is there not some rule of thumb about "set a good example?" Is this where the old cliché comes in "do as I say and not as I do"? The Prin-cess has been so worried about her children and sex. She has an eighteen-year-old son and has informed him that if he ever got to that situation, not that she would condom it—oh, excuse me, I mean "condone" it—he should come talk to her. Do you think she went and talked to him? Not!

They have been at this awhile—you know, keeping it under-cover or "under the covers." I feel just awful for the kids. I just do not understand where their heads are. I do realize, however, that Charm is only thinking with his "little head" and not his "big head." Excuse me for being a little crude tonight, but you have to understand that you have not heard all of this, and I am just a little upset with Mr. Charm and his little excursion from home.

Kimberly had a conversation with Charming, telling him that he was going to end up in hell. "You have broken some of the top ten, and if you do that, you go to hell," she continued. Mr. Charm proceeded to tell her that it is a matter of opinion. Whose opinion? Do these opinions change to fit the needs of an individual? Let us just pick a few commandments just to test this theory and see how it works:

1)   Honor your father and mother.

Does this mean you should respect your parents?

Or does it mean you should honor them with a big party at your convenience, at their house, with all your friends by their swimming pool?

2)   You shall not murder.

This could mean you should not take someone's life.

This could also mean do well in school so you do not murder the English language. Well, ain't youns ever had a teach tell youns that?

3)   You shall not commit adultery.

Does this mean if you are married to your wife that you should not live with another woman? Oh, I know—unless it feels good.

4)   You shall not covet your neighbor's wife, manservant or maidservant, ox or donkey or anything that belongs to your neighbor.

You can do that one all by yourself. Make up what you think works. Now you all know not to cast stones. I understand we all have done things wrong. I just have a hard time with such blatant acts and then trying to justify them to your children that you have tried to raise with morals and Christian upbringing. I won't cast stones, but I think a few big boulders would not be out of the question.

Let me continue with the rest of this story, and you will see where I am headed. After Kimberly tried to make Charm understand that she loves him but this just is not going to cut it, he very smoothly told her, as if this would make it all better, "Un-Charm and I have laid in bed together at night and cried because we have hurt your mother." Now this charming man is telling my nineteen-year-old daughter that after walking out on her mother a few weeks ago, he is sleeping with her mother's ex-friend. Needless to say, I have just about had it with his self-righteousness. This is the man that had the conversation with me that he is almost fifty, and sex is of no interest to him.

He is certainly going through an awful lot and putting so many others through pain just to live in a condom—I was going to say "condominium." You did not let me finish that thought before your minds went there. It must be nice to have someone to cry with in bed. Well, I do have my pillow and my dog. She always licks my face when I cry! At least, she knows how to love someone.

Kimberly mentioned that her wedding keeps coming to her mind. This fall, Vicki was married, and the wedding was really nice. Kimberly looked forward to the father-daughter dance. Now she cannot even think about him being there.

I told her I understand more than she would realize. I began to tell her that I have lost the man I have loved for twenty-eight years as well as one of the best friends I thought I ever could have. I know I have something better coming in life. God will take care of all of us. When the time comes, her wedding will be wonderful. My life will be fine. I rather be alone than be around fake love. There were so many other ways to handle this situation. I've started counseling recently and had hoped to work on myself and healing from the pain. I had counseling tonight just about one hour after this all happened—see, someone does take care of me. I was all set to work on my own life tonight. However, I had to spend time on all this garbage. Now I realize this will take a long time to get over. I do however have to heal myself.

My counselor was in rare form tonight. We do tend to laugh through a portion of these sessions. Sometimes she is so direct and takes something I say and rips it apart in such a way that the only thing I can do is look at her and laugh. The poor woman has her work cut out for her. She has to try to make me respect myself more. Not to mention to get my emotions out in the open. She almost saw me mad tonight. Wow!

I figure she has heard it all. She just sits there and shakes her head. She asked, "Did he really say to Kimberly that they lie in bed and cry because of the hurt they have caused you? What is he thinking?"

I said, "I have no idea." Then she asked why that surprised me so much that he said that to her. I responded with "He has always loved his daughters and has been a good father. What he did was just cruel. I cannot stand him being cruel to the kids." She continued asking questions, "What would it take to make you feel better?"

This was not a good question at this time. You may want to take small children out of the room while you read my response for their own protection. I will try to clean this up a little. I responded with "Can I say anything I want?" She said, "Of course."

"It would take Charm dying on top of NotSo of a heart attack during sex and her not being able to get him off or out from under him to call 911!" Now there have been a few theories presented tonight on shrinkage, but we will not go into those. I really did not have to pick my counselor up off the floor, but I am sure she came close. I continued to say, "Or a pregnancy with twins could really be great too! But of course, I don't really wish that; it would not be fair to the little innocent babies. At a time like this, sometimes things just pop out of the mouth from the cruelest part of the mind.

I also talked to Karen, my sister-in-law, tonight. I called to tell her how wrong we were about Prin-cess. I told her I was going to call my kids, and I would call her later. When I called back, she told me that she had told David and Stephen, my nephews, what was going on, and they were having a difficult time believing it of NotSo. They said, "Well, you know what they are doing." Stephen quickly responded with "I do not even want to hear about it or think about it." David asked Karen who she was having the harder time with: Charm or NotSo? She asked him who he was having a more difficult time with. He said, "They were such good friends, for NotSo to do this to our aunt." Pretty good insight for a thirteen-year-old. He will make a wonderful husband someday.

I wanted to talk to my girls. I called Vicki, and she said that Kimberly had already called and broke the news. Vicki just really did not have much to say. I am concerned about her. She said she did not know what to say. Charm has talked to her the last two days and never told her what he was doing or should we say where he was living. He is totally off the wall. I hope I can heal these kids after the damage these two people have done. I pray for NotSo's kids and hope they will be able to have some good relationships in life. Hopefully, God will help us all.

Please forgive me, God, for using and abusing your commandments, but I feel it was needed at this point—it is important.

Just sayin'—That Emmie pulled off a big one today. It is Saturday, and usually, I played soccer. But this weekend, there wasn't a game. It was sunny and beautiful, and I was ready for something fun. Somehow, Emmie got me to put on a dress and go to a wedding with her! There were some heavy duty sad moments. It was my first wedding since the split. I made it through with a clenched jaw and biting my lip so I would not cry or show my gut-wrenching sadness when the father walked the bride down the aisle. It was just about a year ago that Charm walked Vicki down the aisle at her wedding. Flashback!

Someday we will face what happens when Kimberly gets married. She has some trust issues when it comes to men...due to her father. Speaking of fathers, while at the wedding, remember the flying nun? Well, there was a flying priest. He didn't wear that hat, but his robes billowed out behind him as if he could take off as he flew quickly back and forth across the altar area. He could even sing, but I don't know how he could "fly" so fast without that hat the flying nun wore.

I know after what I have been through, at this time, I am not thinking about getting remarried as I don't want to be a nurse or a purse to some ninety-year-old looking for a younger woman. Gentlemen my age are looking for younger, beautiful Barbie-doll-type women. They are not looking beyond the outside for the inside beauty.

Emmie has a hard time handling my pain, so I did not share my feelings of the day with her. After reading "I Left My Heart in San Francisco," she said she could never read it again. I asked, "Aren't you going to read my book?" She replied that maybe she would do so after we were both happily remarried. Guess I will throw her copy away—***just sayin'***.

CHAPTER 20

Let's Talk Turkey
or
Here Comes the Truth—So Duck

Where have I been? Talk about living in a dream world. All the action of talking to NotSo and realizing where she stands has just made me realize that I was trying too hard to ignore the obvious. There were many lies going on, hidden from our friendship. It was incredible deceit; now it is so real and so very painful.

I am kind of the Gomer Pyle type—"Gool'ee." I cannot believe that people in this world can do something like this. I tried so very hard to give them the benefit of the doubt. I guess I did a darn good job of it because I continued on like nothing ever happened. Who was the turkey in this case? I think we all know the answer to this question: it was me. This has been a very painful learning experience.

If you have feelings eating away at your heart and way down deep in your gut, then the feelings are probably true. I had no idea the toll that it was taking on my heart. I had felt it for months, but tried to ignore the feeling. I continually told myself I was overreacting. I now know I was very much underreacting.

Reflecting back, there was the day NotSo and Charm were going Christmas shopping to buy me a special gift from her, but she needed his help to pick it out. That was all probably true, considering the gift, but I think that the main intent was for them to "give a gift to each other." I had that gut feeling that things were not right, and I made the decision to go up to Un-Charm's house. I had a good reason to be there, but at this time, I cannot remember why I was going. A few things have happened since then, and it blocks some of the lesser important facts. Upon my arrival to NotSo's driveway, I did the usual routine of pushing the button on the garage door opener. Nothing happened. I guess I did not push it correctly, so I did it again and again and the open-sesame button did nothing. I could have thought about the fact the battery was dead, but I knew right then and there that Charming and NotSo were there and up to no good.

I parked my car and went to the front door; the screen door was locked. I had only one thought at this time—they were inside, and no one else was getting in! I absolutely beat on the door with no response. I knew I could lift the garage door because it was disengaged. So I literally ran to the garage door and flung it up rapidly. I felt like I had some super strength. I opened the door into the house and ran upstairs, only to meet NotSo on the landing. I blew past her into the bedroom. That is where I saw "Good Ol' Mr. Charm" in person; however, not in the flesh as you might have imagined.

He was totally clad in clothing, but his always-so-perfect hair was messed up. I just turned around and went back downstairs, shouting, "You just ruined two good families."

Of course, according to them, I had the wrong impression; it was not what it "looked like." I received an explanation that was to satisfy my curiosity and my imagination because everything was cool. I asked why they were there and not shopping, and NotSo said she was upset with her daughter, and they came there to talk. Talking is good; in the bedroom, it is bad. "It was my idea," said Un-Charm, "to go up to the bedroom and lay on the bed and talk." Nothing was going on," she said confidently.

Why did they need to lie down to talk? Was one of them ill? I certainly am sick at this point. Maybe there was a physical problem that would not allow them to sit upright and talk at the same time. I know what it was: all the furniture had been steam cleaned and was still too wet to sit on. I guess it was fortunate that the bed had not been steam cleaned, but I bet it was steamy!

I asked if nothing was going on, why did they have to lock the doors? NotSo Prin-cess said, "Because I thought you might come by." If she thought I might come by, why would she lock the doors, especially if, to quote her, "nothing was going on"? If nothing was going on, they should be talking downstairs, and they could have talked in the car on the way to buy my so-called special present. If this little surprise was my present, I did not like it, and I wanted to return it. Prin-cess said she thought I might not trust them, which is why the doors were locked. No kidding!

After hours of fighting and carrying on, they convinced me that everything was okay. I tried very hard to convince myself that I was convinced, and I continued that process for some time. I think I knew the truth in my heart.

NotSo asked me if they could go shopping the next night because it was so important to her to have this gift for me. Of course, I caved in as always because of wanting to please them and keep the friendship and marriage alive. Look where that stupid move got me this time. It hurts so very much because I know I was suckered—what a turkey!

Looking back, I remembered another little hint that we will call denial number 2. Everyone likes some kind of jewelry. I know NotSo did, and evidently, so did Charm because he bought her a one-hundred-fifty-dollar necklace. I found the receipt for this one-hundred-fifty-dollar necklace at her house. A funny thing—the receipt was signed by the man of charm. Hmmm ... of course, I questioned this act of generosity on his part, thinking if you are buying for her, what about your wife in waiting, you know the one on the marriage license, the one that has been here for twenty-five years. I did not say all that, but I was thinking it. Would you like to hear the explanation for this? "I wanted her to have something special from me. You have a lot of things from me." He responded like that should make perfectly good sense to me. Not! I felt like maybe if he had nothing to hide, he could have bought two seventy-five-dollar necklaces, but even with that equal treatment, so to speak, I knew it was not right.

Don't worry, readers, I know I was just in denial and being too condescending. NotSo said she thought I might be upset if I knew he bought it, so she did not tell me. Really? What could make her think that? Maybe that it was wrong on both of their parts? His giving and her taking? To my knowledge, I had not seen the necklace, but I had previously inquired about one I have seen her wearing often, and she told me it came from QVC.

Since I have not had the chance to view the item of jewelry, I cannot describe it to you. I do hope it is a "choke-her." Confucius says, "If you have to hide it, you are guilty as hell."

Reflecting again on this trust—we could discuss the subject of the car armrest, which would be denial number 3. Here is a real dilemma: a couple of times, Missy Prin-cess went with Charm to take Kimberly back to college because I was teaching and could not go at the time he wanted to depart. You know it was what he wanted when he wanted. He would have only had to wait an hour on me. Gee, I think I get it now! Her school is such a huge distance away; I can make it between thirty-five and forty-five minutes. The reason NotSo rode with him was because he was very tired, and the weather was not great. She was so very concerned that he would fall asleep at the wheel. These last seven weeks, I have taken Kimberly back and forth to and from school after endless nights without sleep and on snowy evenings, and no one worried about me falling asleep. The two times they took Kimberly back to school, I found the armrest in the middle of my front seat up as opposed to down, the position I always kept it in, and I can't remember why they had to take my car. I guess they had a lie for that as well. I questioned that armrest position, and they said they did not move it. I questioned NotSo if she was sitting next to Charm, and she said she would not do that. I am such a trusting person, but I don't believe that story at all. I am catching on.

How about those birth control pills? This is an interesting subject. I hope they will get a kick out of it—literally. It is a whopper of a story and another denial for me. I have lost count. The doctor put NotSo on birth control pills because of very irregular periods, which she did have. Supposedly, they were a very low dosage used as hormones. It is possible, and I am not at all saying this was a lie; however, it is kind of funny to think of what other uses there are for these secret pills:

1) They help you learn to count to twenty-eight.

2) They teach you to distinguish between two different colors! If you're color-blind, you just have to count to twenty-one, and then the color changes.

3) They give you four chances to brush up on your abbreviations for the days of the week.

4) They also teach you responsibility because if you miss one—oops! There is no going back.

Next on the agenda is the note from NSM to Charming that I found. The denials just keep on coming. I was going for a mammogram (which is another story), and I needed the insurance card. I had asked Charm to lay it out for me, but he didn't. About midnight or one o'clock in the morning, I remembered it, got out of bed, and went to his wallet to get it. I felt comfortable doing this because he had me do it in the past. When I opened his wallet, there was a yellow piece of paper in the front slot that had very familiar handwriting on it. I am sure by now you have guessed who it was from … uh-huh— NotSo Much. I had to read it. I had been suspicious at this point. I cannot remember in detail what it said, but in general, it said, "Thank you for a wonderful weekend. I had a great time, and especially for last night."

So what was last night? When asked, they could somehow not remember. Are we surprised? I guess they are not blessed with good memories. Well, they remembered who I was that night. I went to the phone, called NotSo, and told her to get to my house right now. Then I started packing suitcases—mine, which were the wrong ones to pack. When she got there, I let her in and then went in and woke up Charm. He was sleeping in the other room because he was sick with a cold and had been coughing a lot. This was the first time in twenty-five years of marriage that he ever offered to go to another room; I always had to be the one to move. I told him to get out of bed and come in the other room. Un-Charm was asking me why I was packing, and I believe I said something similar to "I have had it with the lies and deceit. I cannot stand it any longer." She said, "Why would you leave your home? He should leave!" She said this so emphatically I now feel that what they wanted me to do was kick him out. How perfect for the two of them. (Note: She probably would have done what I am guessing she has been doing all along, telling her family that I kicked him out, and she is trying to help him. Wait till they read this. I might just send them a free postage-paid auto-graphed copy. I have had many volunteers that would like to go tell her parents the truth. They would fight over the chance.)

I got the note out of his wallet and read it out loud to them. I forgot what else was in the note, but it also included some kind of love like "Love, Prin-cess NotSo Much" with her cute little smiley face she always used. The excuse—and boy, there are many—was she did not remember when she had written it, so she certainly did not know why she had said, "especially last night," to quote her liter-ary genius. There goes her memory again. According to her, she just wrote a note to him, like she has sent me cards. Nothing was meant by it. She just had probably had a nice weekend, and he treated her nice, probably nicer than he treated me. They just could not seem to remember when this note was written or what it was about. Must have been pretty important for him to keep it in his wallet.

Now most of you at this point are saying, "How dumb can this woman be? This is right under her nose, and she keeps ignoring the signs." Not so much. . . they always talked me out of it, and I guess I did not want to believe it at all, but my heart was trying to tell me. My heart hurt more than I ever realized.

Now it is time to clue you in on the mammogram story. Before all of this took place, I had a mammogram come back showing a lump in my breast. Well, of course, stupid me, where else do they do mam-mograms other than the breast! Charm seemed to be upset. I think it was genuine, but I am no longer sure about anything. It was right before Christmas, so we had to go through the holidays wondering. I went for follow-up tests, and Charm insisted on going with me.

NotSo wanted to go as well, but she said she had patients scheduled and was unable to do so. I think she truly was sorry that she could not be there, but at this point, I just can't be sure anymore. I think she really did care then, and so did Charm—another denial on my part, I am sure. As it turned out, it was just a cyst and no problem.

The following December, it was NotSo's turn. She had a lump. She was able to get back in for the other testing before the holiday and did not have to go through Christmas not knowing. Charm asked if I was going to go with her, and I said absolutely, and he said he wanted to be there also. Denial number? What was I supposed to say and I have to say, I thought it to be a little odd. He picked her up at work on his way there, and I met them in the parking lot. I tried to be brave about him being there, but quite honestly, I did not like it one bit! I should have known right then and there, but this was the first of the many denials. My heart ached, and promises were broken as time went on.

Prin-cess was okay; the tests were fine, and that was great. But my heart broke in the parking lot when they got in his truck to go back to work, so I was to believe, and I got in my car and drove away by myself. Things just did not feel right. He was a little too concerned. While NotSo was having her test, he continually asked me questions about the tests. I felt very uncomfortable at the time. I remember it like she was his concern, and I was an innocent fifth wheel. All I know is it was a gut-wrenching hurt, and I tried very hard not to let it do so.

There were so many other things that I now see since I have a clear head. I can see things for what they were. The one day we were at the mall, NotSo and the Man of Charm said they needed to buy me something, so I was to go wait in the car. They really did buy me something. But I did not go to the car as they had requested and expected. Good thing I didn't as they were gone for more than thirty minutes. It would have been pretty cold.

I was looking at puppies. I stood where I could catch them coming up the mall so I could show NotSo a puppy. And catch them I did—walking, talking, smiling, and holding hands. Ready for this explanation from Charm? "I hold both of your hands, but I had just reached down and grabbed her hand because of something she said." So I figured she probably said or sang something like, "I want to hold your hand."

I asked, "And what if someone we knew had seen you?" His reply, "We did not see anyone we knew." Like they would possibly be aware of someone we knew. They were totally oblivious to everyone and everything around them. They were in their own little world. I, on the other hand, was just looking at puppies and was letting the world go on around me. However, I was the one that lost this battle because I took the verbal abuse of being accused of spying on them and not trusting them. What kind of person treats their wife and friend like that—go to the car in the snow and cold and wait.

So those are things that have happened, but this is where you want to duck because this is the clincher. I have told you how the man of charm never supported anything I did. Well, I was director of a music school, and I held a holiday music recital for students of the school. I was able to use a community room at a nearby senior living facility. The manager of the store came and dropped off music stands and equipment. I had asked Charm to come to the event, and he did drop me off at the back entrance, but he would not attend as he said he and NotSo were going shopping for my Christmas present. Don't you see a pattern here? I told him when to come back to get me. The manager came back and picked up the equipment and left. I ended up there alone at the very dark back door. Once I left to see if Charm was there yet, I was locked out. It was cold and snowy and very windy. I waited and waited, and there was no charming prince.

I finally decided to walk to try to warm up, and it was a very long walk up the driveway to the main road. I kept walking, thinking soon he would come down the driveway toward me. I got all the way to the main road, and still, there was no Charming. He was at least an hour late. I thought about starting to walk home while I was standing behind a big dumpster to try to stay out of the wind and blowing snow. It was a good hour and a half after the time he was to be there to get me. When I got in the car, NotSo was with him, and she was laughing, saying I should be really mad at him for leaving me out in the cold. I was not laughing.

Cutting to the chase, I finally figured out later when I found blood on my pillow case that they had been in my bed and must have fallen asleep. The blood was from the NotSo Charming's cut finger. The reason he offered to take me and pick me up—he had control, and I could not walk in on them. I so wish I would have walked home!

Denial was a big part of my life back then. Would it had made a difference if I put my foot down and dumped her? Or him? I don't think so. Things worked out like they were meant to be, but it was so painful.

CHAPTER 21

The Battle Begins
or
I Ain't Dead Yet!

I know you will not believe this, but at one time in my life, I told the dastardly duo that if anything ever happened to me, they should take care of each other. I said if they would be happy together, they should not feel guilty.

I guess, they did not get it. I did not mean that I approved of it while I was alive and well! I think they must have misunderstood. Did they know something that I did not know? Was I dying, or did I just look dead? Did I need more sun and a makeover? My heart might have been dead, but I was still walking erect on this earth. I do not understand why they did this.

Doesn't it make you wonder how they can trust each other after all the cock and bull stories told?

Charming had already told me things that were not true about Un-Charming, and I am sure he told her things that were not true about me. I know him; he did what he wanted to do with no one else but himself in mind. Of all people, NotSo should have known how capable he is of changing the truth to get what he wants. Did either of them have any compassion at all? I can't help but wonder why they treated me so cruelly. I think it is something I will never forget.

The first week that he left, before I knew the whole story, multiple times Charm told me, "I will always love you and take care of you the rest of my life. Even if it means living at my mother's forever. I could never hate you, and we can be friends."

Did he honestly think that we could all be friends? He walked away with my friend, and my friend walked away with my husband of many years, and we are going to be friends? I really did not think a friendship could happen when they were treating me like he hated me.

He did not act like he wanted to be friends as the battle began. You remember the person that was always going to love and take care of me? He did not exist. Once it came time to make financial arrangements, he made a very small financial offer, saying that I could give music lessons in the evenings for additional income. Where had he been for the last ten years? Could he not remember that I had two jaw surgeries and was not able to play the musical instruments? The doctor said it would be best if I did not play at all.

Also, after the muscles in my face had been cut twice, I could not play well enough to help the students. I had a good group of students before the surgeries. After I found out I was not to play any longer, I began giving the students the option to sign up with other teachers because I would have to give up the teaching, but they all chose to stay with me.

Of course, it is possible to teach without playing, but it just is not the same. If you cannot demonstrate how it is to be done, how it is to sound, it makes it more difficult to learn. I knew that through having a teacher that never picked up the trumpet.

I began to think—why should I take this extra job and work evenings because he chose to run away from home? If he wanted to play, he should pay. I spent nineteen years working evenings and finally no longer had to. He should support me, and if he needed to work extra, he could work evenings. He made the choice—not me. He walked out on the responsibilities—the children, the house, and everything. He took what he wanted and booked!

What is it they say, "What goes around comes around"? Many times, over the years, Charm said that people get theirs in the long run. Well, look out, when the long run runs out, it's your turn, buddy.

As things continued, I realized I did not need to say anything to either one of the perpetrators. They had slipped up telling their stories so many times that they have hung themselves.

These perps also had the audacity to show up in church together. I am sure they do not realize how close I came to being there with Kimberly. She would have been devastated. There would have been a double sacrifice on the altar if she had seen them.

Where do they get off being so cruel? The only thing that comes to my mind is the guilt they live with must cause them to treat people so cruelly.

I have done nothing but show love. I respected their wishes for space and time. What I have to say to them is that they are so chicken they could not even come face-to-face with me and let me know how they came to this decision and how they think it is right.

To NotSo, I would have said that I saw a very nasty side of her. I mistakenly felt that she was incapable of acting and doing the things she had done. Where did it come from? She had told me how cruel she had been to her mother as a teenager. But at her current older, more mature age, was that cruelty coming back? Was she regressing? They both had cocky attitudes and were mistreating others. I am sure that they both could give lessons on cruelty and insensitivity.

One night, in a conversation with Charming, he informed me that I did not realize the amount of offers he has had over the years from women, so he would not have a problem finding someone. Gag!

It absolutely amazes me that he can go around town and flaunt his infidelity like there is nothing wrong with what he has done. How does he go places where we had been together and live with the memories? He must remember me. I am the one that he used to tease about the serious face I made when I would drive a golf ball. How could he forget that he always said that was so cute? Does it not hurt him? What does he feel? Is it the excitement of doing something and getting away with it? Someday, it will all catch up with them; the guilt will be unbearable. Especially for NotSo Charming. She always portrayed having such a strong belief in God and Christianity. It is time for them to feel guilty because I am not dead! Maybe my heart is, but not until they double dumped me. They keep kicking me while I am down, and I continue to lay down and take it.

I have made up my mind that I need to sit back and let God do his work, and I will rebuild my life.

CHAPTER 22

In Crisis, I Turned to Those from Happy Days
or
No, Not Ritchie and Potsie

I thought I had been so happy these last couple of years. It also appeared that way to others, so I was told on several occasions. "So what do I do now?" As my heart was in pain, I found myself returning to those that were in my life at a happier time. It is a very strange sensation—something I did totally involuntarily. As I look back now at the years when I played on my first soccer team, I realized at that point I had regained some of the real me. It was quite a group, but over time, we had lost sight of what we had. It was camaraderie. We should have never allowed it to die. Maybe we were beyond playing for the World Cup, but there were other ways we could have remained a team.

I regret not having my soccer friends around. The crisis I am going through is not the reason I feel this way. I have often missed those days. Not only was it great because of those friendships, but it was a good time. I was very secure, and some of what I felt was my real self had come back. I realize now that it has been the loss of that team spirit that has also attributed to the loss of myself and lack of self-worth.

Was it my fault that I did not do something to keep the soccer team camaraderie alive? For once in life, I will say, "No." However, maybe I could have done something about it and did not make a good enough effort—I am not sure. That saddens me because I truly have felt a loss over the years. I want to make the effort to regain that life. I feel I am not the only one who has missed teammates. It was such a sense of completeness for me, and I see it as the time of my life that I had a lot of best friends. No one, other than Charm Man, controlled my life at that point in time. I had fun with many different kinds of people. The neat thing is ... they all were very good people in their own ways. You know, they are soccer legends in their own minds!

What changed these times is a combination of things. Many people went back to work or to working more hours. That was caused by our children getting older. Our children's involvement in activities changed, which caused us to go in different directions. The kids began to go off to college. We were getting older, and the muscles were not so muscular anymore. Most of us lived in a time when there were no high school sports for the "girls," so this was a time to do something we missed out on. It was not playing the sport that was important or that we had missed out in school. It was the team bond. What an unbelievable time we had together. A group made up of all types from all walks of life with all different personalities. We blended and had a great time. I brought soccer people together with my close friends from other parts of life, and it was great.

I think that the prin-cess and her negative and critical nature had something to do with taking me away from the team. I did not see things in this light until recently, and I am continually discovering how I was used at the time, intentional or not. I think NotSo and Charm's critical natures did not allow for me to be myself. NotSo would criticize those on the team and tell me stories that I now know was to pull me away from the team friends because of her guilt of what she was doing behind my back. The real me became buried further and further deep inside of myself.

Now that I see things for what they were, I promised myself I was never going to become so attached to a friend that I could not have other friends. I think that is what NotSo wanted. I am much more aware of being controlled and live a freer life now.

Even though prin-cess was the needier person, the one I jumped in to help, she controlled me. I know that now. I don't know why I was so drawn to helping her; it must have been those lifesaving courses I took as a teenager. When I see someone drowning, I jump in and save them. The only thing is … I am the one drowning in the tidal wave they have caused in my life. Throw me a life preserver; that tidal wave took me under.

Something really interesting hit me as I was sitting here typing. The first time Cess ever got mad at me that I knew of was on a soccer trip to Lake Erie. We had a fun day and spent the night at one of our teammates house by the lake. In the evening when everyone was getting into bed, I made a big mistake of being myself, and I got into trouble. It is funny how much this hurts now that I look back on it sometime later.

I was joking around and could not stop laughing. Everyone else was laughing at and with me, but the prin-cess got mad. I was just totally heartbroken. I remember I was awake all night because I had upset her and had no idea why until the next day. It really hurt. I knew she was mad, but why? I realize she was upset because I would not "settle down." That is where the controlling must have kicked in and taken over. From now on, I can laugh as long and as hard as I want. She will not be there to control me.

I remember a conversation I had with her as our friendship was beginning. I told her how happy I was with my friendships, and I was not taking care of anyone any longer. It was a pressure that had been lifted from me, and I never wanted to be there again. As you know, I was there again.

As our friendship continued, I made a comment that it was hard for me to get attached because I did not want to make my heart accessible to anyone because of the pain. Her comment to me—"Are you ready for this one?" She said, "You don't have to worry about me. I would never hurt you." Hmmm … so just what do you call living with my husband and dumping me? If that is not hurt, please get me a dictionary to find the correct definition. There was so much good in this friendship; I was blinded by the neediness. It suckered me right in. I got caught up in the proverbial web. The thing is she gave back to me in our friendship, so I thought it was all genuine. I am not sure, and I will never know if any of her friendship was real.

It amazes me as to how others saw our friendship. The first response from others is "She did this to you after all you did for her?" I was surprised that people saw that. I must have been in "another world," or maybe this just is a soap opera.

Cess was smart enough to use the rescue gene in me to get what she wanted. So all the promises go down the drain, and off she goes taking my husband and my heart with her. I never had so much trust in anyone as I did the two of them. How do you trust and release your heart to someone ever again? I hope that they have not taken away my ability for unconditional love for people.

So what do you do when the tidal wave clears and you have been swept ashore and left out to dry? You go back to your "happy days."

I have never experienced the feelings I now have ever before. I do not understand where I received the strength to sit in front of these soccer friends and tell them my situation. It took all the courage and stamina I could draw from inside of myself. I never cry in front of people, but I have cried like a baby writing this chapter.

All the promises, the future plans (anyone want to retire to Las Vegas with me?), the love I thought I had, and the trust I strongly relied on have all been taken away. So I rebuild. The soccer girls are a part of the bricks I need to build my life once again.

We all suffer disappointments and losses. We need one another. After all, as Barbara would say, "People, people who need people, are the luckiest people."

We all need those getaway weekends with friends like the one to Lake Erie. It does us a world of good. Maybe it is time for a reunion trip. It is too bad that it took something this devastating to get me to revitalize these friendships. I should have never let the distance come between us. I am just thankful that I have been able to keep my head above water through this, and I can maybe regain a life.

All I need to do is settle things with his attorney, and they will be ecstatically happy. Or will they? It is time to find the other side of me. The one that has been stifled so long by two negative, critical people that took control over my life without me even realizing it. I adapted to everything they wanted me to be—including "out of the picture."

I apologize that this has not been a very lighthearted chapter, but my heart is not very light tonight. Every waking hour I have, I realize another part of me that has been taken away or another lie I have been told. The cruelty that has transpired over the months is just now coming into focus for me, and it hurts like hell. I will now watch my back—help others but never rescue. That is what I have started doing.

Just sayin'—That this has been an awful time for everyone involved, but I am not so sure anyone really understands the extent of my pain. I have ended up with nothing. I struggle with the problem of how I should react to this hand I have been dealt. A few fun ideas come to mind:

Murder—that is pretty heavy duty, and death row is not exactly the Hilton. Being locked up, you can't enjoy the fact that the "perps" are out of the picture. But you do get three squares a day, free education, and medical. And making license plates can't be that difficult.

Dog and cat—a lesser crime would be gathering the neighborhood dog and cat dodo, letting it sit in the sun and rain, then put it in a bag, and put it in their cars—on a nice hot August day.

> Tailpipes—could be stuffed with bananas.
>
> Insurance—leaving messages at all the local insurance agencies with their names and numbers and the need for a lot of new insurance. Better yet, how about leaving their names with the local real estate offices about buying a house. Just think of all the calls they would receive.
>
> Stealing—I could go steal him back, right out from under her nose. But really, who wants damaged, used merchandise?
>
> I would not execute any of the above ideas, but it does relieve a little stress to think and laugh about them— *just sayin'*.

CHAPTER 23

The First Flight
or
On My Flight, There Was No Mr. Right or Even Mr. Left

I found myself on a flight to Baltimore not long after the curtain fell on my life as I knew it. Why Baltimore? It is where my brother Mark, sister-in-law Karen, and nephews David and Stephen live. It was the first time I had flown alone, and it was not without its challenges. I was experienced at the friendly skies, but I've always traveled with my husband and family. Now I am alone, and that is challenging me to keep a happy attitude.

It would not have bothered me to fly alone if it were not for the events of the last weeks. Just seven weeks ago, I was leaving on a jet plane with Charm and NotSo headed to Reno, for what sounded like a fun time, and that ended with me losing my heart in San Francisco. I felt alone—well, there were many people at the airport, but I felt like a quarantined island among the action.

This day was also supposed to be the day that the prince, princess, and I were to fly to North Carolina to meet up with others for a golf vacation. Here I sit wondering if they went without me. How would they explain that one?

As I sat waiting for my plane, I realized that I was at the gate where Kimberly, NotSo, her kids, and I sat waiting for a plane to Chicago last May. That realization added salt to my open wounds.

NotSo and I always had fun visiting family and traveling. Looks like that is over since the man of charm became so charming to her. As I allowed myself to go to the darker side of all of this, I wondered if I would ever travel anywhere or even have fun ever again, but I felt God had a plan for me. At that point, I heard the call for boarding my flight. I jumped up and got in the line to board. As I entered through the plane door, I watched for my seat number. I walked and walked and looked and looked, only to find I was in the very last row of this big orange and tan bird.

As I was walking down the aisle of the plane, I thought maybe this was going to be one of those stories where a brokenhearted woman meets Mr. Right on a flight. You have seen it in the movies. She sits there alone, and there is one seat left on the plane, right next to her. A handsome man of the unmarried variety says, "Excuse me, I believe this is my seat." It is love at first sight.

You could imagine my shock when I was done thinking about the handsome stranger and the lonely downtrodden women from the movies to see I was in the middle seat between ... well, uhh, there is no other way to put it than to say, "two old ugly dudes"—*just sayin'*.

I climbed over the one in the aisle seat and forced my not-so-small body between their even bigger not-so-small bodies with my carry-on tightly clenched between my fingers. On top of this special moment, it was very windy outside, and the captain said we were in for a very bumpy ride—ah, really? He should see things from where I was sitting.

I reached in my purse, pulled out my gray elastic motion sickness bands that usually kept me from getting sick, and hoped they were going to work on this flight. If they don't work, one or both of the dudes might be wearing my snack.

So there I was, one dude with a ponytail, earring, and something growing on his face—or left over from breakfast; I was not sure which. The other one—well, it was hard to tell what he had for breakfast because his leftovers were hidden by his unkempt long beard, and as I turned to look out the window, I noticed the hair in his ears was growing to meet the beard. He smelled slightly of what I thought might have been old french fries. I was stuck for the next hour or so with my arms pushed into my sides as the men hogged the armrests and were hanging over on my side in more ways than one.

My shoulders slumped. I moved my feet to find a place to put them since they both had a foot in front of my seat and thought, *There is no Mr. Right here for me, just Mr. Leftover.* I tried to look to the positive as I did have another chance on the flight home.

As we were taking off and banked left, I could sneak a peek past the ponytail man and saw Kimberly's college. The institute of higher learning, just a few miles from the airport. It made me sad, but every time I would conquer a sadness, I knew I was getting stronger. I knew I was stronger than Charm or Un-Charming as I really could not find guilt on my side. I took new and improved steps every day. Oh, it was bad, but I had to deal with the hand that was dealt to me; I learned that in Reno.

The flight was tossing us around, and I fought not to be tossed into Mr. Right and Mr. Leftover and to keep from tossing my cookies on them. As things got a little rougher in the air, there was one bright spot; right in front of me was a nun. If the plane made a sudden nosedive, I would grab on to Sister Mary Katherine and hold on tight. Certainly, God would save her and anything hanging onto her.

I had a feeling this whole disturbing domestic disaster (DDD) would take a very long time to work out and come to a close. I was so thankful for the people I have around me—in my life, not necessarily at this moment!

As things smoothed out in the air, the curly ponytail dude was sleeping, and his leg kept falling against mine. Ugh, I had nowhere to put my leg so he was not touching me. If I tried to move away, his leg followed mine. I wondered if he was really sleeping!

It was here I made a deal with God: if something happened on the plane, like a hole in the side, if he would suck Mr. Left out and leave me, I would save Sister Mary Katherine.

Trying to keep my mind off the stereo snoring I had in my ears from the dudes, I let my mind wander. I try to use humor to get through every day. Just a couple of days before my flight, I had dinner with a few friends. One of the friends had not heard about my DDD. She was just informed before I arrived at the restaurant. No one said a word about my DDD until she could not take it any longer and asked what was going on. I said that Charm had left and just walked out on me, and at first, I had no idea if NotSo was involved. She listened, but before I could finish, she blurted out—and rather loudly—"Yep, he is screwing her." Well, everyone at the table became silent, except for those coughing as they choked on their refried beans and snorted Coke (as in cola) out of their noses at this shocking statement. They all looked at me, waiting for my reaction. I simply said, "Actually, I am the one getting screwed, but I guess that is all in the interpretation." They all then realized they could laugh. Although I was shocked at her honesty, it is the best policy.

Back on the plane, I was brought out of my reflective state when Mr. Right's hand fell in my lap. Ewww, fortunately, the male flight attendant woke them both up, asking if they wanted something to drink or a snack. They both got a drink. I asked for a Coke and said, "Do you have nuts?" Well, that brought attention to me as the flight attendant threw his hands out in the air and thrust his pelvis toward me and said, "What do you think?" The two men just looked at me. I was so embarrassed, but I have to admit, I got a real chuckle at Sister Mary Katherine's shoulders shaking from laughter at the situation.

I must tell you Mr. Right and Mr. Left did not go back to sleep after that, and soon I heard the landing gear go down. I could not wait to get off that plane. Within a short time, I was safely in Mark's car headed to their house for a little R and R.

The next day, we went to watch my nephews play soccer, as you know, one of my favorite games. I was excited to finally be able to be involved in something they were doing. NotSo and I had planned to come watch them play someday. Well, that day was here, but she was not. I was still wondering if they were in NC.

After the soccer, we came back to the house. And Mark, Karen, and I fertilized the yard. I began to feel better. We ordered pizza and went to Saturday night church. They attended a small country church. It had only nine pews on either side. It was about the size of most dining rooms in a fast food restaurant. The service was informal; in fact, I had to laugh when it came time for communion. The priest poured the wine in the beautiful silver chalice and prepared the silver plate for the communion wafers. I looked up to see him with a yellow margarine container in his hand. I asked myself if they put butter on the wafers, or if this was the pancake breakfast. However, he reached his hand in the container and pulled out the wafers and arranged them on the plate—whatever melts your butter. It proved that God can be worshiped by anyone in many ways. God does not care if there is margarine in the container or a crown on your head (Those of you that are old enough to remember the Imperial margarine commercial just got that).

Some may think your clothes or hairdo are important, but God is only interested in your pure and loving heart.

I continued with emotional highs and lows, as they are unbelievable in this life situation. The hurt is so painful, the loss so very devastating, the fear so haunting, and the sadness so terrifying. I often wonder what Un-Charm and Charm feel. I think the man of charm is elated because he is so physically enamored with NSM. I just cannot understand NSM and her ability to do this. I cannot imagine the guilt she must be living with every day.

I wrote last night till I was ready to sleep, and I woke up early and was unable to stop my mind from wandering into unhappy territory. My mind just races from one thought to another, always recreating the past situations to give me a clue as to what my future holds; only God knows that. Sometimes I find myself so very discouraged and frustrated with the unknown. My only hope each day is that I get another little piece of the puzzle solved of the unknown life I now live.

My Maryland side of the family and I had a very nice day. We took a trip to Frederick for an early dinner at a great restaurant and then took my nephew to symphony practice, dropping him off at a gorgeous old church. We walked around town while he was at practice. The town was very unique, and I think NotSo and Charm would really enjoy this. Who am I kidding? Charm would hate it, and why am I allowing myself to even go there? I know that I will never be traveling with either one of them again.

I found myself back at the Baltimore Washington airport, alone and confused. I have learned by this experience that I can manage by myself. Maybe that is the whole idea of this new life I have been thrown into. I will learn so much, and my hope is that I become a much stronger person. Charm has made it very clear he will never be back or want anything to do with me. I have been parked in the used-car lot of life, and I think I have been sold out.

I had my leftover dinner packed in my carry-on, and I thought for sure that I would set off the metal detectors with all this aluminum foil it is wrapped in. Sitting at the airport gate, I was daydreaming. *Maybe Mr. Right will be on this plane, and the saga will continue.* I scanned the fellow passengers, and to tell you the truth, things were not looking up. My flight was running late. I tried to call my parents from a pay phone—no cell phone. They were picking me up at the airport. They were going to keep circling around until I came out, but they had already left for the airport. All I could do was hope they had a full tank of gas.

On the plane, things went smoother than the ride to Maryland. I had a seat all to myself, so I could get my pen out and write. However, some of the crew was the same. Especially one flight attendant. It was best that I hid from him and didn't ask for nuts. But sitting across from me was Sister Mary Katherine. She must have recognized me because after the snacks were passed out, she looked over at me and handed me her peanuts.

CHAPTER 24

We Did Not Do a Thing Until
I Left Your Mother
or
Bet Me, Buckwheat

What an interesting concept, Charm Man tells our daughters that he and NotSo Charming Woman have done nothing, if you get my drift. Yes, this is correct. You are not misreading the words on this page. They have done nothing. Well, that is nothing until "I left your mother."

You know that would be me. Well, now we all know this makes everything all right. I feel a lot better now about all this, don't all of you? I mean let's admit it, we could all be wrong. Bet me, Buckwheat! "Until" is the important word in the paragraph at this time.

So these two free-spirited, do-as-we-please people desert me, basically told me to take a long walk off a short pier, and the fact that they are saying they never did anything until the man of charm left me certainly makes everything all right. Everything is fine now. I might as well make this my last chapter and go on with my life. No more pain, no more hurt, no more tears, no more fear. I can just be happy now. Bet me, Buckwheat!

First of all, we all know that this is just one of those little tiny— what would you say, maybe you could call it a *lie*.

My attorney called today with a report from Charm's attorney. It never ceases to amaze me how someone hires some expensive attorney to help him and then lies to him. But, of course, not a whole lot does seem to make sense in this situation. His attorney told my attorney that he is trying to slow Charming down and make him understand he needs to give me a little healing space here. Charm tells him I do not need it. I have known about them for a long time. I thought I just understood that basically nothing was happening until "I left your mother!" I get so darn confused through all of this. I mean things change so rapidly. Am I just a little slow on the uptake here?

Why would I need some time to get over this shock? Go ahead kick me. I deserve it! My attorney very kindly proceeded to tell him that while I did have some suspicions, they were quickly denied and that I was told on many occasions that absolutely nothing, zip, zero, nada was happening. Now, all of a sudden, I have known for some time that they were together? You know it is strictly whatever is convenient at the time for him. Right now, it is convenient I have known for a long time. What is a long time? Two days, two weeks, two months? After all, that was the possible time frame he would be leaving for, you know, to think and "take charge of his own life." He was coming back, after the thinking process.

Because it is currently after midnight, it has officially been fourteen weeks, not fourteen days or fourteen months, since he left, and he was now planning on being gone for a lifetime. My attorney told his lawman that I could not even concentrate on making a decision on finances until the present past due bills were paid for and I could have some money to live on. He wanted to approach Mr. Charm one more time to handle these things instead of going into court. I guess we will find out his reaction, or actually, it will probably be NotSo's reaction, and I am sure he'll ask her what he should do next.

The man of charm feels that I should change jobs, make more money, and take care of myself with no help from him. He has decided to take another road in life and leave me at the dead end to fend for myself. Seems like I have emotionally supported him for many a year even when he has gone down the wrong road. I never left him at the dead end alone and unwanted. He feels I can get a secretarial job and make eighteen thousand dollars to twenty-four thousand dollars a year. The only thing about this is I have no secretarial skills. I am not sure where he came up with this one. But I figure it was because I was a so-called secretary at the company where he works. You know, where we met.

The funny thing is my skills consisted of answering the phone, taking messages, helping with sketching in toilets, doors, windows, sinks, etc. on blueprints for homes and going to lunch. I think they probably don't pay that kind of money for drawing toilets, maybe cleaning them! I probably am not qualified for that. He is still trying to take charge of his life and is still controlling mine from a longer distance. I have the answer to solve this problem. He says the secretaries at his company make that much, so I will go down and apply for a job at his company.

What I do not really fathom here is the concept of why he is in such a hurry. He has everything he wants and without obligation. Oh no, maybe she is pregnant with those twins I have had everyone hexing them with. Maybe the lemons are working. I was told that you are supposed to take a lemon, cut it in half, write the name of the person who has scorned you on a piece of paper, put it in the middle of the lemon, wrap it in foil, hide it in your fridge, and forget about it. Whatever that person does to you will come back at them. Yes! Probably not, but here is hoping. The therapy of all this could even be better that when you just are so angry at a person, you could go to the fridge accidentally on purpose and drop the lemon on its head on the hard floor, and you will feel better.

So now that you all put the book down, ran to the fridge, cut your lemons, added the name and wrapped them, and then dropped them on the way back to their safe little fridge space, maybe now I could continue with my story.

What reasons can we possibly think of that he would want this over so quickly? Maybe he wants to marry her, but my guess is she is very impatiently waiting and wanting this over. She does not like living like this, and maybe the whole community will not know what she has done if it is over soon. Too late, they know. They also joined the church—together. Is that not the sweetest thing you ever did hear?

I mean what a loser I was. I could hardly get the man to church, and now he has joined. With her. He probably thought it would help since Kimberly told him they would be going to hell for breaking some of the top ten! He has a roof over his head, someone to wait on him hand and "hoof," meals cooked, even though he never liked her cooking. He has lost weight; he gained plenty with my cooking. I am sure that he can have the remote for the TV anytime his little heart desires; he is in channel surfing heaven! What more could a man ask for? You know that saying, "If you get the milk for free, why buy the cow?"

NotSo probably even let him watch the basketball playoffs. I did not see them. I was writing to relieve the stress and tension of real life since I do not belong in his little fantasy world. I will soon be writing again to let you know if I am allowed to have a little time to "get a grip" or if I had to face up to life and go on at his command like always. After all, he informed his attorney he did not want me to get any money now because I would get used to it and expect it in the final part of this "divorce" according to Mr. Charm. Oh no, I expect nothing after twenty-five years of devoted service, your lordship. Just show me the money. You do have to pay to play.

CHAPTER 25

They Get Happiness
or
I Get a Month-long Period

I just cannot win for losing as they say. This is the third time to write this chapter. I was on such a role, and I decided to listen to some Michael W. And I lost my chapter. As if that were not bad enough, I was at the end of the second attempt when my sister-in-law called, and while I was talking, my screen saver froze. And once again, I lost the entire document.

Here I sit, starting over at eleven thirty-five in the evening, and I have to go to work tomorrow. However, I cannot let this idea escape, so here I sit, trying again. The third time should be a "charm," as they say.

I have been the lucky recipient of a month-long period. The doctor says it is because of stress in my life. Really? Stress? According to the man of charm, I should just move on. After all, I have known about "them" for a long time.

So they are parading around town like the goose and the "goosett" that just laid the golden egg. I have this month-long period and everyone is saying, "Get a grip." Are things the way they appear? Are they happy? Will my period last for life? Will I "get a grip"? Tune in for the continuing saga of *As the World Tilts.*

I have the greatest faith that things are not always as they appear. First, Charm and Prin-cess cannot be as happy as maybe they think. There is a very long row to hoe ahead of them. All the financial end of this divorce, all the people they have to face ... it will eventually catch up with them. What happens when both their bad tempers flare at once, when the puppy love has turned to a lazy old dog. A lot of the passion is physical, and keep in mind that old saying, "The post will break off before the hole wears out." You know as in a fence. There is more than physical pleasure in life. You even get tired of chocolate after a while ... well, maybe not so much.

Imagine, if you will, a place in time, when two people sneak around, lie, and cheat for passion. Then suddenly, they do not need to sneak anymore. Ahhhh ... some of the thrill is gone. Then no one pays attention to them anymore. At this point, they sit in their chairs in their bathrobes, complete with holes under the arms, drink soda pop, watch TV, talk about the other people, and burp and release gaseous fumes. The excitement has depleted. The guilt is still there. So now they have entered *The Twilight Years*.

Charm and NSM are being blinded by love that they probably do not even realize what state they have left my life in. Of course, I know what you are thinking. They know exactly what they have done to me, and I am too blind to think that badly of them. You are probably right, but I have not gotten far enough along to realize it myself ... yet. Before I give them any more credit, I will just get on with my thoughts. This part only deals with NotSo and Charming and not any of my present life, my children, family, and friends.

Here is the way *I* see it. They have no concern for my feelings or what will happen to me—how I will live, pay the bills, where I will go. It was the old "Here is your hat, what is your hurry?" routine.

Summing it up and looking at what got me here:
I had unconditional love for these two people.
But I guess they forgot.
I tried so hard to be what they wanted me to be.
Out of the picture.
I allowed them to control my life.
They continue to do so from another zip code.

I tried to put their happiness before mine.
     I wanted them happy... guess they are!
I wanted to take care of them. I set a fine example.
     They are now taking care of each other.
I am very good at loving people, but I forgot one person, me!
     I start to work on that today. I don't ever want
to lose myself again.

Maybe life will not be all that it is cracked up to be, but maybe it will. What about me? Do I have an ongoing period for life? Does that mean that I will never be PMS-ed again? The perpetrators tell me I have to get a grip and move on as "I have only lost two people in my life; I have many others" according to them. After all, there was still a Lucy without Desi and Lewis without Martin. Can there be a me without a Charm and Prin-cess NotSo Much? Yes, but I need some time to adjust, heal, and be healthy again. They are doing "it." Whatever "it" is. Why not me? I can tell you why. I want to enter a relationship healthy so it lasts. Those two unhealthy people will have to overcome a lot. They have a lot of baggage, and they are not even going on a trip. What they have done to me is like losing a sock in the dryer. Just throw away the "odd" one.

In recent conversations with my daughters, I realize that Charm is lying to them. Why can't he just take the wrap and go on? Both girls have shown him that they can forgive and have a relationship with him. They do not like what he has done, but as I have stated previously, it is important to keep the lines of communications with your family open no matter what. Many feel guilty if someone dies and they have not forgiven the other person. Forgiveness may be there, but forgetting... not so much.

I don't understand the lies Charm has told the girls that he and NotSo did nothing until he left me. Like that makes it right? Not until the divorce documents are in hand and signed. Where does Charm think he is headed with these lies? Heaven?

I believe he is carrying the "Pinocchio" theory a "little" too far. The story goes that when Pinocchio told a lie, his nose would grow. Does he just want a bigger nose, or did he not catch what part grew in the story? It is the nose! The bigger the nose, the bigger the snore. Maybe the story was just referring to nose growth for "wooden dummies."

One of the most difficult things in this situation is the children. I have found that something like this is not any different when adult children are involved. In a recent conversation with Vicki, I found it somewhat disturbing but ended up making me feel better. I am starting to understand them not wanting to lose their father. It is tough for me to bear, considering the example he has set for them and the lies and deceit. I have recently learned that children of all ages tend to thrive on any attention the irresponsible parent will give them. The reason being they are not sure where they stand with that parent. On the other hand, they are very secure with the parent they live with or that has not been the one to leave. Makes perfect sense to me, but what I really see is he will show his real spots—someday.

Positives: I may shrink in size over the years, but at least, my nose is not growing. Menopause does eventually hit, and that long period will end. I am still here, and I will heal. God has something in mind for me when I am a healthy person again. I will stick with the big guy upstairs. I did take those marriage vows to heart, and I would have lived by them, but God does not hold us accountable for things out of our control.

CHAPTER 26

Rip Van Winkle Syndrome
or
There Is No Real June Cleaver

It is a rude awakening to find out you have what I am referring to as the "Rip Van Winkle syndrome." I feel like I have been asleep for the last twenty years, and someone just kicked me and said, "Wake up and get on with your life."

I realize how much of myself I have lost. I have been told that everyone around me over the last year or so felt that I have been happier than ever. Funny, so did I. Maybe I never realized what real happiness is, or my expectations are too Hallmark movie or TV oriented—you know, the "June Cleaver syndrome"? If you think about it, TV sometimes paints a pretty picture of life. Think about the Brady Bunch. Do you really know families that blended three boys and three girls in two bedrooms without more major problems than Marsha's pimples? It just does not happen. There are conflicts and sometimes major behavioral problems.

I was one of those "father knows best" daughters. I never got into trouble in school or did too many terrible things at home other than I had a messy room … you know, the "pig syndrome." I threw everything on the floor, bed, dresser, just wherever it landed. I am sure my mom was very frustrated. Her punishment for me for not keeping my room clean was to throw everything out of my bedroom window. I would open the window, throw everything out, close the window, put on my jacket, go outside, pick everything up, and bring it back in. Then . . . take my jacket off, open the window, throw everything out, close the window, put on my jacket; you certainly are getting the idea, and the repetition would continue. If I was missing anything, like my favorite blouse, I just had to go outside and look for it on the lawn.

Living outside the confines of not getting in serious trouble, I did not learn that we all make mistakes and we can learn from those mistakes. I did not learn from throwing my clothes out the window and picking them up repeatedly. I still have clothes on the floor occasionally—but my theory is I am the only one that has to pick them up. No one has to pick up after me. So I am not hurting anyone else!

Watching shows like *Roseanne* is a little different than watching the *Cleavers*. We never saw pregnancy, drugs, and kids talking back to their parents with June and Ward. Then we have *The Middle*; it is kind of in the middle of the *Cleavers* and *Roseanne*. The Hecks have problems but fit most of today's families a little closer in some ways. Maybe Roseanne Clever would be good. She could be the mother of two children, one boy and one girl, and she works as a secretary. The house would not always be perfect and the kids not so perfect. She might forget to buy the milk on the way home from the PTA meeting that she attended after working all day, cooking dinner, and dropping the kids at soccer practice. So the kids get dry cereal in the morning. This sounds somewhat like *The Middle*.

Oh well, back to reality. All I ever wanted was someone to care about me. We could do things together and enjoy life. I guess it would take a certain person to enjoy doing the things I like to do. Golf, soccer, tennis, woodworking, remodeling, music, plays, concerts, movies, hike, walk, trap shooting, vacations, cruises, Las Vegas, and many others.

So why do I allow people to walk on me? What is it with my personality that I feel I always have to be the one to make everyone else happy? Even "June" handled this better than me. Of course, June never took her apron off to fix the car. Maybe that is where I went wrong.

My counselor wants me to read a book. Yes, I know it is hard to believe. However, I am doing it. There are exercises to do. It is a workout book for your mind, not your body. The most recent requirement was to list positive and negative traits about myself. Then to have five other people to do the same about me. I was supposed to have at least two people that were to be intimate relationships, such as lovers or close friends. Hmmm ... do you think I could get Charm and NotSo to do it for me? Well, I didn't try. I went to my family and my friend of many years, Dee. I then had to compare their answers with mine. It amazed me how similar they all were, but I actually knew myself better than I thought. Both the positive and negative matched up. Some of the negative comments were:

Low self-esteem—Given the recent situation, that is to be expected.

Too sensitive—Okay, I am working on not letting things bother me so much.

People take advantage of her friendship—That has been proven. NotSo Much took advantage of that friendship. I would say she pretty much took everything. There goes my self-esteem.

She needs a buddy all the time to do things with—That ended fast. Now I can do things by myself. I was certainly taught a lesson.

Puts people on a pedestal and cannot see any wrong they do— Charm and NotSo were right up there on the highest pedestal. Wonder if it hurt them as much as it did me when the pedestal came crashing down to the ground. I didn't hear of any broken bones or anything, so it must not have hurt that bad. I guess they are floating on that cloud of love and didn't hit the ground as hard as I did.

Tries too hard to please others—I worked for years to please Charm and Prin-cess. Now you see how pleased they are!

Needs to have opinions—I certainly have some now, but I don't think I should express them in this primarily G-rated book.

Too dedicated to friends—This one I have a difficult time with.

I just do not understand. Why are these such bad qualities? Why is it so bad to be dedicated to your friends? How can you be too dedicated? I guess if you are too dedicated, you are also blind to what they are doing to you. I was so dedicated to helping NSM that sometimes I left my own family to help her. "Sometimes" is okay, but I think I helped too much—it is my nature. She certainly is not leaving her family or my husband to help me—she just helped herself to part of my family.

I allowed myself to give too much, and she allowed herself to steal everything I had to give. Then, all of a sudden, I am no longer good enough, and she is drawing her strength from Charm Man. Good luck to that!

So I understand what I do. I just do not always understand what is so wrong with it or how you can change your nature. I will work to correct these negative behaviors because I want a real relationship, not one where I am used or taken advantage of. Charm ran over me like a tank most of the time. Now he will leave his tread marks on NotSo, and I guess mine will fade someday. I can't allow this to happen to me ever again. A heart only takes so much before it gives out.

I was at the bank the other day, and the teller brought my paperwork back to the drive-thru window. She did not give me that usual "have a nice day" but said "you make a good day for yourself." That certainly hit home. It says a lot about life. We must make ourselves happy. No one else can do it for us. I need to be happy with myself, and then the rest will come in time.

CHAPTER 27

The Stages of Devastation
or
You've Come a Long Way, Baby

It has been more than three months after the perpetrators made their escape.

The time, when you think about it, is fairly short, but so much has occurred. And a lot of pain makes it seem so much longer than when life is cruising along. I have experienced so many changes just in myself, let alone in my life. I certainly have been taking a different path on the map of life. My brain functions are sometimes very scary as to how my thoughts have changed in this amount of time. I find there are so many things I can do now that I could not do in the earlier devastating weeks. I have moved to the level of not only being able to sweep my kitchen floor, but I actually scrub it. I have cooked a meal or two, nothing fancy mind you, but it ain't Spanish rice, which I had made a huge bowl of a few weeks ago and lived on it for well over a week before it got moldy and before I could manage to cook something else. I planted flowers around the yard and made a rock garden to build a strong foundation for my new life and not as a burial plot for the perpetrators. Here is a big one—I have moved my way up from just having conversations on the phone to carrying on a conversation in public with actual people. I went to a local restaurant without checking the parking lot to see if I recognized the perpetrators' cars. I can go out with people and have a good time and not continually discuss certain people and their unkind acts. I am able to have conversations with complete strangers. In fact, I have been acting very weird lately, more than normal. I asked three people to go golfing with me that I had only met once. I just really enjoyed their company and thought we would have fun. I do not get that part of the "change" in me. I either am going off the deep end, or I was like this in my past life before I lost myself, and I am now coming back.

I seem to have more good or tolerable times than bad. I have not recently contemplated a double homicide. I can now put a whole sentence together and sometimes make sense. I recently screwed in a light bulb and washed my car, and I have as recently as tonight completed an entire meal.

A big accomplishment occurred last night when I watched the movie *Con Air*. When I was in Vegas with Charm, his brother and NotSo, we saw them filming the movie. We couldn't wait to see it— well, I waited.

I have made some progress toward some normalcy of life. I sometimes feel like I just might be able to do this. I am setting goals for myself and "plan" to accomplish them! Some are going to be very hard to do, but without goals, you have no place to climb, so you must set them very high. What are the goals, you ask?

To be able to cook a big meal, meat, veggies, salad, rolls, and dessert. Possibly putting in four-foot florescent bulbs, not just screwing in a small bulb. Start back with my woodworking. Maybe build some things for the house. Things I have always wanted to do. I have been afraid to do so for fear of my mind drifting, and I would cut off a finger or something important. Hmmmm, I should have thought of that before Charm left, if you get my drift.

I would like to learn to dance and play softball again. Very importantly is to improve myself, so I never let this happen to me again. I cannot allow it. I need to learn to trust and love again.

I would like to do some public speaking to encourage others who go through a devastating experience to use humor, self-worth, and God to get them through.

I would like to be thin again. At least, thin enough that I don't have to worry about the bloat.

I wish I could be like my friend Emmie; she got a great present when her husband left. She hasn't had a period since that day. Here I am getting more than my share, even month-long periods.

I would like to learn to spell so I do not have to rely on spell check so much.

I need to come out of this destruction of my life with enough money to live on. If it comes down to divorce, I want the TV stations to be there and ask, "Now that you have won this Super Bowl of being dumped and in a slump, what are you going to do?" I would answer, "I am going to Vegas."

I had a funny thought while I was mowing the lawn the other day. I wondered if I could mow words in the front lawn. Little messages to Charm and his noncharming prin-cess. If they would drive by, they would see my thoughts in grass. I won't share what I wanted to mow, but you could probably guess some of my grassy thoughts.

I have a lot to work on, and there is a lot more to come. I will be working on all of it as time goes on. The list doesn't include all those "high" goals I was telling you about. Let me tell you it is very, very difficult to survive through any kind of devastation in your life. You can come through it, and you will need people around you.

Live your life to the fullest now and enjoy. You never know what is around the next corner. God is always with you. Keep him in your heart at all times. I do not mean close to your heart; I mean deep in your heart. Fill your heart with his love and spread your love to others. When someone is in need, help them. You may be next, and you will never regret giving to others, that is, unless you do the overkill thing like I did. I sometimes regret the last months before I was double dumped. I never even realized what I was facing. I was totally numb and did not see things clearly. Now I do. I also feel so much relief.

Emmie spoke to her counselor about me. She has a hard time understanding my reactions. I feel I did a lot of my grieving before I was even dumped. I believe I was mourning the death of a marriage, even though I did not realize it. The hurt I was enduring from Man of Charm and NotSo was unbearable.

I don't know that I will ever understand why I put up with that treatment. I have a lot to learn. Do not allow anyone to treat you wrongly, to use you, or to allow the real you to get lost because of someone else. Be you! I hope you never have to have this pain in your heart or your "other end."

Just sayin'—That I am ready to move on with my life, and I crave the feelings of being happy, loved, cared about, and healthier.

How does someone feel they have the right to pull the rug out from under another person and then, on top of that pain, be so blatant, cocky, and just plain mean about it?

This has taken a toll on me physically. I have a huge pain in the neck, not just Charm and Prin-cess, but I believe it is stress. I don't know what I am feeling that causes me to have so much tension. I have been experiencing a tightness in my chest, which is very painful, along with the neck and shoulder pain. I also have a racing heartbeat—guess I am lucky that I have a heart, unlike others. I could not sleep last night because of all of it.

I usually deal with stress very well. Actually, I don't usually feel stressed. I have a book to write, and I don't have time to deal with physical heart issues. I have enough to deal with my broken heart. People are calling asking if I have more chapters ready to read, I have to get them done.

I want to get away from the stress of work and on to happiness. Something is evidently going on in my mind and causing all of this stress. I try to convince myself that I don't know what the cause is—I guess we all know what it is.

It is kind of a woman's deepest secret to wish that every man would just have one menstrual, not as in singer but as in period. It is kind of the same thing with my situation. I think everyone that delivers this kind of pain to their family should have to suffer the same pain someday. That is all the punishment they would ever need.

CHAPTER 28

Aspirin Cannot Cure a Broken Heart
or
God, I Think I Killed Her

Unfortunately, I recently had a reason to visit the local hospital. I was not feeling well and needed to see what the problem was. I learned something very important. I could not be cured by medicine.

I was in the hospital today. It started when I was on my way home from Mark and Karen's. I had a lot of pain in my shoulders and neck. I felt there was a lot of tightness. It was not the first time, and I doubt it will be the last time. That evening, I could not sleep because of some serious chest pain. I thought I was a little stressed out, and it was muscle tension. I continually had the pain and just could not shake it. I lost two nights' sleep because of it.

I shared this information with my counselor—that I was having pain and figured it was stress. She asked, "What is going on in your mind?" "I have no idea," I responded. Now that is an intelligent statement if I ever heard one. "I have no idea." What am I? Separated from my mind and cannot figure out what I am thinking about? You would certainly think so. Now that I feel totally intellectual, we can continue the latest development in this diary of a broken heart. After much prodding from people who will remain anonymous, I went to the emergency room (ER) complaining of chest pain, numbness and pain in my left arm, some discomfort when breathing, sensations that I was going to pass out, neck and shoulder pain, very tired and some "spaceyness." Okay, more "spacey" than normal.

I was attempting to finish the payroll before leaving work to go to the hospital but was just not able to concentrate very well. My co-worker, Kim, helped me finish, and then I cut out to go home. Kimberly was waiting to take me to the hospital. It is absolutely amazing what your children can do when they want to. She had a lunch packed for herself, a Coke for me, quarters to make calls if needed (we did not have a cell phone yet), and various phone numbers she might possibly need. Keep in mind this is the same kid that cannot remember to unload the dishwasher if I ask her to. I usually get "I cannot remember what you told me to do." Pull the wool over my eyes! I came in the house, found the health insurance card, and used the rest room (where did that come from). We all know it is a bathroom—I was not resting, and off we went.

Upon arrival, of course, I am thinking, *My chest does not hurt. Let's go home.* At the point of entry to the ER, I think the nerves take over, and you are too numb to feel anything. However, this new sensation did not last long. The very personable person at the desk asked what I was there for. I thought a response of "my health" would be a good response. I told her I had chest pain. She asked, "When did this start? I said, "Sunday night." She proceeded to put her pen down, shake her head, and say, "We were open then. Did you just think you could wait it out or what?" I laughed. She picked up her pen, and we continued. I found the way to get a bed in an emergency room quickly. Just tell them you have chest pain. They took my blood pressure, temperature, and said, "Get her to bed 23 right away." And they looked at Kimberly and said, "We will have you check her in." Off I went! Kimberly had to do the work. You know all those questions about you that they ask in order to treat you. It is like trying to call some big executive at their place of business. The secretary asks everything under the sun before connecting you. I always want to say, "Do you need my bra size too?" Remember this in the future; it could be a very helpful source of info. When you enter ER with blood running from your arm to your shoes, hopefully not your good shoes, just tell them you have chest pains. If you have a broken leg, just limp through the doors bent over, holding your chest. You may ask how does this help for you to get your leg fixed? Easy, tell them your chest hurts and then bend over in pain clutching your chest. Then once they have you signed in and take you back to your bed, just mention you stumbled and fell, hurting your leg—in the hospital parking lot. Simple! A different injury, just a little twist to the story, and you are in. Imagination is such a great tool in life.

On to the story. I am quickly hooked up to the monitor that makes all those cute little teepeelike drawings. Mine looked like pretty good ones. Then comes the fun part. Why do you totally have to undress to have your upper body checked? I never said a thing about a pain anywhere on the lower extremity. I have had a couple of real pains in the rear portion of the lower extremity but never mentioned them at this point. This is probably a good time to interject the old mother's cliché, "Always wear clean and unholey underwear." "Unholey" does not mean underwear that hasn't been worn to church. Fortunately, I had recently shaved my legs.

So the blood pressure was being taken automatically, and the monitor is making teepees, and oh, oh, the teepees all fell down. Is this what they refer to as flat line? It looks like three straight lines to me. All I know is that on TV when this happens, half the cast runs into the room to check the patient, even all the "stars" come for this flat line thing. Where was Dr. Dreamy in this "case," or my all-time favorite, James Brolin? Now that would be worth having an emergency room trip for.

Well, I have to be honest. If I leaned over and peeked out of the curtain real hard, I could see a cleaning lady standing there. I guess if I died, she could at least go get someone to move the body so she could clean the room. I am trying to look at this monitor and decide that maybe I just checked out, and I am looking down on myself while I float, one of those out-of-body experiences. Maybe there was a power failure, and the thing just automatically flatlines but stays lit with the backup generators.

I know all the lights are on, and I am just being ridiculous about the generator. But why is it that no one is checking on me? Talk about low self-esteem. I can't even get a trained emergency room staff to pay attention to me when the machine goes flatline! Oh, good, here comes someone. In they walk. Am I alive? What is she doing? Oh, she is hooking up the one connection that came out. Well, I am still alive, but at least, they could have made a little more of a fuss for my self-esteem.

The doctor was in fairly quickly and asked questions. I did not get much time to speak. I learned women still menstruating usually do not have heart attacks. A new fact for my already overloaded brain. Just what is wrong with me? The doctor proceeded to walk out, and all he said was that he was going to give me some medicine. The staff was very nice, and I really do not have a lot of complaints, but I would like to mention that it took the medicine an hour to arrive to my lovely little curtain-clad space. It reminds me of *The Wizard of Oz*, "Pay no attention to the person behind the curtain."

During that hour, I didn't have a clue as to what was happening. There is a man around the corner telling the nurse about the blood in his urine and for them to go ahead and put that catheter in and then told all the stories he had from World War II. The lady next to me had a very upset stomach but had not thrown up. It seemed she was allergic to every kind of medication they brought to help her. At least, she was getting her medicine! The big story is the poor lady that kept moaning and started yelling, "Help me, help me! Oh, God, help me!" over and over again. I felt very sorry for her. I am sure she did not probably know what was going on, so I said a little prayer for her, "Please help this poor lady, God." I never heard another sound from her. God, did I kill her with the prayer?

I hear wheels coming toward me. Is someone finally going to do something? Maybe it is the dinner cart. Let's see what shall I have. Maybe a filet, baked potato, lots of butter and sour cream, and rolls. I will skip the salad if the ticker is going. I will eat the cholesterol. Oh man, it is just the EKG, and they are looking for me. Of course, they have to ask your name, you know, so they have the right person. This is always a fun game to play. They get you all set to have a test and say what is your name. So what do you tell them? Emilia Earhart? I know Annie Oakley? It could be fun to do something like

Taylor Swift or maybe Caitlyn Jenner. Well, it is boring to use your own name. Besides, another name shakes them up a little. Now they are sticking little blue dots all over me and talking about their dates from the other night. So what do they do with these little blue dots? Connect them with magic markers? If they want to do that, they would have more fun playing "dot to dot" with my freckles and age spots. They hooked all the little blue dots up to the machine, took a fifteen-second reading, and said, "Thank you." And literally, they ripped them off my body, and off they went.

Now what? The teepees are still being drawn on the screen, blood pressure taken every few minutes, the lady next to me still complaining about her stomach but refuses the medicine, and Mr. Army World War II is telling stories. Still, no sounds from the lady I thought I was helping by saying a prayer.

Here, I lie, thinking I have no one. Do you have any idea how lonely it is to lie there wondering what is happening to you and know that if this would have happened months ago, both Charm and NotSo Charming would have been there, concerned and caring? I think! I believe there was a day that would have happened. I am not really sure about it though. I guess I will never know what was real and what was not when it comes to them. It is an awful feeling to think that you had this type of relationship with two people and considered yourself happy and lucky and then get a great big "kick" right to the proverbial curb!

Now understand I must explain for my children's sake. I'm not talking about them. I am very lucky to have them. I feel closer to them than ever, and I am very proud of them. Just all sorts of thoughts are racing through my mind. I was at home with chest pains and worried what was wrong with me. But I am more worried and stressed lying here in the hospital, worrying about my life.

Oh no, I think I see George Hamilton coming around the curtain. Never mind. It is just the vampire department taking some samples. Wait till they see that blue blood. After all, my great-, great-, great-, etc. grandfather was a king. Hey, wait this is red; maybe it turns when the air hits it. I guess the blue did not filter down this far into the family.

Now we are up to two tests and some medicine for the esophagus and no doctor, no answers, and they will not let Kimberly back yet because they are taking an X-ray. So where are these X-ray techs? Monitor is still making teepees, and blood pressure is still being taken. My feet are still cold; my arm has stopped bleeding. The medicine did not help. Still no answers, still no sounds from "Help Me." Still no medicine quite right for the stomach next to me. I never ever want to hear another World War II story as long as I live—if I do.

Finally, we are taking a ride to the X-ray room. I hope there are not too many turns. The last time I rode on one of these beds, I got motion sickness and threw up in an elevator full of people. My lovely daughter reminded me of that, thanks. Hope I can do the same for you someday, only in front of your children. The X-rays have been taken. I have discovered that I have a heart. That is probably news to some people, and I think I hear the doctor coming now. As he sits down, he starts explaining that some of the tests are back, and he does not feel I am a candidate for heart problems. So far, things look okay. Well, things are not okay. I asked if it could be stress. He said he was not going to say that at all. So what are you saying? "We still do not really know." But he will be back after the rest of the test results are back.

Well, here is the update—no real answers but no real bad news. The World War II stories are over, and all is quiet on the front. They must have put that catheter in; the stomach still has not found a medication, but now it hurts instead of being upset. Still no sounds from you know who, and I have flatlined again!

As it turns out, the doctor is back and has no real answers. I am to rest and take what Kimberly and I thought the doctor said were big-ass pills. What he said was they were big aspirin pills. So what can I say? I will go home and let the counselor know that we need to work from the stress angle.

Remember I was telling you about those feelings of those special people not being there for me? I was really wrong. No, Man of Charm and NotSo Charming were not there. But many others were. I was in the process of getting dressed when I heard a familiar voice say, "C. R." It was Emmie. She and another friend called every hospital in town until she found out where I was. My parents did that and got no info, but when Emmie called, they told her I was going to be admitted, and she could see me in about a half hour, that I still was in pain, and that they were doing tests. She knew more than I did!

Fortunately, I was not admitted, but I did learn something, didn't I? There was Emmie, and when I came out of the room to the waiting room, there were my parents and several group members with big hugs for me. When I do have these moments of feeling sorry for myself, I get reminded of what I really have, and that is a lot. I had all these people concerned for me, and my original intent was just to sneak over to the hospital by myself, have this checked, and be home before anyone missed me. I got fooled in a very special way.

Kimberly had left a message with Emmie's son that I would not need a ride to group tonight because I was in the hospital. Emmie gave her a lecture about that. I have received many concerned phone calls, and I realize what good friends I do have. I will be all right in life without "him and her." But aspirin will not fix this broken heart, not even those "big ones." Only God and the love and care of the people around me can do that.

My counselor called today to see what happened, and I explained. She wanted me to do some relaxing. Her question to me was "What do you like to do for relaxation?" My answer was "Ah, ah, ah, I guess, if I could come up with an answer for that, it would be writing. I seem to really enjoy that." She continued to prompt me, "Do you like to read, watch a movie or some TV?" "Yes, I can do that." I responded. She continued, "Get a cup of tea, go to the bathtub, take a book, and relax. Get a movie and carry out dinner. Do nothing but relax." I just kept saying, "Okay, okay, okay," all the time knowing I could never relax. I do not think I remember how. I used to take those cups of tea and book baths. Could I remember how to do this? I told her I would try. I am a lucky person to have everyone trying to make things better. So I hung up, went out, and planted some bushes. Was that on the relaxation list? I think it was. I, at least, did come in and take that bath, and I have tried to relax all evening. We just will not mention that it is one minute till midnight, and I am sitting slouched in this chair writing. I will tell you this. I have tried very hard and hope to do even better tomorrow.

Even in the disaster portions of your life, look for the good and positive things. If you try with an open mind, you will find a lot. There is hope beyond hope out there, and you cannot lose sight of the good. I have two very important things to hope for now. One is that my prayers did not kill that poor woman. As you know, my prayers don't seem to work so well, and I really hope that someone can tell me where to buy one of those lovely stylish hospital gowns. If I ever remarry, I would like one for my honeymoon, better yet, I will send one to NotSo Charming!

Just sayin'—That I am a laid-back person. I think that is healthy, but in this situation that I have been victim of, I have to work hard on staying laid back. As I work at it, I am sure that NotSo and Charm are "lying back" but not in the same way. To quote—but I don't know who—"You should never look back." And now I know why; it hurts like crazy. I know I am a better person because as I am working to forgive them, in spite of themselves, I have chosen not to hate but to forgive.

Easy going is what makes me happy. So what if I stand around with my hands in my pockets? Brief story: The one thing my boss could complain about in my review was that I stood with my hands in my pockets. So he demoted me from a twenty-five-cents-an-hour raise to a dime. With that news, my hands came out of my pocket, and I said, "Make it a quarter, or I am out of here." He did, but I said, "Well, at least, my hands in pockets just shows I am relaxed. I am not rearranging the twigs and berries."

So what if I don't wear Liz Wear while planting my garden? I wear my Umbro (soccer shorts) and a T-shirt. In fact, I want to be buried in my Umbro's. I just can't picture myself in one of those pastel, mint green, silky things. I would get all tangled up on my ascension to heaven (I hope), and Umbro's are comfy. I could spend eternity in them. Now if it is cold, I might want a sweatshirt and jeans. My mirrored sunglasses would be a nice touch. I am sure, after spending so much time in a cloudy climate, God will give me a sunny assignment in heaven. I really don't think St. Peter looks to see what designer clothing we are wearing when we hit the pearly gates. I think he might ask what we have done in life to be worthy to enter, not if we stood with our hands in our pockets. I don't think he will say, "Turn around and let me see the label on your butt."

CHAPTER 29

Why Do We Get Out of Bed in the Morning?
or
How to Have a Heart Attack Finding a Doctor

Why do we get out of bed in the morning? Some people would respond by saying such statements as "It is a glorious morning," "I am so very happy to be alive," "I cannot wait to go to work and accomplish great things for the wonderful world," "I am ever so lucky to be alive because I have everything," "The world awaits my smiling face this morning as I go spread cheer to the less fortunate." Or maybe something as splendid as "I cannot wait to serve my lovely family breakfast, do their laundry, clean up after them, not to mention cleaning up the hair balls from the cats." Is this just not the epitome of happiness and a true example of our everyday lives?

Oh, I am sorry, I have not lost my mind. I am just being a positive person, and I am positive I do not want to get out of bed this morning. Only three more days till the weekend. I wonder if I can call off sick today or maybe my poor aunt died—again. I will have to remember what Aunt died the last time I called off. I am just being sarcastic, but I cannot believe I have to get up already, only twenty-five more years till retirement. I wonder who is going to yell or get mad at me today. I don't think I will make the bed I will be crawling back in tonight. Of course, this might be a little exaggerated, but you get the point.

This would have been a "week" for me to stay in bed. You have already read about my little excursion to the hospital, and that was almost the highlight of my week. I cannot possibly tell you everything that has happened this week nor is any of it as devastating as the big double dump I deal with daily, but some of it could be entertaining to you.

Let's start with getting out of bed. Besides that being a mistake, I have been having sleepless nights, and I am very restless due to this pain in my chest. You know the one that is nothing. These restless nights tend to totally destroy a well-made bed, and being entangled in the covers tends to make you fall out of a waterbed. That was the start to yesterday. Today I was more cautious. Yesterday was extremely frustrating. I finally made up my mind I was going to pursue going to a doctor after not resolving this pain in my chest during my visit to the hospital. It takes a major thought process on my part to actually call and make an appointment with a doctor. I always feel guilty for bothering them because there are so many sick people in the world that need to be taken care of. I just realized I cannot continue with the situation I am having here and better get some real help as opposed to the hospital's response of "take this aspirin."

I have recommendations for doctors from friends. Oh, I forgot to tell you. I did not have a family doctor because our insurance changed, and of course, I do not have a list of providers' book, you know the one that "moved" with Charm's desk when he left to think. All I can do is call around until I find a doctor that will take my insurance. First call at nine o'clock sharp in the morning, the highly recommended doctor number one. "I wanted to check to see if you are on my insurance plan. Yes, you are great. Oh, you are not taking new patients." Why, did you answer the question about my insurance is what I wanted to say. Got my hopes up.

Wonderful doctor number two. "Hello. I was wondering if you are on my insurance plan. Oh, good. Are you seeing new sick people?" Long silence. "I wanted to make an appointment." Silence. "Could I make an appointment with one of the doctors?" Then I answered all the forty-two million questions about my health, and I am totally stressed out as she says the doctor makes her own first-time appointments. Well, this is a good concept. I guess she probably likes to be more personal and give the people some extra attention. The doctor will call you today or tomorrow. I was not pleased because I wanted in, but I respected that and said okay. I could tell this was one of those ladies that loved the control she had over these poor people's lives that called in wounded and sick. Think about how godlike it is. She could choose whether people live or die, if we suffer in pain or get relief. What power! She loved it.

So what if I had chest pains? I guess that only works at the hospital for a rapid response. It was good while it lasted. The day continued, and there was no call from this doctor number two. I realized that my afternoon schedule for the next day was going to be open now and would allow more time to schedule for them. I called back after two o'clock in the afternoon and told them of the change, Ms. Choose Life or Death proceeded to inform me that the doctor was not in today. "I thought I made that clear to you this morning," she said. "No, I did not get that out of the conversation when you said the doctor would call me back today or tomorrow." I continued to make her irritated, so I now know she just labeled me as "death." I asked for her to please make sure the doctor would call me tomorrow no matter what. She answered with the fact it would be tomorrow, Friday, or Monday. The next response was "If it is that bad, go to the emergency room." I basically felt like I would be receiving an engraved invitation in the mail if I were accepted as a patient. So does my chest hurt now? You better believe it, and I went out and mowed the lawn, finishing in the dark, trying to work off stress. Dumb thing to do, but it is done.

The next-morning attitude revealed that I really did not want to do this all over again. However, I got up, got dressed, and thought, *Well, at least, I will get into the doctor today and maybe start working on getting some relief.* You know I really dream a lot in life. Dreams do not always come true. Your bubble breaks. All the water does go over the dam. Elevators do not always go to the top floor. The sun does cover over with clouds. Peanut butter sticks to the roof of your mouth and the dog's mouth. Babies spit up no matter how cute they are. The point is sometimes life stinks, and then you die!

So the morning continues. I go to work and just get into things when someone knocks to get in. Where I work, we have two stores together, and everyone for the next-door store comes in through our doors in the morning. I got up. I was the only one there. I let the salesman in and went back to my phone call. Never giving it a thought. No one had been in to turn off the alarm next door, but that did not stop this salesman. He went over and turned on lights, and off went the alarm. I received a call, and the police arrived. Of course, I did not have the proper ID number to prove that I was allowed to be there, and we waited a long time before we could retrieve the number and call off the dogs. That is all right. Today I didn't have anything else to worry about. I just had to go represent my bosses' development company in court that afternoon to evict a tenant for not paying rent. What do I know? I am a musician, not a landlord or even a land lover. So why me? Everyone in that line of work was out of town.

Now picture this. I got chosen to go to court to evict someone. You remember me, the one that is a sap. I lost my husband and friend. Remember caring too much got me there, and I am working on just that caring too much thing in counseling, trying not to allow myself to be that way and using some possible assertiveness for a change. Or at the least not to be such a sap, sucker, weenie—you get the point. And they send me to throw someone out of their home?

I got to the courthouse after dealing with the alarm thing and headed toward the courtroom labeled "traffic court," but I was supposed to ignore that because it was really where I was supposed to be. I signed in and then waited outside the door. My common sense told me that since the court wanted me to sign in outside of the courtroom, someone would come out there to get me when they were ready for me. As I stand waiting, a head pops out of the door and looks at me, then goes back in. It reminded me of that children's toy where you wind the handle and the clown pops out on a spring. Who thought that up? It can scare the poor little kids. Anyhow, pretty soon, the head pops out again and looks and does so a third and fourth time.

The next time when "pop went the weasel" opened the door, the rest of the body followed along through the door and all the way out.

And the full body is visible, clad in pink tights, white blouse, tennis shoes, funky glasses, and a tooth that she can flip out upon command. And the person looks right at me and says, "Are we supposed to wait out here?" I guess I was the chosen one to answer that question. I very intelligently responded like I knew what I was doing with a big healthy "I have no idea." This pink-tight-clad person was my evictee.

As I stood there with my opposition, a little weasel-looking man opened the door and, in this very soft-spoken roar, said, "Any evictions, come in." "That's me," the pink clad tights, flipping tooth lady said.

The little pop weasel guy turned out to be the magistrate. He asked us to sit down, and shortly after, approximately twenty other people filed in and sat down. I was stressed out enough and wondering what I would have to do, only to find out they are going to ask me questions. What do I know? I am the musician, not the landlord. It turned out fine. I did the best I could answering questions, and the pink-tight-clad person grabbed on to me, and I was stuck. She took my ear and bent it in every direction. I helped her to get copies of the papers, and she walked me to my car, still bending my ear. Now that made me a little nervous as I just got this lady kicked out of her home, and she is walking me to my car. (Note: Today, I know better and would have made an excuse to stay in the building, ask a security guard to walk me to my car, or something.)

After hearing her problems, I wanted to tell her what life really was about after my recent events but realized in my heart there was something that told me her problems measured larger than mine on the problem scale, and I had so much more good in life than she probably would ever have. I am a lucky person, but I don't own any pink tights, oh, and I never will. Boss owes me big time for this one.

I don't know what made me do what I did next. Maybe it was being in the courtroom that did it. I ran straight to my attorney's office. Once I arrived, I asked the administrative assistant if I could see the attorney for a minute. I only had to wait a short time, and I think the thing I was worried about was owing her money. I think I needed to get it free from my mind. We discussed that, and off I went to the next adventure. How many people do you know just drop in on their attorney? Yeah, me neither.

Going back to work was fairly uneventful, and coming home was a pleasure. Emmie called, and we discussed taking a field trip to the emergency room as she calls it. She is a kindergarten teacher. Upon my refusal, Emmie called her doctor, which is doctor "no new patients number one." They told her the doctor was not taking new patients, and they were really sorry but highly recommended a doctor up the street. Then she called that doctor's office, and he could not take me until Monday because he was seeing Emmie's doctor's patients because she was sick! After Emmie was finished speaking with the new doctor—as the nurse refereed to him as Doc Holiday—I was in kind of a sensitive mood. I do not show it with anger or tears especially, but I now have this tendency, thanks to my situation, to be cautious and not too trusting. The name Doc Holiday makes me wonder, "Are we talking 'home on the range' here?" Maybe it is like the "one-doctor towns" of the pioneer days. Does he deliver a calf and castrate a lamb then come into the examining room and tell me what is wrong with me? Trust'? I plan on going to him on Monday. They showed concern and said, if he had been my doctor, he would have met me at the hospital. I think I finally ran across a human being. I got through with doctor dealings and was awaiting my counselor's call. I had promised to be home by four o'clock in the afternoon so she could reach me at home.

"The group" was going to the Italian Fest, and I did not really feel like going, so I said, "Let me know what you are doing afterward, and maybe I will meet you." Emmie called and said they were going to see *My Best Friend's Wedding*, and she asked if I wanted to meet them. I said, "Yes, maybe I can get some pointers for my ex-best friend and her upcoming wedding."

I met the groupies at the theater. This movie was very good. We laughed, but I had a hard time with some parts because it took place in the city of Chicago. In the movie, they go on the same boat ride on the river that Mark, Karen, NotSo, the kids, and I took one Memorial Day weekend when we were there visiting. Just some of the scenes were hard, but I made it. There were a lot of funny scenes, and it was enjoyable. Standing out on the sidewalk before leaving, we were all discussing the sequel, *My Best Friend's Divorce.* We thought this was an excellent idea and felt the people in the movie should get a divorce, and then they could go to a divorce group and go to movies together, play mushball, go to Italian Fests, cry together, go to court together, pay alimony, and wonder every single day of their lives what direction they were headed and what the rest of life has to offer. What a great plot for a movie, fact or fiction.

On the serious side, these "groupie friends" of mine have no idea what they mean to me and always will. I wonder if they have ever taken a step back and looked at what they have in one another. It is a very special thing for people to stick together like they have. No matter where our lives turn, we will be there for one another.

I do not know what tomorrow will bring. However, I do hope it will bring some kind of relief for this discomfort I am having. I try to keep life as normal as possible, but tonight was very difficult. I really am uncomfortable and getting very annoyed with this pain. I guess I will go take one of those "big pills" and hope for the best. It has not been my choice, but at least I know I have the best when it comes to friends and a new start on life. Maybe I did not get a vote on my new life, but now, with knowing all the issues at hand, I won the election!

CHAPTER 30

Kimberly Got Dinner, and I Got the Leftovers
or
Crack Those Nuts

I have never witnessed a crueler act than that of Charm toward Kimberly. I refer to his actions as being cruel and unfair punishment.

This man was either out to get all of us, or he could no longer distinguish between fact and fiction. He has always had the typical male selective hearing, but he has also developed a blending of fact and fiction.

He reverts to that "Pinocchio effect" discussed in a previous chapter. As you recall, we were discussing the effects of growth on body parts during the process of verbal fabrication. At this point, I had not seen Man of Charm at all, so I cannot attest to the validity of this Pinocchio effect nor do I want to see the effect.

Kimberly went to dinner with Charm tonight. I got the leftovers. It always seems that is what I get—the leftovers. NotSo Charming gets the main dish; her kids get the side dishes, and Vicki and Kimberly get the dessert. And if there are any, well, I get the leftovers. Eventually, leftovers spoil.

The plan earlier in the week was that all of what was Charm's blended family unit, minus me, were planning an excursion to the zoo. At this time, I will not make any sarcastic comments relating certain members of the family unit being compared to zoo animals. I would not want to hurt the zoo species' feelings. I know you would not blame me and might even expect a comment about apes, monkeys, and snakes, but I need to continue to be calm and relaxed. And I think these comparisons could somehow send me into a hysterical hyena-type laugh.

I just need to tell you that in this whole situation, I feel the worst for the kids. I feel the most compassion and concern for them. It took me awhile to come in from the rain, but as I am starting to dry off, I am seeing things so much more clearly. The kids really got a lot of grief from Mr. Charming!

He was not a good emotional support for them, not unlike what I had experienced in my years with him. Vicki who is newly married, needs to lead her own life. Kimberly is home more and around the situation. She has gotten a lot further than I ever have with him. She can stand up for herself and can express her feelings much more readily than I. Of course, we recently saw that I am unable to express anything I feel. I so badly wish I could share those feelings with others in a more emotional way. I just want to sit down and blow it all out. I've been advised to talk to some of the group members because they would understand my feelings. I honestly gave it a try. I know they were trying to worm things out of me, but I do not know what to say or how to express myself. I really truly do not understand why I cannot say just what I feel.

I believe this problem of not being able to express what I feel somewhat comes from the fact that Charm would never allow me to complete my thoughts when I was talking to him about my feelings nor did he show compassion and feelings toward my emotions.

Kimberly has discovered this painful experience, but Vicki has a different personality and deals with this in a much better way. Instead of insisting on his listening, I would turn to a mime act. I would go into another room, quietly cry, or involve myself in an activity to keep from reacting. I would do so without a word to Charm.

On many occasions, Charming showed signs of quick temper, little heart, no patience, and planned cruelty toward Vicki, Kimberly, and I. He would use us as a pawn in his game of chess. He would tell me I needed to support him against the children and that I was the cause of Kimberly's behavior and disrespect toward him.

The cause was his situation, not me. At this time, he could not deal with looking his daughters in the eye. His treatment of NotSo's daughter was so sickening sweet that it upset Kimberly greatly. I was constantly put in the middle and was so totally verbally annihilated by both Charm and Prin-cess because of my lack of support to him in certain situations. I did not understand. I was supposed to support him and her when she was taking my husband and he was taking my friend. Look, when he moved out, he took his athletic supporter with him. He doesn't need my support.

They are not speaking to me. And they want me to support them? I never realized how I was ganged up on. This was not *West Side Story*! There was no reason to gang up on me. I can't even sing and dance. NotSo wanted me to join their gang of outlaws and protect Charmer and be loyal to him against my daughters. She what? Because I did not do so. That is probably why she had such a distaste for my children. Or maybe it was just the anger and guilt she had raging inside her screaming to get out, begging for forgiveness. Or could it be her ponytail was just wound too tight?

I was so out of the realm of things at this point I could not even see straight. In the past, I tried so hard to respect him and stay on his side instead of protecting the children. I was so brainwashed, brain-dead, brainless, and debrained. I had no clue to the intensity that surrounded me or the snow job taking place right under my nose. I now have so much to learn.

Kimberly and the perpetrators' dinner talk must've been very interesting as Man of Charm proceeded to give Kimberly the electric bill and pointed out that there was a shutoff date, and it was going to be shutoff unless I paid it.

I guess this tin man has not yet made his pilgrimage to Oz for that heart. He continued to inform her that the attorneys said there was so much debt to be paid off that everything would be sold, including the house, and the debts would be paid from that money. Kimberly's response was "So I will live in a crummy place?" Charm asked, "Why?" She responded, "Because on Mom's salary, we would not be able to afford anything nice." That is when Mr. Charm said, "Your mother can get a better job. We know she can." Did you catch that "we"?

I must absolutely have been hallucinating. I swear I heard Charm, on several occasions, say he would always love and take care of me. I do dream a lot. I guess I should wake up and smell the rotten eggs because he is going for the jugular, and I am going to crack those nuts.

That's exactly right! You heard me. I am going to crack those nuts. I had a visit with the doctor today (the visual picture I had of him in the home on the range thing was not too far off because he does play country music in his waiting room). His advice to me was that I needed to go crack some nuts. I was a little taken back by this. You can imagine what I was thinking. But really, what he was saying was that I need to show my emotions a little more. He thought maybe one of those penile whoops—I mean primal screams—in the forest would be good for me. Emmie and I thought cracking nuts would be good. I just don't think I have it in me to scream.

The latest medical-educated guess points in the direction that my chest pain is coming from a broken heart. Isn't that what I said from the beginning? At least, I now know that once again, I did something in a strange way that seemed to puzzle everyone. As far as the report from the test, I am all right. The doctor said relaxation is the key.

So back to the nuts thing. Because I do not have that primal scream in me, I thought about cracking walnuts on the driveway with a hammer. That made more sense to me. If you desire to take this in a vindictive way or read more into it than I am telling you, that is your privilege. I am one heartbroken human, and I tell you that your opinion is yours and not necessarily that of the author. I just feel this could be a good physical way to release some of those pent-up emotions that are not coming out. Maybe it is best said by Peter Paul and Mary, "I'm going to hammer in the morning, hammer in the evening, hammer out love" between Charm and Un-Charming. It's the hammer of justice, and the nuts are going to fly.

Charm told Kimberly while they were at dinner that there is so much debt because I never paid more than the minimum payment on the charge accounts. He is absolutely right. I usually only paid the minimum. The part he forgot to tell her, probably accidentally on purpose, was that for many years, he was holding back more than two hundred dollars a week from the paycheck that I never saw. You can be certain that NotSo saw some lovely parting gifts with that money. I just did not realize they were parting from me. He would cash his check each week and bring me the money. He did not "show me the money." I never saw the pay stubs. On the occasion that I would ask something about the money and why was he giving me so little when he had a raise, etc., he always had a quick answer. He would occasionally spend his secret money on the kids. But I'm sure this last year, it went in another direction.

The unconscious mind—excuse me, I meant the subconscious mind—is a tricky thing. You can forget the facts that can really be important. Once again, they have figured a way to blame me for anything they can.

Sounds like Kimberly's dinner conversation consisted of the little seeds to be planted, grown, and ripen into rotten tomatoes. It was unfair of him to use innocent bystanders that are his own flesh and blood to try to hurt me. I am sure Prin-cess was a little put out that Kimberly did not readily accept her and the "situation." I am sure she is planting a whole crop of ideas in Charm's pea brain and working to get them transplanted in our breaking hearts.

The original intent of the dinner was to plan for the zoo trip. I wonder if they ever got to that through all the crop rotation. Vicki, Mike, Kimberly, and I do not know if NotSo's offspring were originally going to the dinner or not. However, they were to go to the zoo with them on Sunday. Vicki and Mike were to come to my house for dinner last night but instead decided to take some time alone. Newlyweds you know. So they canceled with me. Then they canceled with Charm. She informed him she would go to the zoo but not to dinner.

Kimberly told Charm that she could not bring herself to go to the zoo with NotSo Charming and have dinner with her all in one week. She has not yet accepted this enough to be comfortable with her. I will never accept this or like the situation but will someday be comfortable enough to deal with it.

So she had dinner alone with Charm and then went to the zoo on Sunday with Vicki, Mike, and Man of Charm. That eliminated some of those animal species that were supposed to be attending. I wonder if I was blamed for their extinction.

As I work to find some positives in every day, here are the positives I found for today. I know I'm not having a heart attack—it is just a broken heart. The doctor was home from the range, so I could get an appointment today, instead of waiting till next week. Vicki and Mike came and brought dinner, and we went shopping. Emmie brought the nuts, and I brought the hammers. Kimberly is doing all right and does see that the way things have happened is not quite right. I can still manage to crack a smile, and I know in my heart that God does walk beside me.

Lastly, I sit here eating the leftovers Kimberly brought home from the dinner while looking at the nuts I have to clean out of the driveway and wondering how I am going to pay the electric bill.

CHAPTER 31

Home Alone
or
Sleepless in Ohio

Even the strong ones submit to the pain and hurt sometimes. That is where I am tonight or should I say this morning. Eastern standard time, daylight savings, it is exactly two o'clock on Sunday morning. The pain and hurt is so intense I cannot sleep. I had a good day and accomplished a lot around the house. A friend told me about a book she had read. In the book, a woman had suffered a loss of a son and, I believe, went through a divorce. She made a happy room for herself. I really liked that idea, a room where I could spend time with only the things that have made me happy. No bad memories.

I started the process of my happy room a couple of weeks ago, and I am almost finished. I stained a shelf and had Kimberly and her friends help me hang it. It is five-foot long. I had built it and wanted to hang it in this room for some time. Done!

My day started with me sleeping in a little. I was getting dressed when I received a page from work that they were locked out, and I had to go down and unlock the door for them. I came home and was going to start on my shelf when I ran into a little technical problem. One day, Charm and I were working on cleaning the basement. During that time, Charm Man picked up the shelf and hung it on the studs in the workshop area. At the time, he put nails all the way through it. I asked him how I was going to get it down when I wanted to finish it. With a very smart connotation to his answer, he replied, "Don't worry, I'll get it down."

As I look back on it now, I do believe when we cleaned that area, they were preparing for their big move. So where is he now to get it down for me? Who knows, it is just one more broken promise.

The shelf, as I said, is five-foot long, and it was wedged right against the steel beam and the family room wall. I could not even wiggle it free. The nails were driven so far in that they were actually recessed into the wood. Because of that, I could not use a hammer to pull the monster to freedom. The harder I worked, the more I felt angry. I think I almost could have pulled it off with my bare hands! I got a pry bar and was able to free the one end. However, the other end could not move in any direction due to the positioning on the wall. There was no stopping! Now that puppy was coming down in one piece or a thousand at this point, I did not care. All I can say is it is stained and on the wall still five-foot long and in one piece.

Anger does come out at this point, and I do not yell, cry, and curse. I just get more determined to do what I set out to do and not let them get the best of me. Frustration is very prevalent and makes me want to pick up the phone and say, "Okay, smart"—well, you know—"get down here and do what you said you would do!"

My happy room is very happy now, and I know I will be adding to the treasures. I gathered some of Vicki's swimming awards, some of Kimberly's awards, and some of her artwork. I put the kids' pictures in special places. I have some of my books and my trumpet clock. I covered the chair with my Beethoven throw, even though it was a gift from Prin-cess NotSo Charming, and I have the eight-by-ten picture of our soccer team Michelle gave me for my fortieth birthday. The picture was taken on NotSo's first day on the team. She did not know if she would continue to play or not. She was filling in for a player that was not there and she did not have a pass to play. So we gave her the pass for the missing player, just in case the ref asked for it, and, yes the passes did have our pictures on them. I told her to stand by me while the ref checked the passes in hopes that he would check my pass and not hers.

He did not check. That was our first step to friendship. I think it is very healthy that I can have this picture with her in it in my happy room. Especially since she has caused me so much unhappiness. I just figured the good friends that were in the picture outweighed the one NotSo Good Friend. Besides, Emmie covered her face up with a Band-Aid. I am feeling pretty good about having this room well underway and feeling healthy because I can deal with the picture.

I have had very little sleep tonight. Soon after I fell asleep, I heard a noise, and the dog began to bark. I was not able to go back to sleep as I could not get the not-so-good thoughts out of my mind and hurtful feelings out of my heart. I tried to give them to God and let him deal with all of it while I slept, but that didn't work either.

So here I sit—hungry, awake, and writing. I went out to the kitchen, got leftover decaf coffee, and the last fourth of my Swensen's Galley Boy hamburger from lunch. If you ever come into Northeastern Ohio, hit a Swensen's for a burger. You will not be disappointed. Okay, back to filling you in, and I will try not to spill my coffee on the computer.

This morning, my friend Kay called. We had not been able to carry on much of a conversation for probably two weeks. Every time we would get on the phone, one of us would have to go. That is go as get off the phone, not the other "have to go." It was so nice to talk to her. She is one person I can share my true feelings with. I can say anything, and she can relate and understand. She has had similar "kick me" things happen in her life and is happy and moving on.

Hopefully, I am headed in that direction. I think we talked for about two hours. I was relating my feelings of inadequacy with other people to her. I told her how when I come home from spending time with other people, I would worry about what I said or did wrong. I said that I guess I do not feel satisfied with myself in any direction. I felt better about things after we hung up. Our conversation was fun, and we laughed a lot. So why can't I sleep tonight? Or really, it is early morning.

I can't shake some of these feelings. Lying in bed awake, the feelings just kept popping up, and I can't resolve them to go to sleep. I feel like I will never measure up to what I want for myself or what I think I am supposed to be. Maybe even what I think others expect of me. I have to realize that I am what I am, and I have been this way for many, many, and many years, but I expect to handle all these little defects and get on to being me with a new life. Follow along and see if I can return to being me. How can I rid my heart of the pain? Loving and caring about people is so much a part of my life. It is hard to stop that. God gave me the love I have for people. I guess I just have to learn to be a little more cautious with what I do with it.

I have a tendency to set myself up for disappointment, and in doing so, you know what I get—disappointed! It is just the natural me, and I guess part of the reason I am sitting here writing instead of sleeping with my husband.

I am always under the opinion that because I make people laugh, I think that they are having fun, but maybe realistically, when I walk away, they are laughing at me. I have to get over that worry and thought and move on.

Just sayin'—That now you have read "Home Alone or Sleepless in Ohio," you can see that I have been riding on the lower hills of the roller coaster. It is funny because I am really down that much in my emotions, but I am not where I had been in my previous life before the big dump.

The "Home Alone" chapter gave you a little insight on personal happenings toward myself. I believe I have discovered something tonight. I am just not sure what it is.

Here is the scoop—I took the picture I had told you about, the one in my happy room of the first soccer team and showed it to my counselor. I explained to her that I could live with it in my happy room because of all the good people in the picture. She looked at it and said, "You look like a kid in here." *So I am old now?* I was thinking. But I couldn't say anything because that is what I thought when I put the picture in the room.

I guess what I have discovered is not the fountain of youth but a life that is an unfinished symphony. With any luck, when I get through this "situation," maybe I will get younger looking again! I can see the difference. I have circles under my eyes from lack of sleep and heavy eyelids. I no longer have the sparkle in my eyes or a full smile. I still have freckles and the same nose, and I have gotten my braces off. I had a heart like a kid, but now it feels "not so" young—*just sayin'*.

CHAPTER 32

What Will Be the New Me in Relationships
or
How Can I Do It Right for a Lifetime?

I have homework from counseling. I figured I might as well share it with you. After all, we have become friends going through this together.

This could be very interesting to see how I turn out after this *minor* setback in my life. This is the year of "disaster films."

My homework is that I am to make a list of things I would do differently in a new relationship. All right, I will get serious about my homework. I did run out and get the book my counselor wanted me to read. It is not something I want to read, but I know that she is dedicated to helping me, so I have put myself in her hands. I trust her, and that is a big step for me to trust anyone, and I will do what she thinks is best and work hard. As proof, this chapter is my extra credit.

Here is the list of things I would do differently in a new relationship:

1) I would not let someone constantly criticize the way I do things. I made it real easy for people to tell me how, when, where, and why I should do things. I have always allowed others to tell me what to do, when to do it, how to do it, what to wear, how to cut my hair, and how to act. The reason you ask? Because I felt it made others happy. I guess really,

they had to have control. I do realize now that I was compromising myself. I cannot tell you why I went along with it. I just go with the flow. Time for things to change I guess.

2) Did you know that there is only one way to do anything? That is what Charm said. Yep, that is right—his way was the logical and correct way. Anything I did I was questioned on why I was doing it that way. To get it done, maybe? "That is not the right way to do it," he would say. My question was always "As long as I do it well and I get the same results, what is the difference as to how I accomplished the goal?" His response, "Because there is the right way to do it." Prin-cess was very much the same way. She always had a better way to do things than how I did them, and I was the one that needed to change. I need to learn not to worry about how someone else would do a task and do it as Sinatra would say, "My way."

Let's stray from the subject a little. There is always the right way to do everything correct, according to Charm. Was their action the right way to do what they did to everyone? Okay, what they did was not right, so maybe that changes the rules. I do not even have an argument or fight right according to the NotSo Charming One. She would scream in my face and say, "Why don't you call me an ass or something? I am treating you like one. Yell back at me!" So why would I not yell back? Sometimes I think I am afraid maybe someone would not like me. I did not love and respect myself enough. I now realize how sad it is. But I was not lowering myself to her level. However, with that being said, maybe it is better to let the other person stand and scream and give them no reaction. It obviously frustrates them!

3) Next item on my list. I will not be the social director of the relationship. I have always been that person saying, "Let's go do this. How about we call so and so and see if they want to do something?" Get the point? It should be even. If I waited for Charm to make plans, we would not have gone any-

where. He only made plans for what he wanted to do and where he wanted to go. He usually turned my ideas down.

4) I do not always have to make everyone else happy. Maybe it is time for me to sit back on occasion and let someone else make me happy. However, I have learned that happiness is within yourself. You must make yourself happy; no one can do it for you. I felt I was very happy, and it has been taken from me. Maybe I was making myself happy by working so hard to make everyone else happy. The question is how many times did I use the word "happy" in this paragraph? Too many!

I guess I just feel like this is a crime I have to sit here and think of things I would not do again in a new relationship when NotSo and Charm are just a mile away sleeping together.

I am too tired to do any more now. I guess I will just stop and read my book for counseling. I am sure I will have some "brilliant" ideas tomorrow. Wait! I think I have number 5.

5) This could be the big one. I no longer will surround myself with negative, critical people. I realize more all the time how negative and critical Prin-cess and Prince of Charm were. I have always been a very optimistic and positive person. I've tried to have a good outlook when anything went wrong. They were the ones with the negative attitude about everything. Critical to the hilt. Always saying, "Why do people do that?" or "I can't believe they are doing that." "Why is that guy mowing his lawn today?" It is too wet? Why would someone put that in their yard?" "Why are they golfing? It is too cold to golf." Or "it is too hot." "Why would he buy that car?" The sky shouldn't be blue; the grass shouldn't be green. I heard this type of criticism all the time.

Nothing was ever good enough. Why did I want to be around that? I never even look at those things. I live from my heart and enjoy the moment and the people I am with. I was the one that was the romantic. I like to do special things for my friends and family. I like to give flowers, have hot chocolate waiting when someone comes in from the cold. I enjoy surprising someone with a special gift, just even a small token just to show my thoughts were with them.

Sometimes Prin-cess would surprise me with gifts. I now realize that the giving was done with a different attitude than I had. That is not being critical, just seeing a difference. I really truly am a real romantic. I remember working most the day one Sunday, and this happened more than once with Charm, to make Charm and NotSo a really nice dinner. I set the table and lit candles, had wine, the whole nine yards. No one did it for me. Why do I surround myself with that pressure? NotSo was very good about fixing me something to eat or getting me a drink whatever; it just was when I was at her house and not planned ahead like I did.

It can hurt to think from the heart, but it is me. And how can I be something different? Do you think there are other people like me, or am I just a mistake, a second so to speak, in the production line? You know like when Stouffers puts too much salt in an entrée, the inspector rejects it, and they sell it in the outlet store. I think what I am starting to realize is that no one else really cares. I have all these very deep-seeded sincere feelings that I try to share with music or words, and people are probably just going, "Okay, whatever."

I feel I have two choices: either I can become a brain or logic thinker or I can stay a heart thinker and take the disappointment. Either one stinks, unless I find that other entrée out there with too much salt. If you are there, please stand up!

Last, but not least, I will never save anyone again. I can help a lot of people, but I will never save someone again, like I did NotSo. At least, that is what I keep telling myself. I saved her from the life she had. I surrounded her with happiness, love, my family, friends and took care of her happiness before mine for years. That was obviously not enough for her. She wanted more, my entire life, my husband. I cared, and she abandoned me. She molded me the way she wanted me and dumped me flat on my "donkey." Her actions over the last months are totally despicable. Her goal was to have my husband at any cost. It certainly cost me a lot, but who needs a friend like that? You all know the saying, "With friends like that, who needs enemies?" Her parents had thanked me for "saving her" as they said.

I hope this is a good extra credit project. Maybe I will not have homework over the weekend.

CHAPTER 33

Emmie's Story
or
Chill Out, You Are Okay

I am inspired by Emmie to write this chapter. As you know, we met again back up in divorce recovery group. Her story: Emmie is a kindergarten teacher. In fact, she was Kimberly's teacher. We actually met before she had Kimberly in class. I knew her before I had kids. We had mutual friends, and when Vicki was in the class next door sometimes when I volunteered, her teacher would do things with Emmie's class.

I began volunteering in Emmie's classroom when Kimberly was in her class and continued to do so even after my children moved to different schools as they were older and in the upper grades.

I enjoyed helping her, and I knew she was a very good person and teacher. After all those years I spent in kindergarten, I still color outside of the lines.

As it turned out, I had just recently heard of her divorce and could not believe that I did not know sooner. After hearing, I shared Emmie's story with NotSo Charming. She seemed distracted and did not want to listen. I now know that it was because she knew I was headed the same direction—as she and Charm were making their "undercover" plan of escape.

Emmie's husband left the house, what will soon be one year ago. He was a policeman. Really, he was the chief of police in a small community. He had retired from the department and decided to move in with his "former" secretary. Not an uncommon event; however, he chose to do this dastardly deed the last day of school. Emmie walks in her happy home with a smile of relief. School is over for the summer, and suddenly, she realized half of her things were gone, including the muffin tins! She told me, "He took my muffin tins. Can you believe it?" No, I could not believe it, and as I write this chapter, I am thinking back to my telling NotSo about this. And here, about six weeks later, Charm cuts out on me.

Back to basics. Emmie's husband left her a note and said he was leaving, and he and his secretary are playing "bad cop, bad secretary." Well, the note did not say that, but I did.

What a total devastation—no clues, no instincts, just total abandonment of a life that was good for many years. She spent months crying. Because of the caring person she has been, she was surrounded by people at all times. She was very lucky to have so many and her son and daughter. Her adult son lives at home, and her daughter is married and lives out of town.

Emmie had a lot to beer—no, that is "to bear." However, "beer" probably would have helped. Her husband wanted more and more things from the home, and he would just come in and get what he wanted. She just could not even protect herself; she cried. Emmie even ruined a perfectly good pair of contacts because she cried so much they warped. Much like the ex-cop's mind!

Suddenly, she came to some of her senses and decided the one thing she still had in the house of value to him, now that the muffin tins were gone, was his gun collection locked in a safe in the basement. She hired a man to come and drill the safe open. Too bad, she did not know me that well then; she would not have needed a man to do it!

Those guns were taken out of the safe and immediately put under the washing machine. Many loads of laundry were washed, and the dirty water filtered over and over the barrels of those carbines, which somehow ended up rusted before they were in his possession once again. God does work in mysterious ways.

I, myself, thought that was pretty good therapy, and it didn't begin to take as long as writing a book. The best of all is that in giving him some more furniture, she taped her pictures to the bottom of the drawers. As the tape would get old and dried out, just like the secretary, her pictures would fall out when he opened the drawers. Excellent! I am sure Emmie would not mind if you copy her idea. Feel free!

She just celebrated the one-year anniversary of her divorce and still feels those sad times, and the devastation still lingers. Everyone has those sad times for many years. It is the end of a long chapter of her life. Her children were born because of that time, and you cannot just say, "Get a grip." It just is not that easy. Emmie keeps comparing her "emotional maturity," as she refers to it, to mine. No, no, this is not a healthy thing to do. Everyone is different. She refers to herself as being a big baby. I do not think so. Do you have any idea what it took for her to walk into that divorce group for the first time? I do, been there done that. A baby could not do that. No, babies do not walk; they crawl. Emmie walked in under her own power and maybe with some of God's help; we all need some of that.

To continue, I was not present, but Emmie cried through weeks of the divorce group. It did not matter whether her eyes were "humid" or not. She was there, and that was good. She went that first week and took two friends along with her. The chairs in the room were arranged in a semicircle with an aisle in the middle. As she sat down, she realized there was only room for two of them, and she slid a chair over toward them. The leader of the group came up to her and said, "If I ever need a couch moved or any furniture, I will know who to call."

Of course, Emmie was in her weakened condition, and as soon as she was away from there, she just totally—well, you know what she did—cried. She almost did not go back the next time. She now laughs about the incident. The courage was there every time she pulled in that parking lot. Take credit for that, Emmie; it counts.

A situation arose with the fact her son was letting the "copper" into the house, and Emmie had to protect herself. You better believe she should, and she had to do one of the hardest things a parent could ever have to do. She told her son if he let his father in the house again, he was out. So now that is real strength and definite courage. She risked losing her son, but he knew who to stick with. Thank God, he had the strength also.

So, Emmie, do not tell me you did not cope or have courage. You had the strength and the foresight to help yourself. Because I do not cry, do not compare your strength to mine. I have always been that way. I do not cry in front of people. Not even at sad movies or funerals when others are around. I cry privately, maybe days later. Trust me, you are better off. We do what we have to do. I have my way of coping; you have yours. You said it is so hard for you to listen to music anymore. I went through that. Music is such a big portion of my life, and I decided "they" were not taking that away from me. So readers, remember when you hear those love songs that many times composers have experienced that heartbreak or happiness they lived to write about. This puts a whole different light on the subject. Listen to Michael W. Smith; it becomes habit forming.

Emmie, I do not see God letting go of either one of us because we are not measuring up to his standards of coping with being dumped. I have never read in the Bible a chapter explaining the "Commandments of Being Dumped." In your eyes, those commandments must be very strict:

1) Thou shall not cry more than one hundred fifty-nine tears, or thou are a baby.

2) Thou must have certain amounts of emotional maturity by age levels. If you do not measure up, you will have to stay in the kindergarten room for extra years after retirement until your level is up to the proper grade.

3) If you do not respond in the same manner as others to the crumbling of your life all around, you must pay the restaurant bill for all those who live up to the code.

4) Get a grip. What is wrong that you can't move on? Do not just sit there. Look for men and start new relationships. Who cares that you are not healed. He moved on, why not you? Not!

I think you get the point. There are no rules. Your heart does what it can do and when it can do it. Your head follows along when you are ready. You have done a fine job. You asked me to help you with one situation that you are having trouble with, forgiveness. Here goes. I feel forgiveness is when you can let go and move on productively with your life. Emmie, I have a very strong faith, and I always have. When things came crashing in on me, I never felt so filled with faith and love for God. He was not going to leave me hanging. I was not responsible for this situation, and I cling every day to the fact I know God has something much better in mind for my life. I know you also have a very strong belief and faith. Use it every waking moment of the day. Put your troubles in God's hands before you sleep at night or when you do not have the time or the strength left to worry about things. Just ask God to deal with things for a while. You have things you need to be doing. He does not mind helping you out for a while. You are expected to help yourself, but with his love and guidance.

It is kind of like a free baby-sitting service. All it cost you is a couple of prayers. A small price to pay. Your forgiveness is easy. God forgive them, for they know not what they do. I remember reading that somewhere before! So try it. They do not know what they do. If they had your faith, they could not have acted in this manner. They are to be pitied; they do not have the love and fulfilling grace of God, or their actions would be different. You are blessed with his presence. When you decide to let go, you will not believe the weight that will be lifted from your heart. It is simply amazing, and you want to laugh and cry at the same time. You ask me how I could forgive so soon. I will not be tied down to their pain. I need to refresh myself and feel happiness for myself, my heart, my soul, and my mind. You have to let yourself understand there is absolutely nothing you can do about the situation. The cop and the secretary are in control of their lives. Control your own and let go of theirs. You will then find peace within your heart, and your life will be very full. Trust me, I have not steered you wrong yet. I got you to mow my lawn for me. I must have some kind of power. You are a special person, and God does want to see you whole and happy again. Forgive. Do not compare. Just heal. I will always be here for you day or night.

Just sayin'—That lately, I have been so low that I am doing the limbo with the earthworms. I don't know what to do with myself. I have taken a plunge that would even scare Greg Luganis. Basically, I am afraid. I would kick myself, but I can't get my leg up that high.

But enough of that! I need to talk to you about the two psychos and a psychic. Life is strange, the way it all comes together. On a whim, Emmie had gone to a psychic a few months back. When you are uncertain of your future and feel like you are in a state of limbo, you will try anything legal to get a look as to what is down the road for you. The psychic told her that she was going to have someone from her past reenter her life and that they were a kindred spirit.

Now, we believe that is me. The psychic also told her that she was going to move to another city. She poo-pooed that thought thinking, "Yeah right, that won't happen." Oh poo, it did.

I looked to *Webster* for the meaning of kindred spirit—no, not "poo"—and I quote "kindred, kin, relatives, or friendly." Many "kind" words surround the kindred spirit, and that all "kind of" fits with Emmie's kindness and her "kindergarten" theme. Another word was "kine"—cows or cattle. I fit into that as I am "utterly" lower than cow poo.

But, I digress, the point is how in the world did that psychic know that we two kindred psychos were going to be brought together and end up moving to a different town?

Can't say I believe in all the predicting all the time anyhow, but wow, that was darn good.

CHAPTER 34

My Batting Average Is Below Two Hundred
or
In a Slump Since I've Been Dumped

I was a batting coach for a woman's softball team at one time. I have been told that I have a natural "ball sense." It is just an instinct as to how to respond with the ball. In any sport, there is a natural sense of the game. Some people just have this, and some have to learn it. It is an obvious thing if someone has a natural sense of the game. I had this instinct when it came to batting, and I would give the other ladies on the team some pointers. That is how I became the "batting coach." I certainly do not have the correct instincts for this game of life. My batting average stinks, and I am striking out!

As you have been reading over the last chapters, this has proved to be a very frustrating week for me. Life has pretty much measured up to pond scum. As they say, "This too shall pass." That is great. But if this passes, what is yet to come?

They say (whoever they are), "This too shall pass." But it shall pass right by and maybe bring something worse. I have choices to make now. I can float with the pond scum or improve my batting average with a lot of practice. Today I just wanted to float with the pond scum. Why bother? I cannot get it right. I will never be able to change how I am, and years down the road, I will be right back floating on the pond filled with scum again.

What is wrong with me that I have the feelings I do for people? Let's start with this morning and see where we end up. I woke early after having very little sleep, and I had plenty of time to go back to sleep but could not. I sure did not want to get up. I just lay there, and my chest hurt so badly, but I knew I should get up. I could not stop thinking about my friend Emmie. I knew she was upset last night, and she would not talk to me about what was bothering her before she left my house. I did not force the issue, and I knew what the problem was, but she needed to tell me. I know why she did not stick around to tell me. She knew she would cry, and she thinks there is something wrong with that because I do not cry. She is wrong. If she only knew, I wish I could be more like her in showing emotions.

She ran out of here last night, in a manner of speaking, before we could discuss the arrangements for church in the morning. We usually attend church together. I had planned to attend a different church this morning to hear a choir that was singing. We had discussed this a while back but had not recently followed through on the plans. Emmie called this morning before I got to her and said, "We did not make church arrangements last night." I said that I was planning on hearing the choir this morning at the other church, but I knew she really wanted to attend our normal church because she had not been there for a couple of weeks.

For once in my life, I was actually going to follow through with my plans. Emmie was very down, and I could tell her disappointment, but it was all right with her. As we spoke about her feelings from the previous night, she was just tearing herself to shreds. It was not a good day for her at all. I just cannot fight my instincts. I do not know how I am supposed to do this. Everyone tells me I have to make my own life and do what I want for myself. I cannot help that my life goes in the direction that my friend is more important than hearing the choir. I wish someone could tell me why this is so wrong. Why is it that this weak heart I have tends to get me in so much trouble?

"Emmie, come pick me up. I'll go with you." How else would I respond? It is my "ball sense" in life. I did not feel uncomfortable with my decision at all. On the way to church, Emmie thanked me for going with her. She also said she felt guilty about it. "You do not need to feel that way. I made the choice, and I am happy with it." This in itself is a huge improvement for me. My normal response would have been along the lines of "Oh, please do not feel bad. It is all right. Do not think a thing about it. I really wanted to go here anyhow. Whatever you want to do is fine with me." I realized I did make that choice and not from guilt or pressure that I had to do the right thing. My heart made a choice of caring and concern for someone I do care about. Most of my responses are totally from my heart, and it definitely causes a problem with heartache. I function on guilt a big part of the time, but not in this sense. My guilt tends to be when I think I have not done something well enough. The guilt? That I have to do it somebody's way, or I will not make them happy. Or I think that I am not acting properly, in other words, their way.

I am not sure who decides what is proper, but I am certain that they watch over my shoulder all the time. They are my "guardian guilters." The sermon for the day was about trusting in God providing for you. God sent disciples to do work and said, "Do not pack provisions for the trip. Trust my providing for you." Just take a change of shirt (let's hope they took that clean unholey underwear also) and sandals. They were also allowed to take a stick.

I just went to Mark and Karen's for three days and took three quarters of all the clothes I own. I could have borrowed anything from them that I would have forgotten, and these poor dudes are in the desert with a shirt, sandals, and a stick? This God guy plays by pretty tough rules. Let's hope these guys have enough "ball sense" to get them through.

So out they go to the desert. Now God's point here is to trust him to provide what they shall need. Deodorant and soap would be good. But I think what he meant was not toiletries but the love to help others, and in return, they would get the provisions they would need such as food, drink, and a retread job on those sandals. Basically, what is said is carry nothing except necessities to get from one place to another to care for people and their needs. Rely on provisions from God and grab a stick and go is what the minister is saying.

It seems like every time I grab a stick and go, I get beaten with it! Next time, I am leaving that darn stick at home and taking the deodorant.

I do not see how I change the natural "ball sense" that is in my heart when it comes to other people. I can't help what is there. I figure it will take eight weeks of counseling to just get this one week of life straightened back out. At this rate, I will be living dog years only backward. It will take me seven years to live one year. Who will last longer—my counselor or me?

I think there is a story I need to tell you, something that happened years ago that might explain where some of my feelings come from. I, upon two occasions in life, was very sick, and I lived with a lot of unknown as to where I was headed. Now I know you have, at this point, read the chapter about weight and having my throat slit, but those incidents do not even figure into this. Briefly, as to not bore you with my medical problems, I was at one point going blind and not knowing why. This made it very difficult to drive. Ask my friend Dee; she was brave to ride with me.

Eventually, things got bad enough that I decided to seek out a doctor's opinion. As I quote myself, "I only go to the doctor if a bone is protruding from the skin." I guess this was close enough. I described my feeling to the doctor as looking back and watching myself on TV. I would just all of a sudden lose my sight. I felt really funky and could not understand. Well, here was one hospital stay I got out of the old insurance plan. The doctor sent me to the hospital immediately for tests. I later found out he thought I was the one flying over the cuckoo's nest. I asked on several occasions if it could be the birth control pills I was taking, and all the male doctors said no way. I tried to explain that my cousin had similar incidents, and it turned out to be birth control pills. I was loonier than tunes in their minds now. A nice doctor came into see me one morning "just to talk." Oh, okay, like I do not know what kind of a doctor she was, head check. We talked for a while. She asked many questions and laughed and said, "You are saner than I am."

It was finally narrowed down to the diagnoses being not the proper birth control for me. So much for birth control pills. Problem solved, but the time that you have to live without knowing is so unbearable.

It was similar to my present unknowing situation. The big one was actually being told I was probably going to die. After many tests and a hospital stay, we were into leukemia, lupus. Oh, man, I cannot even remember all the things that were told to me along the way. There were no bones protruding, but man, I was sick. I could hardly function. In fact, everyone wonders how I did function. I had every blood test imaginable. I was like "blood sisters" with the vampire department at the hospital. I think they had a rubber stamp with my name on it.

I had X-rays where they injected uranium in me that was about the price of gold on the current market or maybe market-priced lobster tails. They put me up on the rack and did body scans, bone scans, head scans, checked the oil, changed the filters, and kicked the tires. They did everything they could think of, including sending me to a contagious disease expert. Eventually ending up with a gland doctor. Not a glad doctor, a gland doctor.

I do realize there is a technical name for him, but I am doing the best I can at this hour. He did a blood test that he sent to California. After one month of waiting for this test result, it was finally proven to be a poisoning in the blood known as toxoplasmosis. When this is present, it throws the adrenal gland out of whack, and that is what runs our bodies. Finally, an answer. I have to watch not getting too tired or rundown because I then have mono-type symptoms.

I hope you are sitting down to hear what the cure for this was because you will never believe it. I was put on birth control pills to straighten out my hormones that the adrenal gland threw out of order. Go figure—life is sometimes just pond scum.

The other thing is I probably should not give blood! Talk about life change or the change of life; however, you want to look at it. Thinking you are going to die has a definite effect on life. I found out having everything perfect in the house or entertaining people with everything totally perfect was not where it was at. Having people in your life to entertain was the important part.

I will drop anything when a friend needs something. I guess we already established that, didn't we? I will leave dirty dishes in the sink to go and have a good time or help someone else. Dirty dishes are nothing compared to death. Usually, I am very comfortable with dropping and running to help someone. However, on occasion, it comes back to haunt me. My problem is just when I sacrifice dirty dishes in the sink, that is when someone will come in that does not know me well.

I have a very strong feeling there are so many other important things in life other than everything being perfectly neat all the time. When someone comes to my house, I want them to make themselves at home and be relaxed. What is mine is theirs, and I no longer wait on them hand and foot. I want to spend time enjoying their company. However, I take care of visitors. I make sure I do everything socially correct. I am not a pig, but I am not intense any longer when it comes to dishes, a few dust bunnies, or the cobwebs that have become my artwork.

I have found myself falling right back into old and dangerous patterns that have gotten me in trouble before. I want to care for people.

I have been "pondering the scum" of life today. I have decided I have a very broken heart and spirit. I am so afraid and feel like I am out here all alone with only a stick and no deodorant. I miss having someone that loves me for me, that I can laugh with, talk with, and be my total self without fear. I miss it, but I guess I really never had that, did I? I am so tired both mentally and physically. I am just worn down. I do not know how long my strength will last to continue the fight. People mention to me about all the talent I have. It is in reference to my woodworking, repairing things, music, etc. Friends often ask if there is anything I can't do. I do not look at those things as talents. I look at them as desires. I desire to build cabinets, so I do it. I desire to fix the car, so I do it. But all the talents and desires are nothing in the world without self-esteem and love of other people. If I did not have my love of others, I feel I would not exist as a human being. We are taught to care for one another. I do. But I get beaten with the stick. I guess I just let the bruises heal and wait for those provisions from God.

I had a strange experience tonight. I came home from swimming, tried to write, and could not stay awake. I thought I would get something to drink and try to wake up. The phone rang, and it was Emmie telling me that she and another group member would not be over to watch a movie tonight. I managed while talking to find my way to my bed. I flopped on to it and laid there to talk. After hanging up, I fell asleep. I usually sleep and dream and at the same time hear what is going on around me. I woke up angry, realizing I had a dream about Charm and his jewels and a stick. A total panic came over me. I could not believe I did not set the alarm before going to bed. I had wanted to call the insurance company and doctor early in the morning. Now I am late for work, and I am to let people in at nine o'clock. They are standing there waiting on me. What a fool I am. I picked up the phone to call Emmie to ask her to call the doctor for me while I got ready and made it to work. When she answered, I saw my computer was on, and I realized it was nine ten in the evening. I think I need some rest. Maybe after tomorrow, I can do that.

The choice I have to make is do I quit and give in or go on to try to change myself and make a good life? I guess I will once more pick up that stick, and instead of getting beaten with it, I will take my deodorant and brave the heat of the desert.

Maybe my batting average is not up to par this season, but I can hope for the best next season. Maybe lifting weights off my shoulders over the course of the winter will help my game. I sure need a new playbook to get out of this slump. I know what I need to correct, and daily, I learn of mistakes I made in the loving and caring department. I cannot stop caring, but I will try to do better and learn along the way.

CHAPTER 35

The Tin Man, the Scarecrow, and the Lion
or
Trapped Like a Beetle

I bet I have your curiosity peaked on this one. How could anyone come up with a title like this? Keep reading, do not jump ahead, no cheaters allowed. I have had enough cheaters in my life.

Maybe the wizard had something to do with this story of the Emerald City.

Charm loves the story of Oz, and maybe he should pay close attention the next time it is on television. I could just send him a copy of it and see if he gets anything from it.

Being in the line of work he has been in all these years, the tin man fits him perfectly. As you know, he worked for a heating and air-conditioning company, and his job was laying…out duct work, I mean. He would cut and bend the tin into the correct dimensions and shapes.

Could the story of Oz fit him any other way? Yes, I think so— heartless to a fault. How can he be so heartless? I had him pegged wrong.

Charming has always been such a family man, so it appeared, and now he has deserted us for a newer model family. What he does not realize as of yet is this situation leaves him with a false kind of love and family. I found that out the hard way. That seems to be the way I learn best. I now realize that the care I felt for NotSo, her kids, and her family was not returned to my family, at least on her part. She could not have done what she has done to us if she really was a caring friend.

I truly do believe that you can care for people outside of your blood family. Friends are very important, and sometimes they become like family. You know what they say, "You can chose your friends but not your family." No offense to my family members—*just sayin'*.

The "heartless tin man" now has my friend, and I now have to tell you with all the courage that I have that I will survive. I will be a better person for this, and God will make sure I quit getting beaten with that stick. I feel the tin man has not yet shown all his capabilities of being heartless, and there will be much more to come. I can only hope he makes a pilgrimage to Oz to get a heart before too many days pass. I understand, from this story, that the tin man wanted a heart so badly he was willing to do anything for it. Well, not so much in this story. If a heart is so important, how can a person break the hearts of others so easily without even looking back?

Hearts are not made to be broken, and they are so hard to mend. They should be for loving, giving, and caring toward others. It is too bad that people have the capabilities to break the delicate hearts of others. Maybe the tin man will break loose from of his stiff joints and travel to Oz to get a heart from the little guy behind the curtain. Maybe one day, he will get caught in the rain, and all his "parts" will rust!

Now we have little Ms. Scarecrow! Personality wise, I should be the scarecrow, but the brainless part fits Prin-cess NotSo much better. What is she thinking? She is hurting her children, my children, and everyone involved. How can she show her face in town? The Reverend recently said to me, "You know they joined the church?" I answered, "Yes, I heard, and I figured they would." Reverend said he does not understand how they can do that. My sentiments exactly. How do you do this act of treason, as I would call it? He continued, "They are breaking commandments and coming to church, for what? If you break the rules, why do you come to church. You evidently do not believe in the rules." I responded with "I can enlighten you on this. Charm comes only because Un-Charm comes. I always respected her because church was so important for her. Although now that I am coming out of the dark and back into the light, I realize that she always said she 'had' to go to church. If you are right with God, you do not have the attitude that you have to go to church. You want to go to church. She attends out of guilt." God does not expect us to attend worship because we feel guilty for not going. He wants us to go because we believe and want to follow. The three of us started attending church together in December and were faithful about going.

I had asked Prin-cess why she felt she needed to go, and she said, "I just feel I need to go because I am so thankful I have the two of you." Aha, knowing what we all know now, she did need to go to church? I know that her head was not where it should be—the obvious comparison to the scarecrow. It still totally blows me away when I realize what she has been capable of. I had such a different impression of her, and I am so heartbroken. I learn more every day about what went on behind my back and realize how I was treated. Maybe I am the brainless one. I allowed too much control to be taken of my life, and I trusted too much. My hope is that I never make this kind of mistake again. I was definitely used to get what NotSo wanted. All I can say is "take a hike to Oz!"

As the lion, I already made my journey to Oz. I am walking with courage every waking moment of my life. Probably, even during those few sleeping moments I get as well. I have the courage to go on and try to make a life for myself and a good life with my kids.

I had an experience that does help me get through. Our company picnic was today. It started with golf in the morning for employees and then a family picnic in the afternoon. The employees' golf outing usually consists of most of the men of the company and me. The other women never go. Next year will be different because I will be putting the females of the company through extensive training for the outing next year. This outing is for fun, fun in my eyes, but these guys are competitive. I went to the clubhouse, and they had to make a change in teams due to the amount of people. Upon coming back out, I am sure they were debating over who was going to have me on their team and not because they wanted me. I know I saw them flipping a coin when I was walking their way.

Well, fine, guys! Someone has to take me; you already paid for me. If you don't, I will go tell my mommy you do not play fair. I was teamed up with two men, and off we went. I ended up having a great time and was very relaxed and calm. If you would like to know which team was victorious, I do not like to brag but *mine*! The moral of this story is never give a woman incentive to fight back. Look what happens. Now in all seriousness, it was a good day, and the picnic was fun. Kimberly went with me and was her social self, and I enjoyed having her there. I discovered something. I was the real C. R. today. Charm went to the picnic with me last year and sat there with his arms folded. I even had to fix his plate for him. I allowed myself to be under that kind of pressure the entire time we were there. All he wanted to do was go home. I did what he wanted last year. This year, I had fun.

I came home with prizes from the golf game. But what I really came home with was the fact that I got through this whole day playing golf with men, talking to everyone at the picnic while being myself, and did not second-guess myself. I noticed that I sat on the bench, and people came to me to talk. The young man that worked in the office with me came over and sat next to me to eat. I am twice his age, but he sat and talked to me. I could always talk with the little kids, the medium kids, and the older kids. I guess it is just adults that I don't blend well with. This day taught me that I can function in life. Kimberly said she could see how much people liked me and that all the younger people think I am cool.

Every little positive is a major accomplishment in life. I need positive in my life; it keeps me functioning.

A story Karen shared with me today sums up a lot of what has happened with the tin man and the scarecrow. She was sitting on her front porch putting together a beetle trap. She said they have a really bad beetle problem. No, not Paul, Ringo, John, and George but little hard-shelled bugs. Upon reading the directions, like most women do, she read there were two scents that attracted the beetles to the trap. The first one being the flower scent, the second being the scent of the female beetle. Now this just proves the mentality of the males to me.

Males probably invented the beetle trap, and they knew that only males would fall for that trick. The directions did not say they are attracting the female beetles with the male scent. Probably, that scent would be one of dirty socks out of a gym bag. So Karen proceeded to tell me that her reaction was that these beetles are pretty dumb to mistake a plastic bag trap for a female beetle. She thought this was pretty funny. Her son came out and asked what she was doing. She said, "I am assembling a beetle trap." He asked how the trap worked, and she explained. When she got to the part about the scent, his reaction was "How dumb can those beetles be to think a green plastic bag could be a female beetle?" Her other son came out and asked the same question. However, being in high school, his reaction was just a little more hormonal, as he responded with "How cruel can you be to do that to those poor guys?"

Charm is not unlike those hard-shelled bugs looking for their mates in a green bag. They are trapped without even realizing. Then only when it is too late, they are stuck for life. NotSo, on the other hand, is like the bag—just a green bag—but with the added scent of the luring female taking her prey any way possible.

So we have the heartless, the brainless, and the courageous. We will see how everything comes out and if heartless and brainless make it to Oz. I am hoping for the best in my life. Maybe I will find someone to reassemble me.

Just sayin'—That the "bluebird of happiness" has crapped on my life today. I should have kept my head down and not looked up. Maybe if I had started my day out with my favorite prayer before I got out of bed this morning, things would have been different. "Dear Lord, so far today, I've done all right. I haven't gossiped, haven't lost my temper, haven't been greedy, grumpy, nasty, selfish or overindulgent. I'm very thankful for that. But in a few minutes, God, I'm going to get out of bed. And from then on, I'm probably going to need a little more help. Amen."

I usually do need help throughout the day including today. I started with a good attitude and headed to work. I went in late, so the manager could leave early to spend the evening at the baseball game with his family. Then the men at work were discussing how unfair the golf game was. I had to laugh at them, and I am sure that discussion will go on until next year's game.

Then things got poopy as I found out that some of the groupies met that night and began to argue among themselves. I don't know why, and I decided it was best to stay out of it. I think they forgot we are here to support one another, not to be critical or rude to one another. They are all coming to my house tomorrow night, and I hope their issues are finished by then.

After work, I had a couple of things to do to prepare for the groupies. Vicki and Kimberly were talking on the phone and wanted to hear what was going on with me. I was mad! Mad that their father has put me in this position in my life and the fact I have no control over my life that the perps are still controlling. We talked about their feelings as well. Once again, Charm and NotSo ruined my evening without even being there. My day ended on a sour note, but the talk with my girls was good, and the groupies finally got it all together.

CHAPTER 36

They Kept Promising Me Fireworks
or
All I Got at Wal-Mart was Utter Cream

I saw a sign at a church on my way to counseling the other night. It read "In order to advance, we must sometimes turn around." Turn around? I have been spun in multiple circles. My hope is to stop spinning because I am extremely dizzy and nauseous. Advancing will come soon, I can hope. Of course, it is almost inevitable that I advance because I am about as far back as I can go. I have definitely gone to jail without passing "go!" That's all right. I am not a sore loser, and I can play just for fun, but I feel that there is no fun in this game for me.

It seems they are having the fun. The perps are making up their own rules. I just want to tell them to read the directions and play fair. I can only hope I own Boardwalk and Park Place when the game is over.

A year ago, almost to the day, I was in the same place I am now, driving route 695 headed for Interstate 70 in Baltimore. Yes, I am in Maryland, again. I just left Severna Park and am headed for Mark and Karen's on "Independence Day." Yes, it is the Fourth of July, but I will refer to this as Independence Day because I am starting to show my "independence." After work last night, Emmie and I drove to her friend's house in Severna Park. They live in a beautiful house overlooking the river and Annapolis. When we arrived, it was almost midnight, so I spent the night with them, and now I am on my way to Mark and Karen's. Do you have any clue how difficult it is to write while you are driving "independently"? Do you have any idea how difficult it will be to read what I have written while driving "independently"?

Upon waking this morning, I went downstairs. And Estelle, Emmie, and I went on a walk. Down the hill is their dock and boat. We ventured out there after watching the very long big black snake on shore. What a wonderful view, not the snake, the river. The houses on the river are beautiful, and next door to Estelle and Bill is a civil war house with the big porches. Every home is surrounded by beautiful trees. Here is some real irony for you. No, this has nothing to do with wrinkled clothing. As I stood on the dock taking pictures, Emmie said, "There is Annapolis." I had told her on our venture down about the trip Prin-cess and I took to visit her brother, and we went to Annapolis. I said, "Oh no, I can't believe this. I now realize this is where we were water skiing. We had found this nice quiet spot to do these courageous activities of skiing and tubing, and this is where we came. I was out in that water skiing and tubing looking up at Bill and Estelle's house. NotSo and I discussed what it would be like living in a house on the water. Now she is gone with what was the man in my life that would never take me to Annapolis. I had always wanted to visit. Now I am here staying in one of the houses I had admired from the river, making new friends on 'Independence Day.'"

Charm and I were in this area several times, and I asked to see Annapolis. It somehow did not fit into his agenda. NotSo's brother took me by boat to see the naval academy. We even got to see the cadets playing soccer and fished a ball out of the water for them.

Back to our walk, we walked around the neighborhood and stopped in at Estelle's mother's house. She is ninety some years old and could probably dribble circles around me with a soccer ball. Estelle introduced us to her mom as her friend Emmie and her new friend C. R. Do you understand what she did? She did not introduce me as Emmie's friend but very kindly as her new friend. Sometimes it amazes me that there are real people in this world—thoughtful nice ones.

So here I am driving along "independently" writing and listening to Michael W., lost in my thoughts. Sometimes it was thoughts of how Charm and NotSo abandoned me and sometimes thoughts that I am very lucky. Oh, wow, I have to quit writing while I am driving. I think I made a wrong turn. I must be in Texas. I just passed an Ewing Oil truck.

Independence is something very new to me in some senses, and in others, I am an old hand at it! I have had to be very independent about such things as taking care of the kids, house, cars, etc. I handled all the swim meets, soccer games, school open houses, conferences, etc. Charm Man only went when he wanted to, and if he did not want to, he just flat out would not go. I am getting the hang of this independence, and some of it is not too bad. Some of it fits right in there with that pond scum we have been talking about.

Mark and Karen were going to an auction, and I was to meet them there. Upon getting off the freeway, I came to two signs for the road I needed to be on. I turned left as the directions said. I was driving the Maryland hills and valleys, and shortly after the one mile I was to travel before coming upon the auction, I ran out of road. I actually ran out of road with no warning. The pavement ran into a stone driveway with barrels in it. Whoa, better stop here quick! Returning to the scene of the wrong turn, I realized that both the east and the west went to the right then split. I never did find that auction. Well, actually, I did find it but did not realize it because it was not well marked. I went on to Mark and Karen's house and arrived at the same time they did.

Shortly after lunch, Karen and I took David to the pool. It was so nice just to be able to talk and relax. I know I need to do more of this. I need to practice relaxing.

That night we went to a nearby town to watch fireworks. We stopped at the local ice cream stand and got a cone; well, it had ice cream in it. We pulled over to a parking lot to wait for the ever popular Fourth of July fireworks. We figured that they would begin at dark, as they do in most towns. It would be silly to shoot them off in the daylight.

It was a beautiful Maryland evening. We were relaxing in the car having a good conversation, waiting for those ever popular Fourth of July fireworks, with the fresh air flowing through the windows. We continued to finish our cones, with the ice cream in them. Darkness fell, and the anticipation was in the air, and soon we saw fireworks way off in the distance. I correct that to say we saw the glow of the ever popular Fourth of July fireworks in the distance. They were starting in a different town, and our anticipation was mounting for the fireworks to begin here in this town. They should have started by now. We have been sitting in this stupid car, anticipating these dumb Fourth of July fireworks, in the chilly Maryland night air for one hour. The other town shot off its grand finale, and we are still sitting here.

Maybe they could not find a match or lighter. Impatience was mounting in the children, and the anticipation was dying rapidly; no one was around. There was no more glow in the sky. Conversation was dwelling on why the fireworks were not starting. After all, it would be the unpopular Fifth of July in an hour and a half.

Waiting like that can make you start to ponder about important things in life. You know like, do the different-colored M&M's have different flavors, or do my taste buds just not work? Well, this could be important! I should see a doctor if my taste buds do not work. It was decided that we would take a drive to the location the fireworks were to be coming from to see if there was any action. Seemed like no one had a match, and they all went home, and so did we, laughing about our none-ever popular Fourth of July fireworks night that we were there on the wrong night.

Upon rising and shining the next day, it was the ever unpopular Fifth of July, and it was a lovely morning. Rumor had it we were going to try the fireworks thing again tonight. I hope we see them. I would much rather sit in the house than in the car in the dark with no fireworks.

I was able to help Mark and Karen wallpaper while I was there, and it was nice to do so. They have been so very good to me, and I would do anything for them, anytime. The love I have for them has always been in my heart, but I am able to express it better now, and I love spending time with them.

David and Stephen have treated their old aunt wonderfully, and I enjoy being with them. Even Corky the dog has been good to me. I guess you could say I am telling them how I feel, but I need to let them know in person.

Errands have been run and wallpapering finished, and it is time for church. I kind of like this Saturday night church thing. I love this little country church, and the priest is a totally cool dude. After church, the plan was to catch up on those fireworks an unpopular night later. The plan of attack was to sit at a gas station by the Frederick Keys Stadium and watch from there. We didn't get to watch the game, but they threw in Wal-Mart. I guess that is what you do on the Fifth of July in Maryland. We cruised the parking lot of the stadium with the game on the radio to see how many innings were left.

Mark and Stephen ran into Wal-Mart to get a baseball for David to have autographed at the Phillies game he was going to the next night. I then entered Wal-Mart where I decided to buy the ever-popular udder cream. I better get fireworks out of this tonight or at least darn soft skin. A cruise through Burger King and it was on to the gas station as darkness hit.

This time, we hit a home run. We saw the fireworks, and I had the udder cream. Who could ask for a better unpopular Fifth of July?

CHAPTER 37

Encounter of the Worst Kind
or
The "Bore" and His Sow

I knew it. I have said it all along. I was so very positive. How else would it have happened? I just plain knew it! I had a feeling I was going to have an encounter of the worst kind. The encounter occurred this evening at approximately seven thirty in the evening at a local store in the parking lot. I have had a premonition about this moment for some time now. You may be asking what I encountered. UFOs? Aliens? And what is this about pigs or boring people? Oh, boring people, now you get it. Put boring with people, and you realize what the excitement is about.

I saw "them" together in front of my very eyes. I had talked to a friend who will remain anonymous throughout this chapter as to protect his or her semi-innocence and not to incriminate him or her. In speaking with this friend, I asked if he or she would go to the store with me because I never go there alone anymore. I know this is a big hangout for the boring parties, to whom I am referring the "bore and his sow." I just need a little support in case it happens, and it did.

Upon entering the parking lot, the conversation was in full swing, and laughter was prevalent. And then I saw it, right there with the bug guard staring me in the face—the relentless red truck of Charm. I cannot believe it. I said something along the line of "Oh golly, gosh, gee whiz, I think this red truck could be Man of Charm's. Is that not wonderful?" Well, believe what you want, but we were able to confirm that the truck was Charm's.

What do I do? Where do I go? Do I sit here? Do I go home? What the heck! They are only people, right? I should not be afraid.

Another little portion of this story is that Charming was to take Vicki, Mike, and Kimberly to a baseball game tonight and called it off because he was too sick to participate. So what was this evening of shopping? A lack of participation, a nonparticipation sport, or at least a noncontact sport? I do not think so. This just broke my heart. He cancels on the game with the kids and goes shopping with the sow; he is a bore. Do I sound a little "sower"? Yes. However, can you possibly tell me I do not have that right? He lied to my kids!

Back to the parking lot. In this same parking lot, I had previously found them meeting and talking after work. You know, they were parked way away from the store. You know how that is? You always run into friends at the store parked far away from the store in the parking lot, sitting in the same car talking. Seems like a meet and greet to me.

Here I am faced with the reality of it all, and now I have to deal with it up close and personal. What should the plan be? We continued to case the restaurant and stores that were in the plaza to see where they were. Anonymous found them. This friend anonymously looked Charm right square in the eye. I can't believe he or she held it together and did not do something like stick his head in the freezer, choke him with toilet paper, pour chocolate syrup on him, not to mention other various thoughts that crossed my mind.

All this time, I am sitting in the car wondering, waiting, and watching. Where will they come from? What is taking anonymous so long? What is he or she doing to them if they were found? What will I do if I see them? I seemed fine, but those butterflies kicked up in the area of that Wendy's burger that I just devoured. I glanced in the direction of the door to see the ever so anonymous one coming back to the car.

"They are in line at the check and will be out soon," he or she said. Now they are even controlling the time I can go to the store. There I sat wondering, waiting, watching, and anticipating what my reaction would be. Then "they" emerged from the doors of the store. Why do I keep ending up shopping in these stores? I don't like to shop. There was Prin-cess NotSo Much right in front of my eyes with good old Mr. Charm pushing the cart behind her. Gee, I always walked behind him. When he, Cess, and I shopped together, he pushed her cart for her and not mine. Nothing has changed. It was obvious as they wound through the parked cars that NotSo realized they were in the wrong row and angrily reached back, grabbed the cart, and turned it toward the truck. They unloaded the heaping cart into the truck that, I am sure, in his ever so weakened, sick condition was very difficult, poor thing. I asked, "Should I get out?" "Yes, get out" was the quick response. I jumped out of the car and walked right toward NotSo. She turned and looked right at me.

Man of Charm was rounding the truck to the driver's side in anticipation of driving their little treasures they had gathered "home." His new home, his castle with the flowered wallpaper he hates. It is in NotSo's name and is NotSo's decor and NotSo's possession just like he is!

What was I doing? I had no prethought process on this one. Where was I going? What was I going to do? You wonder too as did my anonymous friend who was witnessing this sudden brave and extraordinary behavior. Prin-cess looked up at me. She was just ten feet away and never flinched, batted an eyelash, or changed the "sower" look on her made-up face. When she looked to my direction, those years of marching band paid off. I did a sharp quick TTR (turn to right). You never saw a right face done so quickly and precise. I turned and quickly made my way toward the store and then stood on the sidewalk with arms folded and hoped they saw me, but it was obvious they didn't. I figured it was because the sun was at my back and shinning in their lying eyes.

Reaching home, after my shopping, I somewhat came back to semiconsciousness. The anonymous one told Kimberly that I was upset and the reasons why. Kimberly was concerned for me as I was for her over the fact that he was well enough to shop but not go to the game. She called the bore, and the sow answered. She asked to speak to her father, and she asked if he was lying about being sick. He said, "No." He asked why? She said, "Did you not see Mom at the store? She was ten feet away from Noncharming and looking her right in the eye." "No, we did not see her. I would be civil to her if she wanted to be," he said.

What does he mean "civil"? Like civil defense because he should be on the lookout for falling debris, bombs bursting. Maybe it is civil rights. No, he was always prejudiced against other races and ethnic groups.

"Do you really think Mom wants to talk to you after all the hurt and pain? Do you know what tonight seeing you together does to her?" Kimberly asked. Mr. Charm claims he was sick and just wanted to get out for a little while. I do not know what to think anymore. I have reached the point of "who cares?" I mean just flaunt your new lifestyle. Do not look back or think of the consequences. They can't see any further than the end of their growing noses.

I did not think going to the bank would be a risk. I was so very wrong. Here it is the day after the encounter, and guess who is at the bank. Don't they have anything else to do in life but go to the store and the bank? Go to another town, another store, another bank, get a life, and stay away from mine! Poor anonymous keeps getting drug into this with me. We were sitting at the drive-thru window when Charm and NotSo pulled up to the ATM machine. By the way, he had the same shirt on as last night; he must be really sick. They pulled away right before us, so we ended up behind them at the traffic light, and Charm Man looked in the rearview mirror and saw me. I just stared right back at him. His lips were moving, trying to disguise the words of "C. R. is behind us." NotSo's neck almost snapped off as she looked in the side-view mirror to see me. That was the longest traffic light in history! They proceeded to turn the same direction as we were going. Several miles up the road following Charm's precise and slower-than-speed-limit driving, they turned off, and we continued to our destination.

He stared so long and drove so slow that I thought he was trying to count the freckles on my face or the gray hairs on my head.

How does this all settle with me? I don't think I know yet. I shed tears that evening. It was about the fact they just dumped me and ran. Rejection any time from anyone hurts badly, but twice from two people you respected and trusted? God does a have a great learning experience for me, and I will come out a better, happier person. I only hope I do not mess it up with the new people in my life. It is only fair, before the completion of this chapter, that I reveal why I used this chapter title. Anonymous said Charm looked like a "pot-belly pig." Being the socially impaired person that he is, I chose the spelling of "boar" to be "bore." Remember the old saying, "You can't make a silk purse out of a sow's ear"? I think I have explained enough, and I feel a little relief of stress without yelling or screaming.

CHAPTER 38

─────────────❦─────────────

Puddle Jumper to First Class in One Hour
or
Peanut Gallery to Cashew Crowd

Here I am on my way to Florida in the blazing heat of August. The August heat of Florida is much more appealing than the everyday heat of Charming Man and NotSo. So here we are—Emmie, Linda, and I—winging our way to the land of oranges and swamps.

When I say winging, I am not kidding. We had to begin our journey by boarding a puddle jumper that, on takeoff, felt like you needed to flap your arms to help keep it off the ground!

Upon arrival at the airport, we were greeted by an empty counter. We were there as expected by the airline more than an hour prior to our flight. Where were they? Turns out the person from the ticket counter was out gassing the plane, cleaning the windshield, changing the oil, kicking the tires, and loading the baggage. Although I am quite the kidder, I am not kidding.

The ticket agent came to the counter apologizing for the delay, and I, with my usual smart wit, had to say, "We thought you were out kicking the tires and gassing the plane." The agent laughed. She asked where we were going, and we said Cleveland (as we had to take the jumper to Cleveland to get on the plane heading south). She said, "Good, Newark is closed." Our baggage was checked in, and we proceeded to gate number one, and we were the only ones there. We knew this was a little twelve-seat puddle jumper; however, we only had a few puddles to jump to get to Cleveland—fifteen minutes' airtime. As we were anticipating our trip and drinking our morning coffee, I wondered if there was a bathroom on this puddle jumper.

Out the terminal window, we could see the ticket agent in the area where the plane would be coming in and parking. You thought we were just kidding, but the agents literally gassed the plane, swept the pavement, loaded the luggage, shoveled snow and spread salt (in season as needed), and directed the plane—multi-talented.

We walked out and climbed the stairs to the plane. We found a very pleasant crew of two welcoming us aboard, including a woman—yes, *woman* pilot—and male copilot or flight attendant. Our luggage was being loaded, and we could watch out the plane window to make sure that our suitcases were among the bags that were loaded. All on, we fastened our seatbelts. I put on my sea bands; the propellers were whirling, and we were ready for takeoff into the wide blue yonder or, in this case, up into the cloudy sky.

In a small plane, you do not fly at a very high altitude, especially between Akron and Cleveland. The view is really comparable to a ski lift or sky ride at an amusement park. I never realized how much farmland there is between these two cities just forty miles apart. This little plane made for an interesting flight. The vibrations, at times, were so strong that I kept thinking the wings were going to fall off. Takeoff was good, and after banking left, we headed north. I wonder what the directions are for this flight coming from the control tower. Instead of the normal follow header 129er they get, go to the third farm, turn left until you see Interstate 71, hang a right, and head north. Follow the downtown exit heading toward the big body of water (Lake Erie), turn left, fly over Terminal Tower, and land in the big area with all those little roads with numbers on them.

We did all that, and we landed safely. It was like watching the landing on a flight simulator as we could see the entire thing from our seats.

Once we were on the ground safely, we were quickly shuttled to the terminal to catch the big plane. We were greeted by a friendly airline employee who told us our flight was overbooked, and we would have to sit in first class, if that was okay with us. I guess we would just have to suck it up and sit in the cushy seats. Charm Man would be soooo envious.

We were properly seated in our plush, comfortable, oversized first-class seats. I am watching the face on the people coming aboard. I recall the same look on my face walking through first class. No one smiles at you; there is just a sort of an angry sneer as you are "checked out from head to toe." I wish I had more gold and diamonds on, or maybe even a name on the rear of my "not-so" designer jeans. If only my fanny pack was from somewhere other than Wal-Mart. If I only could get to my mirrored sunglasses and had a scarf around my neck, they might think I was a movie star.

Truth is I am just like all those sitting in the coach section, just happened to get my name called to be up front. I remember those feelings as I have walked through the first-class section many times to get to my little seat in the back. I am happy in the "peanut gallery" instead of the "cashew crowd." The flight was good and the company good. I sit here feeling I am comfortable and do not have NotSo Charming here telling me what to do and the proper way to act.

Most of the sneering faces were seated except one last sneering lady passes by as her little daughter turns to say something, and the mom quickly responds with "Shut up, Grace."

Now we have our drinks, and the black curtain has been pulled to exclude the "peanut gallery" from the "cashew crowd." This is when Emmie kindly reminded me not to ask Jack, the male flight attendant, if he had any nuts. Good point, been there done that.

Once we were in the air and cruising along, Jack asked if we would like a cheese omelet and pancakes. Bet me, Buckwheat! This normal member of the "peanut crowd" will take whatever you are serving. He then spread a linen cloth over the tray table and graciously served a fruit plate and croissant. That was enough for me. I did not need an omelet and short stack at this point. I ate it though, and it was good. Since Ms. NotSo Manners was not there to control me, let me ask a question. When you eat grapes with the "cashew crowd," do you pull them off the stem and eat them with your fingers? Or do you use a knife and fork? Personally, I like tossing them in the air and catching them in my mouth.

The lady in front of me was asked to put her dog away. What? Her dog? I just thought that was her husband whining! That explains the scratching noise I had been hearing. Let the poor thing out so he can run the aisles and play with the "peanut gallery" kids. Now I hear that "Skipper" is his name, sort of blends with the "peanut gallery." I was just happy his name was not Bingo. My poor dog was "home alone in Ohio."

If you can recall in an earlier chapter, the one about my trip to Baltimore, when I sat between two gentlemen, then you will appreciate this little story. I am sitting across the aisle from Emmie and Linda, and the seat next to me, of course we know, will be occupied. Anticipation fills the air as I wait and watch for the possible bachelor number one, number two, or number three. I think I got number ten and a half. He does not display a wedding band and probably ranges in the mid- to upper fifties. Clad in khakis, a green golf shirt, and Ralph Lauren socks. Maybe he has money, or maybe he is a good outlet shopper, or he probably was bumped up from the peanut section as well. I can't say that our eyes met and it was love at first sight as he has not looked at me . . . yet! The next thing he did was take his shoes off. Ahh, a man after my own heart. I usually take my shoes off on a plane. As he sat there with his legs crossed and his little pony on his socks, I noticed it. I saw it in plain sight; right in front of my face was the hole in his sock. I realized two things at this point: he is not married, and he really was another one of the upgraded peanut shellers.

I decided God puts opportunities in front of us, and I will not let this one go by, just in case it is a plan of God, but I am prepared if God is just using his sense of humor again. He could be a book publisher!

"Are you going to Fort Myers for business or pleasure?" I bravely asked in a non-nosey threatening manner. "A little of both" was his direct response. "Oh, really," I responded. Was that the best I could do? Pony socks responded with "Yes, I am going to buy a place close in the area. A nice quiet area, a beautiful city." Buying a place? Pony socks with holes? Could this be a good mix? Personality was not his forte, and I have been through that once, and once is enough. The holey sock, I could live with, but I need a smile and some sparkle in the eye to make it work for me. Besides, he snorts. There is more to life than pony socks and a possible purchase of a house in Florida.

The landing was safe and smooth; the sun is shining. Skipper made it through the flight without an accident. The snorter is practically pushing me off the plane. No more free drinks, and I will be back to the "peanut gallery" for the flight home.

CHAPTER 39

If I Have Told You Once, I've Told You a Thousand Times:
Never Go to the Park After Dark
or
Never Wear White If You Don't Want to Be Seen

Day two in sunny Florida is coming to a close, and Emmie's sister took us to shopping areas, beaches, a great lunch, and more beaches and more shopping but no more lunch. It was a great day and fun for all. The highlight, of course, for every woman—that is any woman that you could get to admit it—was the noontime main event of lunch at Zoe's. It was a very wise choice—the best french-fried sweet potatoes. I will strive to have more before I head back to the Buckeye State.

Emmie's brother-in-law made crab cakes from the crabs he trapped. Makes sense to make crab cakes from crabs, like I needed to explain that to you. Dinner was great. If you recall in other chapters, I explained my romantic side. We ate at the table with candlelight, good food, and conversation.

What is better after a great dinner than a cigar? A walk to the park down along the river. Such a beautiful evening, warm but not too much, great refreshing breeze, palms flowing in the tropic like air, and peace and quiet. Just as we were walking through the park, we were joking about the cars that were sitting around. What were these cars doing, or what were these people in the cars doing? A joking concern was coming through our conversation, and we were saying we were safe because there were three of us. We were sure we could take care of ourselves. I was walking by the river picking up shells and had every intention of sitting on one of the big rocks on the water's edge when Emmie said, "Make sure you look before you sit down." Look? I am thinking silently, *What am I supposed to be looking for along a very dark riverbank in a very dark park on a black rock?* I responded with "The snakes aren't out at night, are they?" "Yes" was the answer. I did not at this time chose to sit on this black rock by the dark river in the dark park. I ventured back to the picnic table, and we continued our conversation, and I joked about if I did get a snakebite, the other two would be hightailing it out of there. So what happens to me? I can see me on the ground with a snakebite, and all I can see are their tail ends headed the other direction. What would I do? I would have to suck the venom out in order to live long enough to hike a mile back to the condo. If I sat on a snake, venom sucking would be an impossible task and an impossible dream of the chance of one of them helping me out—no takers there! The easy way out is not to sit down.

Sitting on a picnic table and relaxing, I laid back and was enjoying the star-filled sky and river breeze. Linda asked a question of me, and I opened up and was talking. I finally started to share some of my life when there was a loud sound complete with crashing and cursing. We immediately envisioned a car accident, but turning to investigate, we saw a pickup truck bouncing over the telephone poles that were in place to mark the path of the driveway to the park. The truck was bouncing at full speed toward our table. He braked suddenly and slid sideways.

As Linda and Emmie jumped and said, "Let's get out of here." The driver suddenly throws open the driver side door and "threw up" the sash. Needless to say, these very loud and entertaining gentlemen were quite inebriated—one too many, a little soused, drunk as a skunk, three sheets to the wind, or they had been drinking, not to mention driving.

There was a young couple standing close by when this happened, and they went to check to make sure these "gentlemen" were all right. They jumped from the pickup truck with profanity flying. We could not see everything that was going on through the darkness and the trees that we were hiding behind, but we heard someone hit someone else and the voice of a female yelling, "Stop!" We could hear the yelling and cursing and could see them running around the truck with flashlights. Oh, I get it—flashlight tag! Maybe it was Marco Polo with flashlights. It must have been hide-and-go-seek' because we were hiding.

We continued walking along the river staying in the dark shadows so as not to be seen. One of us had white on and stuck out in the lights—not so good. Who were these gentlemen and what were they doing? One thing they were doing was throwing up. The passenger was screaming at the driver and trying to pick him up and put him in the truck. He was on his hands and knees throwing up and then collapsed to the ground. The passenger wanted to drive and kept yelling at the man on the ground to get in the truck.

Something like "Oh, dear friend of mine, will you please come join me in the truck." Yeah, right. He started the truck up, put it in gear, and almost ran over the dude on the ground. I had to feel sorry for the two "gentlemen" as they must not have gotten past elementary school because they could only use words with four letters or less. The intellectual statements that included all those four-letter words were not getting the response he wanted from his friend, so he burst from the truck and picked this swaying, staggering man up and put him in the truck. He was very determined to get out of the truck every time he was put back in.

We had walked a little farther away and decided that we would just head back. We knew we would feel guilty if anything happened, so we decided to get the number of that truck. We were in the process of working our way back toward the truck to retrieve that number. This is where we ran across the couple that had been watching, and they saw us peering through the bushes and came over to talk. She had the name of the truck and the truck number. She had hoped we would call the police. We said that is where we were headed. At this point, we continued in a hurried manner up the street for our long trip back to the condo and a phone. We were thinking about stopping at a house to ask them to call, but this community was made up of many seniors, and I do not mean in high school. Every light was out, and everyone all snuggled in their beds while Junior down the street is throwing up his sash.

We saw what we thought was their truck coming and ducked into a driveway and hid behind bushes and mailboxes. You remember one of us had on a white shirt and was very noticeable. We did not want them to see three squatting women behind the bushes. We are hiding on someone's property, and I figure that is a good way to get the police there because we would be reported before we could get to the phone. I am sure that would bring them to the right area. After crossing to the other side, as in street, we spotted a police car going the other direction. We waved our arms and yelled, and he saw us and stopped. Upon us hustling across the street to the cruiser, the uniform-clad gentlemen spoke, "What's up, girls?" in a tone as to say, "What the heck could these three old broads want from the police department?" His attitude disturbed me being the insecure person that I am. "What's up?" is your park is being torn apart, but the worst is two gentlemen are driving the streets of your lovely town drunk as skunks. Do skunks drink? You know of course that I would never say that, but I did think it—hours later. We quickly told him what had happened and the number of the truck, but he said that would do him no good and said, "I'll see if I can find him." Off he went.

Did we get in the car to go see if he caught the drunk skunks? Yes, but only after everyone went to the bathroom—typical! I do not know if these gentlemen were apprehended or not, but I certainly would not have wanted to be on the road with them or anywhere else with them.

Always remember the lessons I have learned from this experience. Never go to the dark park by the dark river and sit on a black rock with someone that will not save you when the fangs penetrate your backside exterior skin. Never wear white at night if you are going to play Magnum P. I. and never ask a woman to hurry to catch up with the cops without allowing a rest stop.

But having good friends and fun experiences will always provide you with memories forever.

Just sayin'—That this is my last day in the sunshine state, and I am sitting at the pool writing and enjoying the last moments of sunshine while the others went discount shopping. I really have no money to shop with. There are things I need, but it does not matter because I don't have the "green bucks" to purchase them.

I kept Emmie up last night talking. You would think she was too tired to shop. She helped me to realize that we all do have our own personalities, and she finds my lightheartedness refreshing.

How do people exist without laughter? If it were not for my humor and being able to laugh at myself and "others" in a good way, we all know where I would be—down in the dumps. I would exist only in my own world, not in the big world. Why would I want to allow them to do that to me?

Using humor in day-to-day living, even when things aren't too funny, helps us to be healthier in mind, body, and spirit. That is one theory. My theory is that it keeps me from crying and becoming a crabby old person. I am not one to sit in the house and knit all day, watch *Wheel of Fortune* and *Jeopardy*, and then go to bed. Those are all okay things to do, just not all the time. I want to be playing with the kids and experience life. I don't think I will ever grow up. I will not forget this Florida trip. I will remember the moonlight bouncing off the warm water, the night air. I don't want to just stand on the dock and watch the ships pass by. I want to drive the ships!

Make each life moment count, whether small or momentous. Share your time, love, and laughter with others. Be a teacher and teach others how to have fun and laugh while sharing your knowledge and experiences and—more importantly—listen to theirs. Listening and your time are the best gifts you can give one another, you know—***just sayin'***.

CHAPTER 40

The Trilogy: Part 1 of 3
or
The Day Before

Anticipation is in the air. How will I react? What kind of a day will transpire? Will I deal with it or fall apart? Deal with what you ask? Tomorrow is "my" twenty-sixth wedding anniversary. Not many people make it to their twenty-sixth anniversary, and I almost didn't.

Fortunately, thanks to Man of Charm, I made it to the big day. If he had filed for a divorce, I could have been legally separated or similar, but due to the lack of response to the situation, on his part, I am still a totally married woman. I am so lucky to be married to such a thoughtful person. I wonder if this will last till "my" twenty-seventh?

Let's start from here and see what thoughts are surfacing tonight. I have had such an unpredictable day I feel like my heart is spinning in circles and does not know where to stop. I have been told so many good things and have wrestled with hurt and agony. One year ago, Prin-cess made such a big stink out of circumstances about giving us a surprise party for the quarter-of-a-century happy couple! I have decided I just need to vomit forth the inward thoughts of concern she shared in wanting a very special party for Charm and I. Give me a break, how does one's best friend and the "lover" of the best friend's husband fake that so well—thinking Charm and I needed to celebrate this twenty-five-year milestone? How does a person with any compassion do such a thing to another? I am very concerned about what a poor judge of character I am. Why is that? Why couldn't I see the forest for the trees? I now realize why a lot of things were the way they were and how capable the two perps were of manipulation and just downright abusive behavior toward me. What is very disturbing is she could look me in the eye while she was twisting the knife in my back.

We had this great party with friends, relatives, and the trimmings. We were celebrating the wrong occasion. I figure I will have a lot to deal with tomorrow on this first anniversary since my being cast aside like a used car. However, I am sure there are even worse times around the corner. I predict that I will receive divorce papers tomorrow. A little tactical strategy on their part. That starts some of the feelings I am dealing with, and there is so much more.

The thoughts in my head just swing back and forth like a pendulum, but time is not on my side. I have not seen my counselor in a few weeks because of vacations, and it will be another week before I do. I will never be able to catch her up in that limited time we have, and the feelings will pass or be buried by then. I feel I should be locked up with a psychiatrist until I can understand how to change to not allow this to happen again. I already see some of my old patterns coming back to life, and I run when they surface.

Others around me feel so much anger and frustration, and I almost feel like I have to be the calming effect. In the past weeks, I have met with the reverend. I took some time and did some personality tests. Today was result day, and I kept him laughing with my answers. That's what I am here for, to keep others laughing and happy. It turns out that I am what the test sums up to be a "golden retriever." Great, now not only am I a used car, but now I am a dog. So do I take that as a compliment or not? He said it was a compliment, but golden retrievers can get into a lot of trouble. Think about the comparison. Upon command, a golden retriever will dive into the icy cold water and retrieve a dead duck in its mouth—no questions asked, with no concern to its self. That is just the way my test came out. I dive in, no questions asked with no concern to myself and no problem carrying that dead duck between my teeth. Here is the team of NotSo and Charm Man happy with themselves sending me in for ducks, and all I have left are feathers between my teeth.

Golden retrievers are summed up as being patient, loyal, deliberate, team player, serene, protective, relaxed, and biscuit lovers, to name a few. And I am house broken!

I had a real rude awakening of my personality traits today and a real urge to chase cars all the way home. It certainly makes a lot of sense when you read about the personality traits as to why I was on a leash and did not even realize my limitations in movement. Other traits I suffer with are casual—that explains the Umbros—relaxed, friendly, and informal; and that explains the hands in the pockets. To continue, there is submissive, seeks attention, likes to have stomach scratched, hates fleas, and is irritated by insensitivity and impertinence. I would like to ask Charming, "Is it really too difficult to reach down once in a while and give a little pat on the head and an occasional good girl, good girl? After all, I obediently waited all day for you to come home, and your slippers and paper were by your chair." As a golden retriever, I am steadfast, reliable, stable, softhearted, and a good listener; and I never talk back and only interrupt with an occasional bark at the mail person or paper person. So now, and only now, have I realized that I have been muzzled, hit with a paper, caged, left home alone, and deserted by a lion for a beaver.

That summed up the test, and the results were discussed and analyzed with the idea of improvement to not let people just pat me on the head and move on. I am the victim. As I am working to improve, where are they? Rolling over and sitting pretty? My work will pay off in the long run, and they will still be roaring at each other and chewing on trees with their buck teeth.

The upside to all of this is that I am okay and that I just have to watch out for myself a little more. There is some good. I also received a letter today from Estelle. If you recall, I spent the night at her house in Maryland over the Fourth of July. It was such an uplifting letter for me because of her appreciation of my faith in God and my trusted friendship and care for Emmie. I do have that care for Emmie, and together, we will overcome the situations our men of charm have put us in.

My job now is to try to put the feelings and fears for part two of this trilogy aside to sleep tonight. We will see how successful I am at that, and tomorrow will be the test. God will be with me, and I do have a lot of caring people around. Faith is such a great reward in life. If you have total faith in God and his system, you can't lose. Your heart will take over and help you to revive your full potential. Please remember, if you see a golden retriever, reach down and give her a little pat on the head—we need positive attention and reinforcement.

CHAPTER 41

Trilogy: Part 2 of 3
or
The Day Of

Why did I get out of bed today? It seems like I have said that before in another chapter that asked that question. I should have called off work. After all, I do have sick days coming, and I am sick! Sick of Prince of Charm and of NotSo Much and their cocky attitudes and self-centeredness. Sick of dealing with legalities of this chosen life and sick of unpaid utility bills. This is where normally someone would say, sick of life, but I am feeling like I am regaining life. That is a very tough aspect of life to deal with right now. It means that possibly I am pulling it together in the face of devastation, but where does the anger, resentment, and all the feelings of hurt and abandonment go? If these feelings continue, what happens when they all surface?

Emmie almost had a sobbing person on her hands three times in the last few days. What kept that from happening? Am I afraid in general to cry in front of others, or am I concerned to let loose in front of her because of the possibility of her past resurfacing? I can't let loose on her. After her kindness to me, she does not deserve a crying, blubbering, sobbing, delayed emotional person around.

So should I have called in sick and stayed home? After all, I could get away with saying I was sick as a dog being a golden retriever, you know. What would I have done all day, home alone on my twenty-sixth anniversary? Probably cry alone. A twenty-sixth anniversary only comes along once in life—for most people. I suppose, if I got remarried, I could make it one more time. If I really hustled, I could do it. I would be seventy-two on my next twenty-sixth. I technically could still make a fiftieth. I would only be ninety-six. I would not be able to do too much about it, but the thought would be there. My goal is to have Willard Scott show my picture for my one hundredth. I bet Willard would like that too. Think about how old he would be.

The day started at work with me calling the electric company to make sure they had received my paperwork that I had sent in to apply for assistance in paying for my bill. I was told that they had not received it, and I was set up for shutoff. I had to pay the minimum today, or it would be shutoff. Like I have not been shutoff from enough already. I explained that I could not get there due to work and was told that I had to or a shutoff would occur. I said, "Fine. I will live without it." Where did that come from? I have never talked to anyone like that before. I had just had it and was upset with Charm that he was doing this. I had to ask my parents to go pay the bill. I immediately phoned my attorney, and as soon as she got in the office, she called. I had my boss telling me, in no uncertain terms, to haul Charm's rear into court and also to get my attorney in gear.

I felt like I was in the middle of a twister. It was only eight thirty in the morning, and my whole twenty-sixth was already becoming a disaster film in 3-D, Technicolor, and Dolby surround sound.

Well, if you have figured anything out about me, you are wondering how Ms. "Lackofassertiveness" is dealing with standing up to the electric company personnel. I will not keep you in suspense any longer. It only took me a half hour to call and apologize! Well, I felt better.

The good things of the day were my parents did pay the bill, and that helped. Emmie showed up at my office with flowers and a nice card to make my day a lot better. This helped the twister subside immensely. Group members called to see if I was doing okay, and I started to count my blessings.

I had my annual preseason soccer dinner in the evening. What would I do without those crazy soccer friends? They always make me feel good. I was told that I looked good and had that sparkle back in my eye. My team members will never understand what it meant to me to hear that.

Among the team, the groupies, and Emmie, I made it through this disaster in waiting. Emmie and I talked on the phone till midnight and solved the problems of the world. It is good to have friends, and I will never allow myself to be pulled away again.

CHAPTER 42

Trilogy: Part 3 of 3
or
Lower Than a Snake's Belly

In this trilogy of the anniversary, I made it through the day before and the day of, and here I am the day after. It has been a bummer since five fifteen in the afternoon, and at this point, I am well beyond the day after and skipping to this day.

I was doing very well. I went to church and came home, cooked three meals, made cookies to take to my counselor and the office gang, did some cleaning, and started writing. I had not been writing more than several minutes when someone knocked at the front door. Kimberly was expecting friends, so the thought never entered my mind that the knock had my name on it. I went to the door to let Kimberly's friends in, only to find an older gentleman asking for C. R. As you know, it is my nature; I trust everyone and never gave a thought to this gentleman being the bearer of divorce papers from the ever-so-thoughtful Prince of Charm.

It is Sunday afternoon, and a man comes to my door and says, "Is C. R. here?" Of course, my normal reaction is "That's me." He says, "Here, I have something for you." I was already in the process of opening the door. I took the papers, and as I pulled my hand back, I felt like it had been bitten off by a shark. I knew by the feel of these papers what they were. How does one live with themselves delivering papers such as these on a Sunday afternoon?

Upon first walking to the door, I noticed a minivan in the driveway and a woman sitting in the front seat. I never gave it a thought other than I instantly was trying to figure out who these people were. I was thinking they must be someone I know; maybe they were from the church. The church of no consciences! The woman in the passenger seat of this delivery truck from hell was watching the whole time, just staring at me. I wonder if she ever received such papers. If so, I can only hope some witch sat and stared at her. It was like they were on their Sunday bye-bye ride and just decided to have some fun on the way home. Just what kind of people do this for a living? I think NotSo Prin-cess and Prince could be capable of doing this kind of work.

I immediately walked to the kitchen looking at these papers, not able to comprehend anything at the moment, let alone this legal mumbo jumbo with all the words blending together in front of my eyes. My mind was not able to unscramble what the meaning was. Kimberly was close by; she too thought it was her friend at the door. I came out with some words that got her attention, and she realized this was not a friend at the door. I think I probably said something along the lines of "There was a nice old gentleman at the door, and he very kindly handed me these papers on this very pleasant Sunday afternoon. It was so kind of him to bring his family with him to deliver these to me. I think it was such a nice gesture on your father's part to have these papers dated on our twenty-sixth anniversary." Sarcasm, *just sayin'*!

What am I to feel now? His attorney will not return my attorney's calls, faxes, or answer her letters. And all he said was he was trying to get Charming to give a little more money until we could come to an agreement. Yeah—and peanut butter tastes good without jelly. So where does the blame of cruelty belong in this case? An unannounced divorce delivery? The deceptive, inexcusable, nonanswering attorney? Does the cruelty lie with Prince in requesting that my attorney not be contacted with his intentions? Was it NotSo saying, "Do not let her know it is coming. C. R. always enjoyed surprises." Your guess is as good as mine. I can't even fathom the cruelty of these two special people that once were a part of my life. What happens to people? Was I this kind of person who is always present in their lives, or I could not see how well they could use me?

Kimberly was appalled at her father's lack of sensitivity and his outright unkindness. Her descriptive nouns were flying through the air as she ran to call him not only on the phone but every name in the book. Fortunately, he was not at his happy home that he claims he pays six hundred dollars a month for, according to these newly released papers. I was able to tell her not to mention these papers or anything on them to him. She wanted to let him have it and could not understand my reluctance for him to know the papers were in hand. I told her that she could vocalize her other gripes with him but not mine. Meanwhile, my father walked in on this mess. He was leaving a car for Kimberly to drive. As soon as I finished talking with Kimberly and dealing with the papers, I took him home. On the way across town, I passed the infamous red truck with Man of Charm behind the wheel. He was the man that said he would always love me and take care of me. What happened to that loving family man? His whole tune has changed from Dolly Parton's "I Will Always Love You" to "Liar" by the Sex Pistols, no pun intended.

His acts have hurt his children. People often say, "At least, your kids are adults." It is not any easier with younger adult children than with small children, just different.

I went a few rounds with my punching bag. I have now made a gym in my garage that includes a forty-pound long bag. No, I am not referring to NotSo Charming but the punching bag. It does have her picture on it though.

I called a friend, and we had a good talk, and she was encouraging me to call my attorney and leave her a message as to how upset I was and to please call me. But then she remembered who she was talking too. I wish Emmie was here, but she was on the road coming back from her daughter's house.

I feel so alone and so very violated. I feel like my life is still controlled by perps. I don't know what will happen to me. I know I am not really alone, but it sure feels like it sometimes.

Emmie called as soon as she got home, and in a very spirited voice, I heard a kind "Hi, and what are you doing?" I asked her to come over, and she did. I just asked—right to the point, direct, no hem hawing.

Kimberly had a fight with Charm, and he tried to dig deep to see if I had gotten the divorce papers. She did not crack. He has no idea what he has done to his daughters and what he has lost. He told Kimberly that she would have to accept NotSo if she wanted a relationship with him because she was his wife. Hello, here I am— chopped liver, dirt beneath your feet, jam between your toes. I was just a speed bump in the road to the life they wanted. At least, Kimberly takes nothing from him and dishes some very mature thinking his way. He can't keep up with her. He has lied so much and gone back on his word. I feel very badly for my children. It must hurt them so much. He had promised them they would never have to accept Princess of Uncharm to have a relationship with him, and now he says this is his wife, and they better learn to live with it? What parenting book did he read? I think Dr. NotSo Spock had something to do with it!

Emmie was listening to the day's events and was supportive. I wish I could have cried it all out, but I couldn't. I believe God will take care of me. Emmie assured me that God had a better plan for me and that there is a reason I am going through this. The unknown is what I fear. My faith will not falter; it will continue to get stronger, and I will use this experience to help others in time of crisis. Charm and NotSo can break my spirit but not my faith. It is the one thing out of their control. I saw a sign the other day that stated, "It isn't over until God wins." Well, back to the punching bag!

CHAPTER 43

The Battle Does Hurt
or
Out with the Old Lioness, in with the New "Lie-oness"

How soon the love and the dedicated years of service are forgotten. After all, most people get a gold watch after twenty-five years of honorable service. I have served honorably, without even a mention. This is what happens—the good is forgotten, and the anger and guilt mount until the only action is a cruel one. Why is this? They got what they want, so why do they inflict so much hurt and pain? All I can say to them is "You got what you wanted. At least, be fair, own up to your actions instead of spending all your energy inflicting more pain." In my book, if you walk out on your family for a new one without a care for the old one, why don't you try to work out a suitable situation for everyone instead of trying to beat us to a pulp?

Here is the recent situation. Charm has filed for a divorce, as you have already been informed. Now the fun part is that he expects me to pay his attorney's fees. I know you are laughing. We all did too. He claims I caused him this expense. My guess is that he thinks because I did not come back with a counteroffer to his offer, he blames me, and he just wants out. Now keep in mind that I just wanted to get my utilities paid for; then I could think about the rest of life.

However, Mr. Charming would rather see his daughter and wife—umm, I am still his wife—sit in the dark, with no water or gas to heat and cool the house, than try to help us out so he can have what he wants. Makes sense to get angry at us! I am struggling to keep these utilities on, and he is struggling to decide which fancy golf shirt to wear on Saturday to the course.

Life does not seem fair at times, but I do have a theory. What seems unfair at this place in time could turn out to be a blessing in disguise. There are reasons for everything in life. It just takes a lot of patience to wait it out, and then God will provide at the right time. God will provide for Kimberly and me. The thought is I need to work as hard as I can to keep things running properly and the love to continue in my family.

I am now faced with the problem of finances, and this will be a rough one. I feel if he is now a permanent client of NotSo's establishment of pleasure; she can provide for him. She has done fine on her own for three years, so take care of what you "bought" because, in my mind, he will come with a huge price tag. I do not make much money at all. In fact, it is considered poverty level. Mr. Charm, as you know, marched in and had me sign the tax return checks and said, "I will pay the bills, and you pay the utilities. I am going to an attorney tomorrow!" I stood in disbelief with emotions flowing through every portion of my body and was making no sense of anything. He then left, checks in hand, without even thinking of how little I make and how I was going to live and support Kimberly. That is not true. He has thought about it a lot. At least, he has all the ideas for my life and what I should do with it!

Let's have a little history lesson, a look back in time of the life of Mr. Charm and C. R. The mentality was that women don't work and men do. Women take care of the home and the children, and the men are the lions, the king of the beasts, and women are the golden retrievers. The lion struts home proud of a day in the jungle but tired and hungry with a nasty growling tone to his loud roar. "What is for dinner?" he roars. Do you know how many times I have heard that roar in twenty-five, now twenty-six, years of making the den a home? The problem was not only the roar of what's for dinner but the disappointment when it was not good enough for him. The "I had that for lunch," like I could suck that info out of my thumb, or "You know I don't like that." But the absolute loudest most biting roar was the ever-so-piercing "I am not in the mood for that." So make me a list of your moods and nonmoods because I cannot guess these things. So he wanted me to stay home and not work. "Women," in his mind, were to do the home and kid thing, but I could never measure up to his standards, and I evidently still do not.

The recession in the building trades hit us. He, Lion Charm, was worried about his job and rightfully so. However, in his manly way, he said to the den keeper slash cub raiser, "You need to get a job to help out. Go to the local fast food place. Certainly, they would hire you." Hold the phone! There is nothing wrong with working at the fast food restaurant, but I seem to see this control thing here. He tells me to get a job, where to get a job because they will "hire" me, like no one else would, and he would probably like to tell me how to flip the burgers and to ask, "Do you want fries with that?" We all know I will not do it logically or correct. He is right. I would probably put the mustard on before the catsup. Maybe I would hold the pickle and not the lettuce. I feel like my ego, at this point, is dirt under his paws.

Now we update to nineteen years later. I have worked. I taught music lessons, taught band in private schools, and was church choir director. Charm never lost his job, but my income sure helped to pay for the growing cubs' swim team, soccer team, band and orchestra, and trips with those groups.

He always said that it was good for me to work to help out with the cub's extracurricular activities. True, but now I am paying for his "extracurricular activities," and so are his cubs!

"My job is the important one," he would growl. "It pays the bills." That was according to this superhuman. We could do without the extras for the cubs, according to him. According to Mr. Charm, he had all the stress, and what he did at work meant something. Here I am again—chopped liver, jam between his toes, you get the idea. There was never a listening ear for my day's events or even any kind of help offered when I had a problem except for him being critical.

Control—he always had that. He had me by the neck, and he did the usual roar as I coward down and said, "Yes, Your Highness, King of the Jungle!"

He continues to want control of his life, as we heard earlier in this story, and he continually controls mine and the cubs. His idea as far as my money issues is that I can change jobs and also work a second job in the evenings to support myself. I do not recall choosing this life.

I remember it being chosen for me. He still wants to decide what I should do with my time. Do not forget those secretarial skills I supposedly have. With my skills, someone would certainly offer me "less" than minimum wage. I never finished school. Someone came along, proposed, and said I did not need to work because that was the man's job. In my eyes, it still is, so get busy and do your job. Honor those vows. If you are going to break the "until death do us part," you could at least respect the promises you made to God. I followed the love, honor, and obey part, so you could at least have enough respect to honor the part of in sickness and health and when you are unfaithful! I have been sick, and I have had health, but I do not have your honor. You made all these promises to God, and you figure he won't care. Not! You could at least be decent in your abandonment of love, responsibility, care, concern, and money. You chose, with help I am sure, to be cruel. Why? We all know why, but we want to hear it from your li-on lips. I deserve an answer to that question, and I also deserve a face-to-face explanation from Prin-cess NotSo Much.

To move on in this totally incomprehensible saga, how does a family-oriented man change his tune and sing so off-key so quickly? He wants his lie-ness in the den barefoot and subservient to his working life. Twenty years ago, I had the skills to work at a fast food restaurant. And suddenly, with the flip of an attitude, I have "secretarial skills" and skills coming out my ears. I am Lioness, hear me roar! That is his logical brain on hormonal lust. I went from no talent to sudden superhuman in just a short time frame and as a convenience to meet his needs to serve his new lie-ness.

I think my anger is beginning to surface in this chapter. I sit her typing like faster and faster, hitting the keys harder and harder.

Whew, I need to take a break! I even disturbed my dog Precious (I did not name her) because I was making so much noise typing fast. "Be glad, Precious, that you do not have to go through this. The worst problem you have is that you have to go outside to use the bathroom in the snow and cold." Wow, here I am talking to the dog. I guess that's all right as long as I don't hear her speaking back to me.

Back to the business at hand. The lion can use his logic to fit any need for his life. He always has been able to make the logic flow the direction he needed to substantiate or justify the direction he wants to go. He would very much like to follow the direction of—well, we will not go into what he is following, but it is not his brain or probably not even his true heart. The part that still follows the typical lion logic pattern is the big C word—*control!* He loves his control, and I am sick of it. If he wants control of me, then he should move his mangy lion tail back where it belongs. Oops, too late, the den is closed for repairs of a crushed and broken lioness's heart. He wanted me to pay all the utilities, but he had them all switched to his new den address, except for the phone; he had his name taken off that one.

Upon occasion, he feels the need to send me a utility bill, and he manages to send it the day before the shutoff date. I see a pattern here. He is trying to break me, but the more he throws at me, the louder I will roar. I no longer will tolerate his control. There is no excuse for him receiving the bills, opening them, and then sending them after the shutoff date in snail mail to me. Take the responsibility. Your first lioness has squatter's rights and will no longer be your prey.

Hold old on tight, Charming Lie-on, because there is a tropical storm coming through the jungle, and its name is C. R. There is no stopping it now. The high winds are going to blow and take some of that wind out of your sails, not to mention the torrential downpours that will dampen your spirits. The lightning will shock you back into a reality check, and that deafening crack of thunder will make things sound differently to you.

Most importantly, watch out for that large hail because that will dent that shiny coat that you are so proud of, that ego and cocky attitude. It is too bad you chose this path. I am sorry for you. You are the one that has to answer to God and live with yourself. You got off the path of God and onto the path of the great hot place below. I know your feet will burn when you are walking your chosen path. Just remember, the people there want ice water! You have plenty running through your veins. What's that, Precious? You're jealous that Charming is petting another dog? Oh, boy, now I am hearing her talk to me! Oh, by the way, take that comment any way you want, but Prin-cess does have a dog.

Just sayin'—A few words of wisdom. After rising in the mornin', think of the fact that you got up, not that you have to get up!

Do not look at breakfast and say the coffee is cold and the corn flakes soggy. Think the coffee is almost warm, and at least, I don't have to chew those hard crunchy flakes.

Savor the tiniest of accomplishments and do not dwell on the failures and mistakes. Without them, there would be no accomplishments.

Be positive in your life. Uplift yourself. Do not wait for others to do it for you. Relax and appreciate what you have.

Do not be a complainer or whiner. Nothing good comes of it. Complaining only makes you more miserable. The more you let negative responses in, the more you hurt yourself.

So what if it is hot? It is not cold. If the sun is in your eyes? It is not cloudy.

Hi there, this is Precious, and I'm taking over for my owner while she isn't looking. I have some positive thoughts to add. If it is snowy, at least, she does not have to go outside to the bathroom. If you have a hole in the yard, at least, you don't have to dig one to bury a bone. If your bone is half eaten, at least, you still have another half. Oh, oh, her she comes.

"Precious, what are you doing? Not only have I heard you talk lately. Now I see you have been writing. Get away from my computer. You're slobbering on it."

Boy, you walk out to the kitchen to get some water and come back to find the dog etching her thoughts in ink. I think I better get some sleep—*just sayin'*.

CHAPTER 44

The Comeback of a Lost Person
or
Eat Lead, Sucker

It is fall and time for that local support group to have formal meetings again. I went tonight along with Emmie and Betty from my group within a group. Seventeen new people joined tonight, and their hearts are very much filled with the pain of divorce. Where does all this come from, and why are so very many marriages falling by the wayside? No one seems to respect this institution of marriage. We know some people that belong in an institution for the havoc they have caused. It was sharing time again, and now here I am in the position of new strangers looking at me while I try to put words and thoughts together to form complete and meaningful sentences. I was a nervous twit knowing I would eventually have to speak. I want to speak. I want so very much to help others through their pain. My goal is to do public speaking to help people through tragedy in their lives. Isn't that a riot? I can't talk in front of seventeen strangers, and I want to be a public speaker. Emmie and Betty spoke first being longer veterans of the group, and then it was my turn, and I was severely deficient in the thought area. Emmie said things so well and so relaxed, and then old tongue-tied gets a shot, and I blow it big time.

I am finally starting to realize this new life I have been thrown into can be happy and successful. I do not want to backtrack and worry about the way I react or whether I said or did the right thing when I spoke to those newbies in the group. I made it though and was able to shake off the fear that I did not do the speaking correctly.

The next day was counseling, and while I was parking my car, my pager went off, and it was my attorney. I went into the office and asked to use the phone and called her. What better time to have to face what was coming than at the beginning of a counseling session.

Picking up the phone receiver, I dialed the number that has been etched in my memory, and my attorney answered the phone. She knew right away it was me and said, "C. R., I got the temporary court orders from the hearing, and he"—he being my new sparring partner in life—"must continue paying the current marital debts and you alimony. You are to pay the utilities and take care of your expenses." Numbness filled every inch of my body and brain. My words stumbled forth to say, "This is good, isn't it?" She said, "Yes." Finally, Charm has to be somewhat responsible for his actions. Prayer does work! I chose to live at the right hand of God, and he does take care of me. I try to follow his lead. This God dude can be a nice guy.

I am off the phone and a little shaky, not really knowing what to think. My counselor came around the corner and said, "Come on in." I walked in and said, "That was my attorney calling with the court orders." "Do you want to talk about the orders or the day in court first?" she responded. I am still numb wondering how I even walked in here on my own two feet. I think this is the first time I was speechless in her presence. She continued to pull the information from me, and I still was not sure what to say. "This is good," she kept saying. "You can pay your bills and feel a little more secure." I sat there in this stupor thinking this is good; he finally has to take care of me like he promised when he walked out six very long months ago. "C. R., he has to be just losing it," she continued. "You are allowed to be happy. He has to take some responsibility finally for what he has chosen to do to you." I told her that the worst part of this court thing was the fact that I felt like it was NotSo and Charm against me. I said, "Why do they have to be so mean about all of this? I did not do anything to them. So why are they out to get me? It is like let's get her before she gets us. Well, gotcha!" This is all starting to sink in now, and I am starting to feel pretty good about this decision.

One of Charming's favorite sayings came from, I believe it was *Lost in Space*. One of the robots would say—and for the very first time in my life find it very appropriate to use—so "Eat lead, sucker!"

I got in my car; and drove to Emmie's school to leave a note on the dash-board of her car (which she never locks). I sat in my car, the one that Charming has to officially make the payments on, writing the note which said, "We are going to celebrate tonight; I am buying dinner before group." Not knowing for sure if she would see that note, I called her home phone and left a message, "Just in case you did not see the note in your car, I wanted to tell you I am buying dinner tonight. We are celebrating, and all I am saying is you have to pay to play!" I received a message from her when she reached home stating that she assumed this was great news and that she would love to celebrate and to give her a call. That I did. I did not tell her the news over the phone. We met at the restaurant across the street from "the house where NotSo and the Prince live." Emmie could not wait to hear the news and was very happy for me. What is funny to me is that she was really happy for me; it was not fake or a have-to kind of thing. I think she showed more enthusiasm than I did. I felt really good. I saw a caring that I had not been shown in quite some time. Emmie does not show her feelings sometimes, and she is very difficult to read. I am not always sure where I stand with her. She makes me work to try to figure out her feelings. Challenge is good in a friendship. Her comment was that there was no one that deserved it more, and that was directed in both Charm's and my direction. A twofold observance. I hope she knows how much I appreciate her. She accepts me for who I am. I enjoy Emmie's company, and she gives me the impression she enjoys mine. Sometimes we need each other to talk to, but it is a two-way street.

I do see light at the end of the tunnel. There may be a few road-blocks between here and that light, but I now see that construction will end, and the real C. R. will come back fully rebuilt.

Just sayin'—Happy birthday to me. It is the first birthday I "celebrate" since the duo took a hike, and I am going to celebrate with a murder. No, I am not going to murder them. I am going to a murder mystery play with the group. I might, however, pick up some tips, on murder, not as in money.

At the murder mystery, we were the "clueless eight" as we were terrible at murder. That is a good thing. We had all the right clues, but we were clueless. We had the answers and no idea who committed the murder in this play. They leaned on me to have a clue as the musician of the group because we thought the piano figured into the murder. Well, I know music. I could have pounded out a song, but I don't know murder, at least not yet. We had a fun evening even though we were lousy at murder mysteries. We celebrated two birthdays. We did the singing, candles, presents, coffee, card reading, and more. I had worried about this evening. I am not very good at being the center of attention. I anticipated that I would be nervous, but I got on a roll with the jokes and having fun. The gifts had a lot of thought behind them.

I came home and placed my gifts in their appropriate places in my happy room. I lit the candle from Shelly. Jim gave me a cat's meow, the purrrfect gift. Stan was thoughtful with the music box. And Mo, although her cards were a little bit on the nasty side but funny, gave me a beautiful miniature Christmas tree for my happy room. Betty's book, *How to Play Better Golf*, will come in very handy for next year's game at work, and her best gift was that she thought I was in my thirties. Cindy hit the nail on the head with the book *Writer's Market* to encourage me to publish my work. Emmie had given me a beautiful music box earlier in the week, and this night, she gave me a plaque that read "Where a door closes, somewhere a window opens." A very inspiring thought. Maybe at the next murder, we won't be so clueless—*just sayin'*.

CHAPTER 45

When Is It My Turn?
or
Why Do I Always Come in Last?

It is my fault that I never win, and I always come in last place. I know that. The problem is that I give until it hurts, and then it is too late to correct the situation that I created. I actually train people to use me by catering to their needs. Then when I do something not in line with my character, their impatience with me comes to the surface. Then I am stunned, hurt, heartbroken, and devastated. Maybe "devastated" does not really fit here in a normal heartbroken day. "Devastation" is a Charming and NotSo Charming thing.

Maybe "disappointed" should replace that "devastation" thing. Disappointment creates a lot of hurt and pain without total destruction of a life—sprinkling just a few damaged parts along the way. I do not even have a clue as to where to start this story. There are so many things bouncing around in my very cluttered but empty mind. I am not sure what will come out and what will stay in there, entangled with the cobwebs of other unvoiced feelings. Pretty soon, that stupid chime clock that Charm has requested for his new abode will be striking its opinion that midnight has arrived. I know that I cannot even think about sleeping until I get these feelings out and printed for posterity or simply because I have to spew them forth. Everyone else, with any sense, is in bed and not available to hear my complaints.

Go ahead and chime away, clock. I am going to finish this, no matter how long it takes. My punching bag got a work out tonight. I put on music, "Can't Touch This," and punched dents in those pictures hanging from that target. I do not know if the pictures are a positive action for my anger or a negative action for my heart, but I am positive that I had a lot of negative tonight, not to mention sore knuckles.

My day was a very confusing one. I am doing some work for a friend, and today' job was ripping insulation down from garage walls. Emmie was there and helping our friend in the house, cleaning up the mess from the painters and plasters working there.

This could become a sideline for me. That would mean that Charming Prince would get his way and control me. It would be a second job like he said so kindly suggested that I get! Although after the event this evening, it could be a first job because my boss is not happy with me. I have an idea that I would like to go through with that has to do with repairs and other items people need to have done. It would mean I start my own company, and maybe that is where this leads.

Emmie and I were trying to decide what to do for Labor Day other than labor. Originally, we had discussed going to an amusement park, but things changed from there to a possible bike ride with a friend and her children. Then the bomb dropped. The big *S* word. You know the *S* word, the one I try not to say too often especially in front of my daughters or Emmie. Sometimes if you say it, they take advantage of it, and then you are stuck! Well, Emmie kept saying it, and I could not say no, so off to Shopping we went. Do you know how many golf courses we passed on our way to the outlet mall on this beautiful sunny weekend? To go shopping, oh, man, I cannot even say the word. The thing is we had a good time, but I don't want that to get out to Emmie, or I will have to do it more often!

Upon our arrival back to our lovely city, we decided to do tag team lawn mowing, and that we did. We mowed Emmie's lawn and put her mower in the trunk of her car, and we first hustled off to the video store. We picked up a movie and cheese sticks from Papa John's, and it was start your engines and mow.

Emmie began in the backyard, and I continued my new tradition of mowing the front yard in a V shape. Victory starts with a V. I have not yet been victorious, but I will be. However, the real reason is because if Prince of Charm drove by, it would really tick him off that I did not mow the lawn in the north to south direction with a five-inch overlap, exactly three inches high, and I only mowed it once! I did have other options of letters in mind or words that I could carve out with my Lawn Boy. However, I chose not to use those words even though one of them rhymes with grass. Recently, a lady in the area was arrested for mowing an obscenity in her lawn. A better choice—use one letter.

After tag team mowing of both lawns, it was on to pizza, movie, and paperwork. Emmie did her schoolwork, and I did bookwork. Kimberly came home, and I could tell the mood was not a good one. I asked what was wrong, and guess what she told me? It had to do with the lack of money and sorority, and what was she to do? This is what I said, "Ask the lovely kind people that caused this, not me." Well, honestly, I did not say that, but I wanted too. The guilt hit me, and I felt awful that we were in this situation. I know she is not trying to make me feel guilty, but it does feel like all the guilt, pressure, and responsibility lies with me instead of the parties in question! Prince leaves and does not take responsibility for his actions.

I sit here writing to ease my mind as there is no one I can talk to at this late hour, and there really is not many I can talk to. It is hard to talk to my kids about this situation. Vicki is upset enough, and she has started her own life with Mike. I can't burden them. Kimberly is in college, has her own life, but still has an involvement financially because of school. She gets more hurt thrown at her each week. My parents are angry, and sometimes my mother is in tears complaining about what Prince has done to her! It is a long distance to complain to my brother and sister-in-law, and the one person I spend most of my time with, Emmie, I cannot tell everything to because she cannot tolerate my pain. So tell me, who do I have left?

I do not think Charm and NotSo are interested in hearing my problems, and I do not want to burden all my friends and their families with the situation. Then there is my counselor, but I am sure she does not want a call from me at twelve fifty-two in the morning. God listens but does not give an immediate response, and if he spoke back to me at this time of night as I sit alone, that would scare something out of me. He will answer in his own way and time like most men, but I will be more patient with him than other men.

Kimberly is strapped for money, and I do not have two nickels to rub together. My fears right now are not based on living alone but being financially stable. The guilt I now bear is terrible as I don't have the money to pay for counseling, and that is sad as she is such a help to me. How can I quit? She is comfortable to talk too, and I feel like I cannot go back because of money. The two perpetrators put me in this position. I owe the counseling group money, my attorney money, the electric and gas company money, the water company, and the list goes on.

NotSo and Prince are cuddling at night with each other, and now she not only has my husband but also my checkbook, so to speak. Can I sue her for vandalism of my heart?

CHAPTER 46

D-day Cometh or C-day or the Day, Whatever
or
Round 1: At the Sound of the Gavel, Come Out Fighting!

I am sure you get the picture. Tomorrow is round one of this legal aspect of my new life. You know, where you go to court, and no one cares what wrong has been done, short of murder. It will be an attitude of show me the money, and we will divide it up. It sure would be nice if the courts went back to listening and remembering the sacred vows and the responsibilities one person has to another. No one ever has to be held accountable for the pain and hurt they cause anymore. Now I sound like an old grandmother saying, "In my day, I had to walk three miles to school after milking thirty cows that all gave sour milk because of the tornado we had the night before that I had to cut up all the trees that fell down before I walked those three miles to school—uphill both ways."

My point being, our society has grossly mistreated the human kindness values. There is a certain loss of the world God had planned for us. He had great plans of us caring and sharing, and we abuse his thoughts and only want the rewards. The intentions have to be right before there is a reward.

Tomorrow morning will prove to be the starting block for my future. I have a somewhat calming effect over me. I have felt that way for a couple of months. My attorney cares about me and will do everything possible to help me be independent in my future.

I feel like I would like to run and hide from everyone, but that would be not so smart. I have to face it sooner or later. I have allowed everyone to take my time and my efforts, and there is nothing left for me tonight. NotSo and Charming take so much from me, and even when I spend my weekly time with my counselor, they have control. We are so busy dealing with the weekly problems caused by them; there is no time to update myself for self-preservation in a devastating world. I don't want to be watching everything I do and say. I shouldn't have to deal with all the financial crude. I did not choose to leave; Charming did. He should be bending over backward to take care of the "first family." The work pressure is becoming intolerable, and I feel very picked on. "Picked on and controlled" is the very essence of my feelings.

The loneliness tonight has become unbearable, and there is no relief. "Loneliness" is probably not the proper definition of my current feelings. A huge sadness, with a sense of taking three steps forward and sliding back four. There is the feeling of never being able to deal with things properly and what I really feel that I am not supposed to say is "I can't do anything right." I hate these feelings. I thought I had come along way, and I seem to have stumbled. Sometimes I am standing high a top those blocks, and then some days, I am stumbling all over them. This is not a day for standing on top. I actually have allowed myself to stumble the entire day. My feelings have declined.

Just sayin'—That I am sitting here at two thirteen in the morning feeling lousy. I am lower than a septic tank and don't want to bring others down. Of course, at this hour, there is no one else around to bring down! Living daily with Charm and Prin-cess just drains me.

I had counseling earlier this evening, and she asked me to tell her what made me most angry about the dastardly duos (my words) fleeing. That was easy, the pain they caused my children. That hurts more than anything they could do to me. One instance I thought of was the time Charm and NotSo took Kimberly back to school, and they had a huge fight, and I stood up for him! Not because I thought I should but because he and his what was to be his future bride (I just did not know it at the time) told me I had to support him.

Eventually, I found out that most of the fight was about Kimberly asking him what was going on between him and NotSo. He left that part out of the conversation when he told me about the argument.

Kimberly and I eventually talked about it, and I told her I was truly sorry. I continue to have flashbacks. I have very vivid pictures of the day I left my heart in San Francisco and things that have hurt my kids.

On the way to counseling, I passed another church sign that read, "It is not over until God wins." I am hopeful he wins in my life. Last time I came this way, the sign read, "Forbidden fruit makes many jams." Ain't that the truth?

The tin man and his scarecrow have certainly made a lot of "jams" for my family, but we will get out of these sticky situations and be stronger for it.

CHAPTER 47

The First Step toward Legal Termination
or
Walking through the Dog Poop of Life

My job requires many extra hours during the month of September, and it is here! I am finding there are not enough hours in the day to get everything done.

The musical instrument business is busy once school begins. Tonight, I had the hardest program of the year, and the preparation during the day was extremely stressful. That's not to mention the actual evening of rentals, parents, kids, kids test driving all the instruments all at once, the questions, the reactions of parents, the continual competition between companies, and the many decisions that have to be made immediately with no turning back. The fall rental season is the support for the business for the rest of the year. So I would say these few evenings are very important to a lot of us.

The saying "If it were not for bad luck, I would have no luck at all" sum's up my day. Today was the first court date of this "charming" divorce. That is right, my worst band night and I have eight o'clock in the morning court. Did Man of Charm choose this date on purpose knowing how tough this time of year is on me? Did he figure I would be too tired to fight him? Our county court is in Akron, and I have lived in this area all my life and still cannot confidently get around Akron. I can take you anywhere you want to go in our state's capital of Columbus but not little old Akron. The city confuses the heck out of me. I must do this court day by myself. I just have too. I cannot be late, so I allowed extra time because I was uncertain of my capabilities of finding the place, the parking deck, and the room in time. I surprised myself and went right to it in all three cases. Why? If you remember, I was the support system for NotSo's divorce, and I made several trips to this oh, so holy place of matrimony and unmatrimony.

I was seated in a chair in the waiting room before the lights were on—seven thirty-five sharp in the morning before the bailiff, the judges, the attorneys. I think the janitor had just finished emptying the trash from the day before.

While sitting in the quiet of the darkness, a thought popped into my already-overwhelmed mind. There are not many places that, on any given day, has so many future single men per square inch. After this is over, I think I will just come here and sit, listen to the conversations, and figure out who has the rich ex-wife and make a move for him! There isn't even a cover charge.

Since I was the first one in the room of dematrimony, I chose my seating to get just the right angle where I could get the best and first view of Charm as he entered this room he had put me in against my will. I chose a seat on the end of the row where I could view all the entrances. This way, he could not slither in behind my back and show his fangs. I waited and waited and waited till finally one of those future single men showed. He sat one chair over from me. His wife must be slithering in also. The lights are on, the bailiff seated, and other officials and dematrimonials are filtering in. My mind and stomach were anticipating the slithering in of the man of charm and the expectations of his reptile counterpart slithering along beside him. Every time I heard footsteps or the elevator doors open, my stomach would turn over.

Now twenty-six minutes have passed, like the twenty-six years of marriage, my attorney walked in, and I finally saw a smiling face. Fortunately, she came in before I saw perp number one—the other party involved. We were called into the room of dematrimony, and there he was, the one that decided that my life was going to change, the person that thinks he can play God and control my life. I would not look him in the eye. I have seen too many moments of lies and betrayal in those eyes. I wanted no part of looking at that pain again. I felt that if I looked him the eyes, the hours of training on the punching bag would prove beneficial. A few jabs and upper cuts would probably not help my case. After we were all seated and a little chitchat went on over the magistrate's overgrown poinsettia on the desk, the bout began. Round one was my attorney and her report of Charm's pursuit of his girlfriend and abandonment of Kimberly and myself.

According to Charming Man, that was not abandonment. He felt with what was going on between them (code for what was going on between the sheets), it was better for him to leave.

Hmmm ... what was going on? His attorney must be wrong. Remember, nothing happened before he left me. All that happened afterward. The falling in love and living together all happened in just three short weeks? Hmmm ... somehow, I find that hard to believe.

The financial points came out, and we were showing his deception of income, and they tried to explain that I should make more money. We presented the fact that I have been responsible for the house and Kimberly, and they pointed out that he had bought her some clothing, whoopee! We presented the fact that I could not pay the utilities, and they rebutted that the utilities and groceries only totaled four hundred dollars a month. I should be fine.

We continued with the cost of counseling that I need due to the loss of my husband and friend and the physical pain I have been caused by the stress. This just went back and forth with these little items. Even the dog was brought into the picture, and I just sat there deflated. Just put me up on the rack, rotate, balance, and spin me. I have absolutely no control over my life. My attorney was sitting there, telling the court that Charm claims he pays six hundred dollars a month to NotSo Charming for rent, and since he has been informing his children that she is his wife now and his honorable intentions to marry her, she certainly would not kick him out if he did not pay rent. His first obligation was to his first family. Look at that, I made it to the first family without even running for office.

After the little exchange of "who done its," we exited back out into the cruel world. How am I supposed to continue my stressful workday when my life is being directed by everyone but me? Now I have to wait a week for the decision and hold off the utility companies for a little while longer.

I realize this is just a business to the courts, but this is the rest of my life, and there is a lot of emotion to this entanglement of finances, heartbreak, betrayal, and slithering reptiles.

The previous week, people kept asking me how I would feel when I saw him. I couldn't answer their questions, but I can now. I felt like throwing up. I know I don't want anything to do with him. I feel like such a failure in life to have misjudged so wrongly. Their overwhelming deceitfulness seems to be so much fun to them. I wonder how I could have been so stupid. I think I am still very numb, and I can't even have thoughts on how I do feel. I can tell you once again about the support system I have surrounding me. So many people wanted me to call them after my time in court. There was no time to talk to everyone. I made the choice to stop at school and leave Emmie a note that it was over for the day. As I walked through the office door, I found the school secretary on her knees in front of me, begging my forgiveness for her unintentional recent rudeness on the phone. She then, after returning to her feet, had a big hug for me. She called Emmie to the office, and I was able to talk with her. I spoke with my parents, Karen, and eventually Vicki. Neither one of my children knew of my court date. I did not want them to worry or be put in the middle. I was preparing to leave my office to go to the rental program when, much to my surprise, Mark walked through the front door of the store. He had driven down from Cleveland to see how I was and had to drive right back to catch a flight. I was thrilled.

After a very long evening of stressful musical instrument renting, I was back on my own turf when a car pulled out of a gas station in front of me. Rounding the corner, I realized that it was Charm and Un-Charm. I started and ended my day with him. My friend Debbie, Emmie, and I had a quick cup of coffee at Mickey D's, and homeward bound, I went. My poor dog had not been outside since noon, and I expected to come through the door to see her standing there with her legs crossed. She greeted me, and I sent her out. Of course, she did not come right back, and I was out roaming the neighborhood in the dark and in bare feet through the wet and muddy yards, quietly calling her name so as not to disturb the neighbors at this late hour.

After locating her, I headed back to the house, and that is where the second title of this chapter reveals itself. I stepped in the dog poop with those bare feet of mine—what else could I have expected on such a poopy day?

After scraping the do-do off the feet and jumping in the shower, I checked the answering machine where I found calls from my fellow groupies, just checking on me. I have to tell you that bad luck thing—"If I didn't have bad luck, I'd have no luck at all"—can be true, but I see that the support and faith I have outweighs that old bad luck. God has truly blessed me with so many wonderful people and a strong nature to perceiver and hold my own in the face of challenging days. I know I have more rough days ahead, but I can do it with the strength of God and the many people around me.

Someday as you are walking through the reptile house at the zoo, look at those snake eyes and see if you recognize them, but more importantly, do not allow your bare feet to wander through the dog poop of life.

CHAPTER 48

I Just Do Not Belong Anywhere
or
Reach Out and Touch Someone

Tonight, my feeling is one of a total sense of not belonging anywhere with anyone or anything. You are thinking I am nuts and that I just told you that I have so many supporters. You are thinking that I belong to a church, a soccer team, a garden club, and an alumni band. I have a job and a family. Card group is always there for me, not to mention I am a proud member of the divorce group and so on and so on. You get the point, or maybe I should.

I do have all the previously mentioned areas of belonging. However, my heart sometimes overflows with feelings of emptiness and aloneness. I can sometimes be surrounded with loving, caring people and somehow be all alone. Maybe, and I think this is probably a definite, I was alone even or especially with Charming and NotSo. I now realize they are not capable of sincere caring for another person or the God-given unconditional love for others.

I am learning so much about people. I am better about looking into the inward person instead of the misconception they portray of themselves on the outside. We as humans can portray ourselves differently when we do not want to allow others in.

What brings all these feelings on, you ask? The love I have recently been shown. Now you are totally confused. I have gone full circle from explaining how lonely I am to how much love I have just seen. When you go through downtrodden situations in your life, you can become a little mentally complacent, have feelings of displacement or summed-up "displacent" or out of your ever lovin' gourd.

Here goes the explanation of this weekend that has brought my feelings to the surface. Emmie, who I often accuse of only hanging around me to get her name in my book, and I went to visit her mother. She lives in a very small town in southern Ohio. This is where Emmie was raised, not like vegetables but homegrown in a small two-bedroom house, sitting on the side of an Ohio hill, across the river from Wheeling, West Virginia. My friend Dee was homegrown in a very similar town on a ridge in Pennsylvania. It is like a duplicate, same people, same church, same simple lifestyle that breeds kindhearted people with concern and caring for others. The "bake a pie and take to a neighbor," church social, bingo-playing, loving people.

Everyone knows everyone's business, but when someone needs something, the town is there for them. Sounds like these small-town hearts might be just what God had in mind as his people.

Our journey began about one thirty in the afternoon from Emmie's driveway on Saturday afternoon. We headed for the southernmost route with the fastest speed limit, known as Interstate 77. What a "bottleneck" of traffic we were stuck in. Who made up that term to describe traffic anyhow? Why can we not just say, "A lot of traffic was stopped on the highway, and we could not go anywhere fast!" We sat and talked at a much faster pace than our car was progressing forward. Not one angry or negative comment was said; there was not an ounce of impatience. This is a new concept for both of us. We have lived our married lives with impatient, negative reactions to any situation that did not please the Mr. Wonderfuls of our lives.

Once we were through the traffic "jam" with Mickey D's french fries in hand. (The diet starts Monday, possibly this week. But if not, some week or maybe a Tuesday. Oh, we might as well wait till after Christmas or before spring break. Well, sometime.) I regress, we were "on the road again" and at full speed. I drove the first leg, and Emmie drove the portion with the hills, dales, curves and hills and hills and curves and curves and hills. Oh wow, good thing I have my sea bands on.

This quaint little town does sit on the hillside. There are so many little towns so close together you can spit a watermelon seed in one and harvest the melon in the other. I have always wanted to live in a place with white picket fences, families walking to church as the bells ring, and everyone knows "one another." However, I left out the part where you park your car in the basement. No kidding. When you say, "Where is your car?" The answer is "in the basement." I saw it with my own two eyes. Yes, I did have my contacts in.

We arrived after being "semi" slowed down when the big coal truck turned over on the curve outside of town. Upon our arrival, we were greeted with a hug from Emmie's mom. Throwing our things in the house, out the door we went to visit neighbors. Emmie's sister was having a birthday party for her daughter, and we were all going for dinner shortly, so we could not visit long. Emmie's mom lives almost at the bottom of the third hill below the second ridge, before the river, and after the fifth holler. Her sister's family lives at the top of the fifth hill, second holler, past the third ridge on the twelfth curve. In the words of someone who was raised on flatter ground, one lives at the bottom, the other at the top. To sum it up, a person that gets car sick does not belong in a town like this, but in other ways, I do belong.

I have two lovely daughters, but they have their own lives, and I wouldn't want it any other way. I have my dog; she does not talk back, but she doesn't eat pizza in bed and watch old movies. Well, she would if I let her. There is no one to say, "Hi, honey, I am home." However, I don't have to listen to complaints about the menu for dinner. There is no one to help me take my necklace off before my soccer game. Never could get those things on and off by myself. But there is always a teammate at the field to help. There is no one to laugh with while watching old Lucy shows, but Charming only ever made fun of me for watching them anyhow. More than anything, there is no one to say "I love you" to or hold me when I cried. Of course, once again, he only made fun of me for crying. I feel that is a part of the reason I do not cry in front of others now.

Charm always told me that he loved me. In fact, he usually did not hang up the phone without saying those three little words. Evidently, he did not mean them. I would like to hear those words with meaning.

Arriving at the birthday party after getting up the hill and over the river and through the woods, to sister's house we went. You have already heard about Emmie's sister in Florida, but this is her much younger sister, by twelve months.

Sylvia and her husband John have a daughter and two sons. Dinner was good, and I used one of my ploys to get out of the dishes—no, not the bathroom. I went outside and played football with the kids and kept them busy.

Sylvia liked that arrangement; she would rather do the dishes. I could not have felt more welcome in this home, and even unconfident me did not feel uncomfortable or out of place, but I have been made to feel like family.

Waking up the next morning, we were ready for the walk "down the hill," past about three houses to the little quaint church of this quaint little hillside town. Everyone was talking about the upcoming big event of the next day. A big little town celebration for one of its own. This town claims the hometown rights to four famous athletes. One recently becoming a baseball "hall of famer." That is what the excitement was about. The highway, which sits at the bottom of the hill and running through town, was going to be renamed in his honor. Everyone was making their plans for tomorrow, and the bells tolled, not for me I hope, but for church to begin.

This was the same denomination that I attend at home but done hometown style. Maybe this is what God had in mind. God says "I love you" to all of us in different ways. This was a different way but a wonderful way. The choir consisted of thirteen people, not many, but there were probably only twenty-five in the congregation. The average age was probably, well, let's say, Medicare is the most popular health insurance. Everyone was there and doing their job. There was an organist and pianist. Most churches in my area can hardly get one or the other. The acolyte was the only one present for the children's story, and he also sang in the choir, his age probably averaging around ten. His name is Jerrod, and Jerrod's claim to fame is his unbeatable three ribbons, just won at the pumpkin fest for his prized sunflowers.

The prayers and concerns were next on the agenda, and in keeping with the spirit, the minister asked for any prayer request or concerns. The congregation was silent when a little voice spoke, "I have a hamster." I must have heard this wrong. Someone in pain must have said, "I have a bad hamstring," or maybe it was "I have a ham, sir," inviting him to dinner. I was right the first time, "I have a hamster." The minister asked, "What is his name?" "Sam" was the little response. We prayed for the sunflower awards and Sam the Hamster; he is one of God's creatures too.

Little town USA has not lost sight of God's love for all of us; maybe it is time the rest of us follow and realize everyone does "belong" as one in God.

I told Emmie she has a very loving and caring family. I know, I have a sense of belonging and only because of how comfortable they have made me feel. There is nothing more meaningful from someone than a genuine hug, the old "reach out and touch someone" theory. That was proven to me last night. I was given hugs by the whole family, and I did not feel they were token hugs. The feeling was real and the sincerity genuine. Feeling a part of anything right now is very difficult for me. Recently, Emmie has certainly made me feel a sense of belonging. That is what I need to keep sight of. Remember the positive versus the negative. This is it! I have to make it work.

God is giving me all the right pieces to the puzzle. I just have to choose if I want to be patient and find their proper place or force them into a place where they do not fit correctly. Looking back over the six-month period when I have been patient and trusted in God, I fit correctly into this new life of mine. When I force the pieces, life does not fit correctly for me. I am finding the patience most of the time; however, the slipup comes when I feel unwanted or alone. Emmie said one of the nicest things anyone could ever say to another person. When I feel that sense of not belonging, I dig back in my memory to the positive and pull out "C. R., I feel God gave me you."

Well, Emmie, God gave me you. With you, I received a bonus of your very kind and loving family. Do not ever lose those hometown values. The little town on the hill might have made me car sick but helped to heal my heart that part of the pain lost forever.

CHAPTER 49

This Day Cannot Compare to Last Week
or
Sitting on the Cold, Hard Toilet Seat of Life

I am happily reminiscing back to one week ago today and what a great time Emmie and I were having in the casino at Niagara Falls. In some ways, it seems like an eternity ago, and in other moments, it seems like just hours ago.

We had a great time the whole weekend. The weather was good, the casino fun, the falls beautiful, the casino fun, the shopping good, the casino fun, the food good, especially the meat loaf, the casino fun. Should I go on?

Here I am a week later and down in that valley again. I question everything. My counselor's assignment to me this week was that I am to have fun and relax, and that is what I was doing. Also, I was absolutely not to analyze! Now let's analyze what she meant by that. We have already talked about how I analyze everything I do and say, so I don't need to repeat it. I know I spend too much time in the worry mode, but I am scared to death over my life. I am worried with relationships, my health, my old job that soon I will get the nerve to resign from, my new job and if it will be everything it seems to be. I worry about the holidays and how I will handle them. I mean this just goes on and on. In these last seven months, my life has just gone bonkers.

Today started off on the wrong foot or whatever. I woke up very early but could not get out of bed. I mean, I physically could not get out of bed. My body was in working order, but my mind would not allow my feet to hit the floor. Honest, I tried, but I have had two awful nights, and I think the old body went on strike and refused to respond to my commands. Plus, it was cold out, cold house, warm bed. What choice does a body have? I just spent two very confusing and frustrating nights. My counselor has just confused the heck out of me, and I have been in a major tailspin ever since. I am not going into the conversation we spent the whole time on, but I certainly am in a stupor. Needless to say, I was getting a very late start and not desiring to move anywhere near a fast mode or even medium. I finally made it out of bed and went out on the road for work. My heart and mind were in totally different directions and not necessarily good safe directions. There is too much time to let sad thoughts in when you are on the road. I fought hard and did what I needed to do, and things just went wrong.

I received warm welcomes at the schools, but there was something about me that I could not get myself turned around. I thought about calling in sick. I felt awful. I tried thinking about pleasant things and what I have to look forward to in life, but nothing was good. I finally found something to zone in on. I remembered that Emmie said her pumpkins were rotting. I know to most of you out there in bookland, this is a normal Halloween happening. But we are talking that it is still thirteen days before the spooky holiday and rotten pumpkins in a classroom filled with kindergartners—not so much!

These kids want their pumpkins, and they do not understand the effects of rotting in a classroom and what they do to the air content, not to mention the increase of the gnat population. So I decided to stop and get two new orange round, or sort of round, vegetables—or are they fruit?—for the classroom. I decided to deliver them to school instead of waiting till I saw Emmie the next time. I walked in to the office so as not to disturb the classroom, and here I was with a box of two very heavy pumpkins in it and am told by the secretary to just take them to the classroom. She said, "Emmie will get a kick out of them." *Or maybe she will kick me out, one or the other* is what I am thinking. This is where I need some improvement. I am still nervous about these situations. My stomach was a mess the whole time that I was driving to the school and walking in. I seem to live in fear or the anticipation that I will never be good enough or doing things correctly. I wish Emily Post was my sister, so I would always be informed of the proper etiquette. Emily, where are you when I need you? I delivered the pumpkins, and I lived through it, but I probably should have chomped on some Tums. While in the classroom, Emmie said, "Please go out in the hall and see if the little girl out there counted her corn correctly." Excuse me? What was she talking about? What would sister Emily think about this some little girl counting her corns in public? I mean wouldn't you have to take your shoes off for that? This is school. shoes should be on your feet, not to mention tied properly so there are no tripping accidents. I meandered out into the hallway, and in front of my eyes is this little girl on the floor counting her corn, with her shoes on.

So what is my job in this counting corn adventure? You might as well know that it was candy corn. My thought was *You count it, honey, and I will eat it.* There were all these little paper bags lying on the floor with numbers on them. The first object was to lay the proper number of pieces of candy corn on each bag to match the written number. The second object was to get them to do so without eating it! This job was better than the alternative of changing and redressing the wet pants on the one that waited just a little tooooooooo long before telling the teacher. I can sympathize with this scenario. My mom always had to wash the first-grade generic jeans because I, more than once, had to wear them home. I knew I had to go. I was just too afraid to ask the teacher if I could go to the restroom. It was an embarrassment to admit that I actually did have to use the bathroom facilities; that is private. No wonder I am such a wimpy adult. Dr. Spock would probably blame my failed marriage on my first-grade wetting problem. I did get it under control by the second year of school.

Back to corn counting. This little girl got her corn counted and with just the proper timing. Teacher Emmie came to double-check how we were doing with counting and taught me that after counting we, but not me, got to take three, count them three candy corns to eat from the clean bag. No kidding, there was a bag with clean sanitary corn. The container with the previously handled and counted corn in it was officially labeled "dirty corn." I helped the rest of the little corn counters that had to be tested. All left their shoes on, and I think even I got the hang of this, but I never got my three pieces of clean corn. After all, would that be too much to ask? I did bring new sort-of-round orange vegetables.

To continue my adventure of the day, I was off to my house to have lunch then go into the office. I had a lot of thoughts, and the conversation with my counselor was still prevalent in my mind, and my thoughts were rotating around. I continually tried to throw these thoughts in another direction, but I kept floating back there. I want to let go of the thoughts and eat, without getting distracted and spill chili on my clothes.

After lunch, I headed for the office, and there are two notes from boss lying on my desk. The little notes stated he wanted me to do some filing, and then I was to call him and leave a voicemail to let him know what stops I made on the road and who I had seen. I did, and then I went on to do my real work. I am always so behind because my things never seem important to him, so he gives me other jobs. I reached my point here. I had just about had it when I decided to take a break and hit the old bathroom. How many times have I gone to the bathroom in this particular restroom? Well, I never recall over the years that both seats have been down, so why would I have looked before sitting on that very hard cold toilet seat! There I sat, tears streaming down my cheeks. Don't get smart, the cheeks on my face, not the ones on the seat. Why did I cry? Have you ever expected one thing in life and ended up with something else? I expected a wooden seat with a hole in it, not a hard surface that was cold and had no hole in it. That is how some days go in life. There are the great days when everything goes right, and then there are those where you plop down on the cold hard toilet seat of life.

CHAPTER 50

Friendships and the Alternatives
or
Stop and Smell the Roses, but
Watch Out for the Thorns

I definitely was not myself at counseling. The highlight of my week was finding a copy of the song "Going Through the Big D" to read to the divorce group, you know my teammates and athletic supporters. The line from the song that caught my attention was "I am going through the big D, and I don't mean Dallas." Shows you where my week has been. What can I say? I found it amusing.

Late at night is when I take the time to be thankful to God for what I have—that is right now. I realize that I never want to lose anyone again. You know what it will take on my part to make sure that it will never happen? It will take a lot of hard work and a lot of analyzing, whoops, I mean relaxing. I sit here at night writing, and I have such a drive to do so. I think this God guy wants me to write this book for some reason because some of what I say does not come from me.

I am beginning to have a sense of relaxation in my evening. I just have some things left to express, so here I am working toward that goal. I sit here in my happy room looking around, and there is a picture of Emmie and I at Epcot or "Epecot" as my mother-in-law used to say. Emmie and I took the time to enjoy life that week. She smelled the roses and missed the thorns. Her organizational skills were still flowing, but she seemed to be able to keep them in check long enough to let down and enjoy what she had around her. I could certainly use some of those skills, and I think she could certainly share some. She has plenty. If she gave me some, there would be a little more room for living life. I am not criticizing her by any means. I am saying don't sit in an organized state in that rest home, be out telling your grandchildren the fun and experiences you had in life. Last night, she said, "I don't know, C. R., where this life is going, do you?" I said, "I do." She did not ask what I knew that she didn't. I do not know where that answer came from. This life is headed in the direction for her and me as two people that have been devastated in "the prime of life." Well, we are not that old to come back kicking and screaming to find there is a great life out there. I am jumping on that train to happiness and independence instead of codependency, and I am dragging her with me even if she is kicking and screaming the whole way. Our *ex* loved ones are doing what makes them happy, supposedly. Well, there is no "supposedly" about it. I am on a mission to seek my happiness.

God reached down and picked Emmie and me up and set us in each other's path on the way to a new life. He did not say we had to stop to talk to each other. We had the choice to walk around each other and continue on, but I was not going to take a chance and go against his plan even though I knew I was risking my already-destroyed heart and opening it up for more wounds. But he also knew if I stopped and took that chance, I could receive a great friend. I am glad that I chose to stop. Sometimes we are in the same direction and sometimes in the opposite direction, but we always end up in a similar path when needed. There is a lot of good left in our lives; let's not miss it. Relax and take the good. After all, I can count candy corn.

It is nice to have someone to share the simple things in life like raking leaves and having a bowl of soup. I do not ask for much, but I never did get my three pieces of that candy corn.

I read an article the other day about getting through the winter blahs. It said play. Jump in a pile of leaves, bounce on a bed, bundle up for a walk on a beach, be a kid, and take in the simple things in life. It did not even mention shopping! It is best I stay away from that activity! It is the best therapy for anything—be kidlike.

So, Emmie, I am here for you when you need a listening ear, when you feel fearful, feel alone, or need the dirty corn counted. "Friends are friends forever, if the Lord is the Lord of them," to quote Michael W.

CHAPTER 51

Where Is This Life of Mine Headed?
or
The Wind Tunnel between My Ears

"Confusion" sums up the madness I have been living with this week. How do you describe "confusion"? Let's Google *Webster* and see what is written in those profound pages. Hmmm ... the only thing it says is that it is "the act of being confused." Okay, let's look up "confused." Found it right under the word "Confucius." Ahh ... I never connected "confused" with "Confucius." A smart Chinese philosopher's name appears right above "confuse"—"to mix up, put into disorder, to mistake the identity of." That is what *Webster* has to say about it, and that is now the official explanation of my life, summed up in a neat little eleven-word package sitting right below "Confucius."

What do you think the Chinese philosopher would say about my life? Probably give up fortune cookies. Confucius say, "Woman left in the dust better get the vacuum cleaner out of storage." No kidding, there is a lot to clean up.

Right now, before I can sweep up after the first mess, I am on to a second mess to take care of. I am going to change jobs. What am I? Nuts? I have a lot to overcome, and then I decide to start a new job? I think, just maybe, I should have a CAT scan to make sure there is a brain in my head. What would Confucius say about this one? "Woman with empty head has room for much error." Or is that air?

Well, Confucius or not, I am starting a new job. All I have to do is tell my boss. That will be the hard part, but I have to. The pressure I endure from him daily is too much to handle. I have been told for years about his personality, and I never could see it. Must have been this wind tunnel between my ears. After dinner with friends where the boss continually paged me over and over, I see how things are, and my friends, attorney, and counselor strongly recommended I move on.

I have been left in the dust by Prince and his ever so lovely adopted wife—NotSo Much. Now I see after being out from under the control of those two control freaks that I like my freedom, and my new motto is "controlled no more." So to my boss I say, "I will no longer allow you to keep me under your thumb. I made a phone call, got a new job, and will be telling you as soon as I get the courage." Confucius says, "Motto good—your courage stinks!" Maybe I could write fortune cookies for a living. Heck, I will go for the whole enchilada and become the female Confucius—Confueta.

I did give this a lot of thought, and I am concerned about my future. However, I am very concerned for my mental state at my current position. I feel I need to relieve the stress I am putting on myself by accepting the treatment that I receive. I have to accept that blame for allowing people to "use and abuse me," my old motto.

I am just spinning in circles all the time. My life changes so much it is like a boat caught in the wake of a ship—up and down, up and down, side to side. Confucius says, "Woman with confusion should take Dramamine."

I ask God many times a day, "God, what are you doing with my life? Where am I headed, and where will this all end?" And God says, "Your guess is as good as mine." I know there is a happy ending in sight for me. I continually have a sense of peace within my heart, and the only explanation I can concur with is God. He is right here beside me and will not leave as long as I continue to talk with him.

My new job sounds good, and finally some good things are happening to me. I think a lot of good has happened. Many times I question how I can feel this way after being "left in the dust." I am allergic to dust, so I must fight to rid it from my life. I will make a clean sweep and make the best of these newfound situations.

Whole chapters of my life have ended, and I am like a top spinning on a table, wondering when I will quit spinning and topple over and fall! There have certainly been some very rough moments, hours, days, and weeks. But I am here, and my head is still above water. There seems to be signs of some assertiveness, and I think I am encouraged to keep on keepin' on. I will be starting a new job, and I will actually have people to help me, and I will "control" the situation rather than letting the situation control me. I am working to develop new ways to cope in life and hope to never allow myself to be in any of these positions again. More importantly than anything, I have revitalized my closeness with God and have discovered a truer relationship with my daughters and my friends. What a trip this has been. I guess my situation summed up as Confueta says—gotshaftbutcominback!

I am not giving up, and I will tackle this new job like I did the old one and everyone I have had, with a lot of heart and energy. I hate quitting anything. I am not a quitter, but the situation warrants this ending in order to make a full and happy healing recovery for myself and those around me. I have so much.

Charm and NotSo Charming always made fun of me when a situation would happen that was out of my control. They thought because I did not allow it to control me, there was something wrong with me. I very rarely get mad or lose my temper. I don't look at the negative side. I search for the good side of the situation and can look at things optimistically. They said I lived in a dream world. I lived with love and with confidence in God. The codependency book I read finished with the letting-go process. Letting things go into the hands of God and make the best of everything possible. I am learning that the more I release things into God's hands, the more I receive in my life. I do have a good opportunity, and I will give it everything I have. I am surrounded by love, and I intend to return that love.

My favorite Michael W. quote, "Love isn't love until you give it away," still stands tall in my book. There are all kinds of love and many ways to show the feelings. Intentions are good, but plain old caring and love from the heart gives way to much happiness.

However, Confueta has her opinion too. "Woman who gives away all her love and cannot receive has wind tunnel between her ears. Woman who gives away all the love she has and receives what comes back is of happy heart."

CHAPTER 52

The Longest Day
or
Dinner with the Animals

It is done. I officially turned in my two weeks' notice. Well, as officially as I could, without boss being there. We were to have a meeting, and boss never showed up. I waited. I wanted to turn it in to him personally, but I could not wait any longer. It had to come to this. It was Friday, and by leaving it on his desk, I thought I would hear from him over the weekend. When I had not heard, I thought I would be facing him firsthand and first thing today, Monday. I got ready and went to work, and on the short drive, I sucked it up and said, "C. R., you have to do this, and you have to do it with confidence and make him respect you." That I did, but it was not at all what I had expected. I was at the door well before my clock-in time. I gave the two weeks' notice, and here I am to finish those what will prove to be very long weeks. I see boss's truck there and am surprised but thought to myself it is time to face the music, and they are playing my swan song. I put my key in the door, only to find it would not turn. I know it is cold out, but it cannot be frozen. "Frozen" was not the word for it; it was a changed lock. Boss had received my notice and changed the locks. What an awful feeling to have given so much time and effort to a job and the persons around you to only be mistrusted and locked out. I immediately responded by saying to myself, "Fine, if that is the way he wants it to be, then go ahead." Maybe I used different words, but you can make up your own. I got to my car and remembered that I am a guilt-laden person and knew this was not going to be comfortable for me to just leave. I went back to those doors and knocked. The door was answered. I walked in, and boss met me with a smile on his face. "Do you have a minute?" I asked. I knew I should be humming that swan song, but I walked back to the meeting room with him, and there we were face-to-face. The whole conversation is not important and was fairly simple; however, the outcome was that boss did not think that I was coming back. I said, "I was giving a two weeks' notice." I am now on an unscheduled vacation. It is perfect extra days off in October. The snow is flying lightly. It is obviously freezing, and I get extra days off to do what? Laundry? It hurt to think that he thought I was the kind of person that gave my notice and did not come back to fulfill my obligations.

I do have a meeting with him on Wednesday to go over what is owed to me, and I have a feeling that the fat lady has not sung yet. The important part of the day is that I stood up for myself without feeling intimidated. I had moments today of wondering what the hell I was doing, but it is so very good for me to be away from this added controlling force in my life. I never knew that I was so controlled. I thought I was just being easygoing and not making waves. Well, I am not only going to make waves but huge tidal waves. So get a lifeboat, Charm, NotSo, and Boss. Sink or swim! It is time for little Ms. Codependent to grow and expand her horizons, and I am not speaking bodily. The brain, the experiences, the assertiveness, and not to lose the love and care for others that has always been such an extremely important part of my life.

Do you really understand how much work it takes to change from this codependent state that has taken mega years to get here? My counselor will probably retire and have to pass this old codependent on to someone else. I plan to fight all of this and make it through coming out a much better noncodependent person.

Once I was released from my place of employment, I began to start singing "Born Free." Maybe this is my swan song, but that fat lady still has not sung. Wednesday's meeting is not far off. I best go into training and prepare. My feelings at this time are very confused, seems like a permanent condition anymore. I do not even know what to feel, think, or do. I chose to clean out my closets of all things. Remember Emmie's theory that "life is choices." I hate that!

As if life was not sinking enough, my ship ran aground tonight, and my rudder has been broken and my propeller bent. One of the men from group asked Emmie and I to go to dinner tonight and we "chose" to go to that local Mexican restaurant. If you recall, this is the site where my friend decided to express to the world that—let's see, how can I put this just a little kinder. She basically expressed that Mr. Charming was involved with Ms. NotSo Charming in a somewhat close intense situation that married people do in the privacy of their own homes. It should not be so greatly abused and expressed so openly to others that it is happening in a very adulteress manner, and sometimes people refer to the act of setting a screw in wood with a screwdriver by the same term. If you did not get that, consult your dictionary or ask a teenager; they will explain it to you. Onward, as we entered this local establishment of food, we were talking, and as we were seated, Emmie and Stan were on one side of the booth and I on the other. I was the absolute lucky recipient of the seat facing the entrance. They wanted to hear my story of the day about my ex work when my attention was caught by a person standing at the entrance. I was looking at the familiar jacket, stance, hair, etc. and telling my tale of the day, and that was no fish tale when Emmie, catching that my eyes were connected off in a distance, decided to turn and see what I was glaring at. Her head spun around faster than the girl in the *Exorcist*, and she was speaking words that were bouncing around in my somewhat numb ears, "That's her." So who is "her"? I knew who "her" was, the "ex-her." Well, she is not an "ex-her." She is still a her, but now she is not a "good her" or even a "Ben her" but "Charm's her." You got it! NotSo Charming was the recognizable jacket that my subconscious—or maybe I should say semiconscious state—was viewing. I do not know who was shaking more, Emmie or me. What a sighting this was. "Her mother" followed, then "her father," along next with the ever-effervescent "her Charm."

How was I supposed to eat under these circumstances? Man, I was not sure if my ice tea was shaking from the coldness or my nerves. I can't believe it was not just dribbling down the side of my mouth, not unlike the effects of Novocain. I am sitting here watching the "her crowd" when Charming starts to walk my direction with "his and hers" coats. He walked right past me and never even noticed me sitting there. I even looked at him right in the face, and he looked right at me. Out of sight, out of mind.

Maybe I should offer to buy their dinners for them, *not*. Stan felt maybe he should send them a round of drinks. Pretty funny, huh? Well, how did I really handle this uncomfortable situation? This dining in the Lie-on and Lie-oness den of life? Fortunately, I had two of my athletic supporters with me, and that always helps. Emmie and I could laugh about everything imaginable about this situation. Stan the Man thought we were funny, but on the other side of the laughter, I was a little shaky, a lot heartbroken, and hurt.

We were there first. I had comments to make on the fact that I know for sure that this is at least the fourth sighting of Charm at this restaurant since the transposition of loyalty and love, and he hates Mexican food. My only hope was that he has learned to like the beans because of the snow in the air; it would be too cold to leave the bedroom window open tonight.

Well, enough of some of my wishful thinking tonight. The important thing is that I am happy, and NotSo and Charm have developed new talents upon their recent rejection of me. Yes, it is true. They have grown in their acting abilities. Once they had discovered that I was there, and that discovery was only because Emmie continually turned and stared at them—gotta love her. Anyhow, they decided to play this to the hilt. NotSo put her bashful look on her little sour face and laid her head on Charm's shoulder, not to mention levelheaded Charm putting his loving arm around her and squeezing her in a loving manner, just not hard enough in my opinion. The show was for my benefit, and I hope they recall this action when they someday get the torpedoes of life sent their way, when papers are signed and my ship comes in.

So all in all, it was quite an experience of life today. Things just seemed to hit all at once, and I do not know what I will be capable of handling and what I will not be able to deal with. I always deal with things very strongly when I am in the middle of them, and I fall apart later, and then I am lost in the shuffle. Meaning, no one understands about me keeping it all inside and the surfacing procedure. You could kind of compare my life to a submarine. I dive, dive deep, and lay on the bottom for a long time, and when I surface, I surface with all tubes open and ready to fire. The problem is by then I have been on the bottom so long that everything is rusted and will not work. I was all set in life, and the torpedoes sunk me quickly. I came out of that and started to mend my wounds and patch the holes in my stern, but I now have a whole new set of battles to overcome.

I was really starting to become happy. I was enjoying my new friends and not only as life preservers but real friends. Now every day is so very painful. I have had so much pain thrown at me these last two weeks that there just cannot be room for any more.

I had another one of those month-long periods, and I am *sick* of it! I am so up and down, and I still grasp to that positive, but the rejection factor is hanging over my shoulder all the time. I found I cannot handle rejection, and I probably feel rejection where there is none. I do realize life can be a struggle, and every road we take teaches us something. I am just tired of the bumpy winding roads and am ready for the expressway of life. I will hang in there, and I will continue to follow where the big guy upstairs wants me to go. I need to sever the old feelings. Each time there is a sighting, it will get easier and smoother. I have horrible pain when it comes to seeing Prin-cess's parents, and the feelings for them are not gone. I cared about them. It hurts deeply that there seems to be no concern for me from them. How can they sit there and look their daughter and Charm man in the eyes and talk and laugh in front of me? I know all the right answers, but I still feel the pain.

I just wish that I could be shipped out to another location and learn to swim again. Maybe that is what God is doing to me in a manner of speaking, but I have not gathered all that info in my brain yet. Locked out of my job, I felt like a criminal. Charming's arm around NotSo Charming, I felt a hurt of a blatant act of inflicting pain. The facing of the parents was a heartbreaking pain of loss, and without the laughter, I would not have been in control of those combined areas of pain and heartbreak.

There is a lesson to be learned by all of this. It is an important lesson and one I hope is not too late. God wants us to care for ourselves, be ourselves, but his hope and plan for us is to share our care and love with others. If we cannot do this, we really have nothing to hold on to in life. We have nothing to gain by being selfish or uncaring. Life is too short and totally unpredictable. This lesson I am learning only reinforces that we should put others and the quality of the life we lead foremost in our hearts. I have tried to be someone I am not, and I will never be able to not be the codependent person that wants others to be happy first. But I can learn to semicurtail my obsessiveness, and the natural feelings will then float through, and that is what I need.

Everyone is different, and we all live with pain, but there are all those good things about each one that is so worthwhile putting time into finding. I recently tried to change myself and found it does not work. I am going back to the old C. R., the one that relaxes and wants to enjoy what good things I can extract from life and people. I have to face my fears and reduce the tears. I will turn my life around, and it will be a better and happier life because it will now be my life, my "choices" (I hate that) and following the plan that has been set for my path in life.

I apologize for getting off the humorous side of all of this long day and the meal with the animals, Porky and Bessie. I thank God every day for giving me the ability to laugh at this life, but I sometimes have to release some of those torpedoes, or I would sink.

Just promise me you will try to put a little more happiness and faith into your life. When you are running by those roses in life, take time to stop and smell them. That few minutes of your time could make someone else very happy or could give you a little different outlook on life. The time you take to call someone may just be the most important thing of their day, or maybe the card you sent in the mail brightened the day for someone. Simple things in life give the most absolute pleasure. Love is one of those, and if you love someone, make sure you take the time to pull those thorns off the roses before you give them away!

Oh, by the way, I did eat some. I decided to just consider I was at a dinner show with all the acting that was going on for my benefit. The three of us finished our meals and walked back to the coatroom and retrieved our coats. I did have thoughts of doing something to their coats, but I didn't. I went out a back door through the kitchen, and Emmie and Stan proudly walked through the restaurant and out the front door.

CHAPTER 53

Analyzing Life
or
Life Is Best with Balanced Hormones and Good Athletic Supporters

I have been failing miserably! All I want to do is have fun and live my life and not deal with all of this. My life and even my hormones are in total "limbo." This could be a new group dance, "hormone limbo." My jobs are not settled. I have no idea where I will end up in this divorce thing or if I will have turkey on Thanksgiving or order a pizza. My health is unsettled, my hormones imbalanced. I am disappointed in the outcome of something that was very important to me. I am scared to death of relationships and saying and doing the wrong things. I do not know where I will be living or what I will be for Halloween, but at least, I do know who Mannheim Steamroller is, unlike some people.

It was a very long day today especially for Mo because she was on the phone with me until midnight thirty. Everyone is all snuggled in bed, and I had this sudden burst of emotions that just needed to be put down on paper for posterity. I think I have been totally drained of every ounce of energy I ever possessed. I continue to find it very difficult to roll out of bed in the morning, and the stress of deciding whether to be Grumpy or Happy for Halloween is tearing me apart. Those are the leftover dwarfs, and it is down to Emmie and me to decide who is who. She said she would be Grumpy, but if I were Grumpy, I could just grunt and not have to speak. Then I would not have to analyze everything I say and do. Why did she say she would be Grumpy? Did she figure I would not do it? Was she being nice and letting me be Happy? Since I am no longer to analyze things, we are looking at it from a different angle; it is "anglizing."

Actually, let's get to the point of my emotional outpouring before I "anglize" it to death and change my mind. Who are these people that want to dress as Snow White and the Seven Dwarfs for the big Halloween party? They are a strange and loving bunch. Of course, look who is calling them strange. None of them are sitting up at two o'clock in the morning "anglizing" and being "limboed" in life and hormones. These are people from very different backgrounds and families. Some from little towns, northern cities, western states, men and women together in the same sinking ship with different life vests holding them afloat.

Some are being held afloat by family, church, and friends, but mostly we do it for one another. I know a major portion of my life vest is made up of these seven people.

While having a very long "anglizing" conversation with one of the team on the phone—I like the team "anglization" better than "group"—I was warming up my computer to express my thoughts. Those thoughts were that none of us would be a team player if it were not for our exes or soon-to-be exes in our life. You know, the Dopeys out there. Well, sorry, but prince charmings or Cinderellas they ain't!

I am very proud to be a team member in this organization and at this world series time of year. The team that takes the honors in my heart is this one. The ones who have been the best "athletic supporters" a team member could ever have. They are "very comfortable" to be around. Most importantly, these athletic supporters do not scratch themselves in public and hang in there and are supportive. They are there any time for anything, no matter how big or small.

In all seriousness, I do analyze the position I am in and realize how very lucky I am to have been thrown into a situation that allows me to experience such genuine love and care from seven totally different people. Look at this mixture of people. There is actually a man that built a gate over his sidewalk. That's nice you say. It's a great gate, just no fence! The mailman of the group loves every big dog shirt you can buy but boasts about his eight-pound dog. Most of us have grown children, but fortunately, one has little children, so I have someone to play with. One of us is a nurse with grandchildren, another a community leader with creative ideas, and one of us is a teacher with a dog that talks to only one rock, and the other a mother of five children who loves pumpkin stories. Everyone has different experiences and tastes in life, but the blending of ideas for entertainment has provided me in one summer with things I have wanted to do for years. I just never had that person come out from under "his" rock long enough to gain a little culture or let loose with some fun. You know the type person that thinks Mannheim Steamroller is just a piece of road machinery.

I am no longer afraid to be myself when I am around them, and I actually risk being a fool now and then. This is like being from a big family. We fight or get "Grumpy" among ourselves, but no one better hurt one of our loved ones, or they will pay! We protect and care for each family member as an equal, and love is never at a loss. I thought my whole life was lost when the big transposition of love took place. I actually gained seven new family members to love and care for. At least, none of them will steal my husband! Some of them even know who Mannheim Steamroller is!

I do believe that no matter where our lives lead us, there will always be that family bond, the one common bond we all share—the splitting of our family units that gave us one another. I never want to lose touch, and I always want to know we will be there for one another's pain and celebrations. Who would ever think eight strangers with eight different sets of ideas, goals, ambitions, and talents could end up with so much compassion and care for one another?

As I go through this change of life, possibly in more ways than one, there would not be anyone better to share the painful times, the happy times, and my love. God has put them in my life to cry with and laugh with. Some changes in life do not require hormonal therapy but work best with strong athletic supporters.

CHAPTER 54

The Care Receiver and the Caregiver
or
Headache: the Pain of Fun

I have been talking about the anticipation of starting the Stephen's Ministry program at church. A brief synopsis of the program: interested members of the congregation apply and interview to start training to become a Stephen's minister. This training enables them to actively participate in being a support system for the minister, Stephen's leaders, the congregation, and anyone needing help in a crisis situation.

The minister felt that I may not be ready to handle situations due to my recent crisis. He asked if I would let him read some of my book. I gave him several chapters and hoped for the best. My disappointment was very hard to take, but I had to have the faith in these leaders to know what was best for the program. I had heard in June about the program and anticipated the start for months. Something the minister read must have made him feel better about my healing process. Or he just feared what I would write about him if he did not let me participate! I received my letter of acceptance and was thrilled.

The program began tonight, and I can't wait until the next class. I approached the evening with a little nervousness and, as always, sat back quietly not saying much. However, I felt a comfort among these strangers and semi-strangers. What happened to me? Is it the Halloween moon or maybe some witches curse; it could just be the brownies, pop, and coffee served at class. I was relaxed and participating.

Our letter of acceptance included our first assignment, which entailed taking a material item to class that was very meaningful to us. I took part of this book. I have strengthened my faith in God, and I have realized what wonderful people surround me. I just added ten more people to that list of good people in my life, and they are the leaders and participants of Stephen's Ministry.

I do have to explain, however, that I came home with a painful headache, and it was not from stress or discomfort; it was laughter. What better way to learn how to help people than to be able to laugh and learn together. I know I will remember what I learned and experienced. I will remember much better because of the fun I had doing it.

We were asked to get a partner, and we were going to role-play situations as to put into practice what we had learned this evening. Never expect me to act and be serious all in the same time frame. The partner I had I knew we were in trouble from the get-go. Imagine sitting back-to-back in chairs and pretending to be calling each other on the phone to set up an appointment to meet. When one of our fearless leaders says, "The phones are ringing." I thought I was on a telethon. "The phones are ringing. Send in those donations, and our next act will be performing on stage shortly." I said, "Hello." My partner said, "Hello, this is Barb from church." I said, "Hi, Barb. How are you?" We were history. She almost fell off her chair, and I thought I was going to not be able to swallow that swig of Coca-Cola. We then had the knock at the door and the acting out of the visit and the "Sit down. Would you like something to drink?" It was all downhill from there. We could not look at each other. We were turning our backs and shaking with laughter trying to hide the fact that we could not hold it together. We eventually gained our composure and managed to play the parts of the care receiver and the caregiver. We did fine, but I guarantee we will not forget what we learned tonight.

Just maybe I learned a lot more than what was written in the books. I learned there are those good people out there that want to give of themselves. They want to extend their faith and love to others, be it friends or strangers that need the kind heart and love of a warm hug. God did give me this opportunity, and he has a reason for me to be here. I will give it my all to follow his reasons. I will laugh along the way, but don't worry, "oh, fearless leaders," I am extremely serious about the reasons I am involved in this magnificent program. If my life had not come crashing in all around me, my friend Emmie and I would not have had gone together to church that Sunday. I not only gained a great desire to participate in Stephen's Ministry, but I also regained a great friend. Things do happen for a reason. We do need to have all the unconditional trust and love in God when we do go through crisis. But this is a full-time need that we should continue to work on constantly. He will lead us down a good path if we continue to walk with him.

So here I stand with my shirt, sandals, and that darn stick I keep getting beaten with. No deodorant and no soap, but here I am in the desert with my faith in God to provide those provisions that I will need to go out and help others. The provision of three great leaders is quite a pleasure, and they are going to do a great job. I anticipate one of the best ministry programs around will be ours due to the people involved. To quote once again, my favorite, Michael W., "Love isn't love till you give it away."

I am going to pick up that stick and go. Leaving my daily necessities of life—hair dryer, food, hair color, food, makeup, food, Nike's, food, Umbro's, food, deodorant, food, and most importantly Coca-Cola! I will give my trust to God to provide for me and that I will not get beaten with that stick.

CHAPTER 55

How Should I Feel?
or
The Windshield Wipers of Life

As I am driving along on this cloudy, rainy morning, the dreariness presents a sense of sadness. However, I suddenly found myself having a moment of feeling secure and content. Where did that come from?

I hate dreary days. And how could I possibly be secure and content within my current situation? My feelings and thoughts fly through the air like boomerangs—constantly circling my head until I reach out and grasp one. Then I do not let go until it all makes sense.

I proceeded to drive toward my soccer game, and all of a sudden, I caught one, thought that is. "I am happy." How can I be happy when my life has fallen apart and I have nothing? I must be delirious; maybe I already played that soccer game and was hit on the head. I am having amnesia. That is the only explanation I can come up with.

I continued my journey to the game. The windshield became a little foggy, so I turned on the windshield wipers. As the glass cleared along the path of the wipers, I noticed I had clearer vision; the fog from my eyes was lifting as well. Remember that San Francisco fog? I think it just lifted, and I suddenly realized I was becoming my own person. I have never been there before! What took me so long? I guess my heart got in the way. That is the only way I can explain losing myself.

I began thinking about the fact that throughout my life, I lived in a controlling environment. No one controls me now. Man of Charm has to pay to play, and I can now have a little freedom. I am somewhat beginning to crawl out from under his thumb. I am feeling that sense of independence, but I am also scared to death. There are emotions boomeranging all over.

As I arrive at the field, I realize this is the game. I did not already play it. There is no concussion. The feelings of happiness and some freedom are real—no amnesia. The clouds are just rolling in, and the sky is dark and dreary, but I am lit up in my emotional field.

All this thinking has been wearing me out. I better get my head into this game. The game is different every week. Not because we play different teams but because of how different I feel each week. I used to dread coming to the games before, and I never figured that feeling out because I loved to play the game. Now that the windshield wipers have cleared the fog from my eyes and continues clear during the game, I realized NotSo Charming was a real downer, and I had not been enjoying myself because she brought me down. Way down where she was and looking at things the way she saw them. I had left my "positive" nature in check and was being someone I was not. Her "critical" nature and attitude swept me up and took me along for a ride. Maybe that is why I play the sweeper position on the team. I am good at being swept up. I never left the field upset at my own players, but that is all that Uncharming wanted to talk about after a game on the way home. She never left a game saying she had fun. There were always the things that went wrong coming from her brain and not the good or the fun of the game. My mouth does not usually function that way. Now I know that my thoughts and brain were acting "under the influence."

Not only is the fog lifting from my eyes, but the rain has subsided, and the sun is out. The realization is that I am having fun with the people around me and the game I am playing. This is fun, just like when I was a kid. I have acquired confidence in myself playing this sport, and no one criticizes me. What a wake-up call.

There has not been a week that a fellow team member has not said how well I am playing. These "kids" are telling me how well I am playing. The funny thing is it comes from relaxing and enjoying the game. Today, one of my teammates walked over to me after I made a play and put her hand on my shoulder and said, "Since you have lost that 'dead weight,' you have become a lot faster." No kidding, I have become a lot of things since losing that "dead weight" but mostly just myself.

When the game was over, it was time for the fun part, breakfast! I was sitting on the bench drinking water when one of those younger people on my team said, "You play better every week. I just cannot get over it. You are playing so well." Wow, I am also enjoying this more every week. I no longer dread going. I look forward to this game. It is so much more fun than those that Charm and Uncharm have been playing.

CHAPTER 56

Geriatrics Is Not Generic
or
The Determined Weeds

I cannot say enough about this Stephen's Ministry (SM) program and the people so dedicated to share their hearts with others. The feelings I have are inexpressible, at least to the extent I would like to express them. How do you meet people, virtually strangers, and love them in the same day? This has not only happened to me with these SMers but with the group also.

There are many of us that spend far too much time looking in the wrong directions in life. As normal humans, we tend to criticize and analyze everyone's lives—but our own. If you have never walked in another person's flip-flops, you don't have the right to criticize or be judgmental. You already know that I analyze everything to death or at least did, but at least, I am coming out of that part of my thought process fairly rapidly.

Our SM training tonight was focusing on the geriatric crowd and what possible situations and changes could occur in the lives of the elderly. There are so many issues to deal with as we grow older, and there are so very many plusses as we grow into our golden years. We were asked to choose a person that we respected and would want to be like in our golden years. The first person that came to my mind was Mary, Emmie's mother.

Why? Here is the story. Emmie and I headed down that southern route again this past weekend. Our purpose was to replace Mary's basement steps. On the last visit to the "little town USA," I walked down those steps and have worried ever since about her safety. We packed all the tools we thought would be needed for our special weekend mission and headed south. Upon arrival, we found we had only fifteen minutes to get to the lumberyard for the wood and hustled there so we could get started on our rebuilding process.

The rebuilding process sums up this chapter very well. Those steps were cracked, splintered, split, and "separated lacking support." Sort of sums up where both Emmie and I have been in recent times due to our partners' untimely escape from our partnerships. We rebuilt those steps and, in the process, rebuilt a little more of our lives. Emmie was so proud that she hammered nails, pulled nails out of the rotted wood, and used the drill. I was happy with her efforts and dedication to the project and to me. She hung tight with me to help in any way she could. Is that not what God wants from us as his loving people, to hang in there with others?

Our sense of accomplishment cannot be measured except inside of ourselves. The work was done together with Mary helping and Emmie's sister Sylvia's hand in there also. I taught Emmie the real way to pound a nail, but only after I harassed her greatly that she pounds like a girl. Pounding is kind of like getting a grip on life. Grab hold tightly at the end of the hammer and give it all you've got. We had fun and I immensely liked the spirited smile on Emmie's face when she accomplished something new. But I must ask you, have you ever worked in a basement where a car is parked? Makes a great place to lay your tools.

My reasons for wanting to emulate Mary in my older years are those of seeing the determination she has to continue her usefulness in life. At age eighty-three, it would be real easy for her to just sit down and allow us to do for her. Instead, she was right there with us. She did not want us to do this work for several reasons but now boasts about how many times she goes up and down her new safer steps with the secured handrail. That is what I want out of my future years. New, safer, and secure steps in my life. As we spoke recently in SM, just take little steps and little goals and accomplish slowly. These little steps will build to make bigger steps and permanent ones, safe and secure ones.

This lust for life was seen in Mary's determination to be useful in our project. I would not discourage that spirit for anything. Maybe we youngin's should look up to the older generation and see what they have to offer. Suck in their knowledge, spirit, and advice before they are gone and it is too late.

As a Stephen's minister, I need to be able to help the elderly understand their usefulness, and in doing so, maybe I will learn my usefulness. I think Emmie learned that there is a satisfaction that goes with a labor of love. A very important part of that satisfaction is a growing friendship that goes deeper than the worn surfaces of those rotted steps of life and helps us climb higher away from the split and splinter life we had. Glue won't hold these steps of life together very long, but working together out of love for God and others will take hold for a lifetime.

These SMers have that kind of commitment to God and his loved ones. They will be able to reconstruct and help others rebuild their lives.

We laugh a lot in class, but it eases the tension of the pain we need to learn about in order to assist others in experiencing God's love for all of us. The course my life has been on is phenomenal. I have gone from being devastated to a realization of the wonders God has given me in life. I have climbed up out of the basement and into the upper level of life. I have gained friends and love. I am now becoming strong enough to excitedly look forward to the probability of Emmie and I joining together to purchase a duplex and to start fresh, moving from the memories of our present dwellings. I tend to sometimes slip into worrying about those little petty things that irritate us in life but know that it is so unimportant in the big scheme of things. I feel sorry for those who cannot pull themselves up and experience the total unconditional love that God gives us and the feelings and inner peace that comes from loving others unconditionally. This love is like a big circle. God gives us his love, and when we choose to give it away, it comes right back around that circle to us, stronger than ever. When we give this love, we are never alone.

We travel through life with a sense of spiritualism as one with others. The experiences that we share together with others is never wasted; it only makes us grow. Our lives are touched by so many that it is impossible to conceive all the love there is available to us. My circle came back around to include Emmie, and no matter where our lives lead us, she will be a big part of my circle.

Our discussion tonight at SM involved gifts. The giving of gifts to our care receivers and the acceptance of gifts from them. It is a problem that will face us. People sometimes will want to give us gifts for being there. I have already experienced this with Mary. She always wants to buy dinner or lunch for me when I do things for her. Her thought pattern went from not wanting us to build these steps to "I don't know how to thank you." I do not want her to spend her money on me or give me gifts; however, making peanut butter fudge would not be out of the question. I seriously am so thankful God has given me gifts that I can share with others, and that is all I need. It was mentioned during our discussion that when you go to your care receivers, even stop and pick dandelions to take to them. Of course, this lead to many jokes and much fun.

Take weeds to our care receivers. How ironic. Just to show you how important and strong dandelions are, sitting here in the midst of the Ohio winter, I have a dandelion blooming beside my deck. Maybe weeds are not so bad after all. Is that not what the caregivers are? Just common weeds in the big garden of life—delivering a burst of sunshine to someone in need of some brightness.

CHAPTER 57

Over the River and through the Hills
or
Motion Sickness Turned to Happiness When I Hit Bottom

I bet this title has you going. I know I have had quite an upheaving of events over the past four days. Emmie and I were off to her mother's house again to celebrate Thanksgiving. The traffic was congested, and we decided to take a somewhat-alternate route. The route sent us out of our way and farther than anticipated, but we eventually got back to the freeway of life and once again on our way.

Our dinner stop was an exciting one, at the local country KFC, and we were then headed down the path of curves, swerves, and hills. I never get motion sickness when it is dark out, so this should be a breeze tonight. The conversation we have had so far has been a very intense one about God and forgiveness. Real lighthearted subjects, huh? Emmie and I have the music on and the conversation going strong; the hills and valleys were our designated path, just like life. But those curves, ugh, certainly are prevalent, at least in my stomach.

Our life paths have been changed, but that happens in life, and there is that reason we will someday realize. To quote Christian writer, Philip Yancey, "Faith is to believe or trust in advance what will only make sense in reverse." Thank God, we are not going around these curves in reverse; this is bad enough. Well, Philip has the right idea in my book. This will all make sense someday.

Recently, at the SM seminar, an example was given of a falling rock. You know the "watch out for falling rock" signs along the road? Well, that is what happens to us sometimes. A huge boulder falling hits right in front of our car; we slam on the brakes just in time to avoid colliding with it, but we have to alter our path. It changes everything you thought you had wanted to have and the future you thought you would enjoy. You adapt, meet new people, and change with the flow. God is beside you walking hand in hand. There is a lack of self-esteem and a frustration of the reverse plans, but you put your best effort forward at this point to realize the positives. Positives being the friends you would not have had and the opportunities that would not have presented themselves.

Forgiveness has to be a part of this life in reverse; it is a positive. Not forgiving is being struck with grief. Let go of the hurts in life's unexpected losses, and those boulders in the road will become pebbles. You cannot change the pain, and you have to absorb it into your life, but learn from it. I have had many good things happen, but still, I am not seeing the purpose in all of this pain inflicted on all of us. I do so strongly have the "faith" that there is a better life at the end of this path that is filled with an overabundance of curves and swerves. My stomach, on the other hand, has no faith at all of making it to the straight, flat, path ahead of us in that southern town.

Emmie and I discussed the beliefs and feelings we have about God and forgiveness. That darn forgiveness keeps popping up. We have come from different backgrounds, but both possess a firm and strong faith in the big guy upstairs. Our conversations are good. I find all people do not have the same picture of God, life, and love. No one is totally right or wrong, and we all have our hearts in the right place. Emmie has her heart in the right place but does not realize it all the time. She has so much more love and care inside of her heart than she can imagine. She just does not realize that she can trust yet. That day will come. God has given me the insight to look far within others and not let exteriors get in the way. Where was this insight when Prin-cess came into my life? I guess I would certainly be in a different situation had God's timing been a little different. I guess that is his prerogative to decide when he will bless us with the good, the bad, or the ugly!

Emmie has a fear of the power of God, and I feel his power is to help us not to be feared. My God has an unconditional love of his earthlings. He loves us enough to allow us to make choices in life that sometimes hurt him. That is a love incomparable to any other. We do hurt God, but he very graciously accepts apologies and likes to see his children grow with their learning experiences. He must be loving the growth process that Emmie and I have been going through. We certainly have had enough learning experiences!

This path we are going down is chock-full with these darn curves. I think this is not good, the way I am feeling, I mean. "Emmie, my stomach is like riding in my throat." "What can I do for you?" she asked. "Nothing. Well, maybe pull over when you can, and I will get a Coke out of the trunk. That usually helps." I realize that her mind was spinning with a thought of where in the "hollow" is she ever going to be able to pull over, but she politely responded with an okay. Shortly after she found a little church to pull over, thank God! I bailed out of that car. What is wrong with me? I do not get car sick at night, this is night, pitch-black night in the hills, curves, valleys, hollows, or whatever that we are going over to get to "grandmother's" house for Thanksgiving. I just do not feel like singing, "Over the river and through the woods," or in this case "Around the curves, through the valleys, and up hollers." We are close to the river but still not over it. I got that Coke, did the burp thing and fresh air, and back to the passenger seat, strapped in and ready for more around and around we go action, and all I want to do is stop!

This sort of ended our God talk, and I was just talking to God, *Oh God, Oh God, bring back my stomach… It was still back on one of those curves before the 'Church on the Brink of Upheaval.'* This ride felt like from here to eternity, and my "friend" Emmie seemed to be having fun. Emmie kept laughing. I mean we have had a lot of laughs together, but I have never heard her laugh this hard. I did not know or care what was so funny. Does she entertain a comedy club in her head, or is there something I am missing here other than that deer we just missed on that curve? As a matter of fact, I was missing something here other than my stomach. Emmie had said to me several times, "Just three more curves." Then after several swirls around and around, it was "just three more curves, C. R." and once again. With my head in the clouds and my stomach swirling, "just three more curves, C. R.," and again, "C. R., just three more curves." Just what is she laughing at? Does she always laugh at sick people? Ahh, I think I am starting to get it now. She has been saying three more curves for the last twenty curves. Her explanation is that it depends on your perspective and your definition of how big a curve is. Too big in my dictionary, and I was just telling you about all the good in her heart too!

Finally, we hit the bottom, the straight and narrow, the flat land, and I could not wait to get my legs on the ground once again. Emmie is still laughing as we parked our Dodge sleigh in front of "grand-mother's house we go". I couldn't wait to go in and head straight to the bathroom. Finally, we were in, and I was on the bed waiting for the twists and turns to quit.

Those turns took a while to get out of my system, and as soon as I got on my feet, we were off and running for a fun evening. However, it meant once again climbing the hills in the Dodge sleigh and maneuvering the turns. The lesson here is don't count on darkness being a plus. Wear the sea bands any time there is motion.

As bedtime rolled around, we were once again involved in a discussion of the serious nature. This time it is that forgiveness subject. Should I forgive—I don't mean Charm and NotSo—I mean Emmie for laughing at me in my time of desperate despair?

Okay, so she was pretty funny. I now can laugh, but what about this subject? I find forgiveness is a very profitable act. God is the only one that can deal with the acts of perpetrators that have inflicted pain in our lives. Emmie and I cannot do a thing about it. I find the act of putting this all in God's hands has made me stronger and able to continue to take care of myself and my kids. This act of forgiveness does not make what has happened right; it just clears the path for us to heal and advance to that better life awaiting us.

The next morning was filled with the smell of all the usual turkey day scents, and I think I am on the "road" to recovery. Food is becoming of interest to me again. The house is filled with "gobblers," and what a nice warmth there was and a sense of love. After the traditional "stuffing" of ourselves, we took a walk up the hollow, for real, and then ate again only to take another "ride" to see the lights of Oglebay Park." This was quite a sight, and I had quite a good time. Then we were off to sister Sylvia's house, and that is where we were staying for the night. Shopping till we drop is our motto for the day, and that we did on this busiest shopping day of the year. There is a lot more to be done, but I have faith that it will get done. You know Emmie and I will make it through all of this, and adorning my sea bands, I made it through the curves and swerves comfortably coming home. Maybe there is a sign here. We could look at the dependency I have or my stomach has on those sea bands, and we could learn a little lesson. It does not hurt to lean a little on something that will help us—God, one another, and love.

I had a very Happy Thanksgiving and came home to a wonderful surprise. My three kids had the tree up and decorated for me. The important thing is that they spent the day together and had a great time in helping. Their relationship with one another is very important. Emmie and I had a great time, and I am glad I could be the source of her laughter and enjoyment! I sometimes cannot understand myself. I question where my feelings come from. I have always been one to really feel life.

As a musician, I have learned to open my heart and let the feelings out. It is the only way to really feel and express the music. I may not be playing with a full deck, but I have played the cards that I have been dealt. I have worked my way up to a full house, and I am on my way to a royal flush, no jokes please.

Emmie, thanks for sharing your family and the time with me. Thanks to all of you for the care you have shown me and for making me feel such a part of the day and sharing your lives. My only hope is that someday I can give back to you what I have received and that those curves get straightened out before I come back.

Just sayin'—That I know I have a strong faith, and I really do know who is in charge of my life. I know I have a lot of control in what

I do, but God is the CEO. I am trying hard to put the pieces back together, but this puzzle is the hardest level I have ever attempted.

I should have listened to my gut and heart months ago when my heart sunk when I looked at NotSo and Charm Man. I thought he was being nice and cared about her. He cared all right—more about her than me. What they did to me and my kids never crossed my mind that they could do such a thing. I thought they were better than that. Goes to show you I am a poor judge of character. Don't I feel stupid? *Just sayin'!*

Tonight was the once-a-month card bunch. Which is funny in itself because we never manage to meet once a month. We had a lot of fun, but I was asked the question, "In your heart, you knew right, C. R.?" I said that I now believe that I did, but at the time, I did not believe it. However, I think I felt the deceit and the cruelty, and somehow, even though I didn't think I was, I was not believing their lies and excuses. I thought I was.

We now know they "lie" in bed together at night and cry over what they have done to me ... ha! I "lay" in bed at night and hope that God hears my pain and has a plan for my future happiness. Even though there is not an answer yet, I believe my thoughts do not fall on deaf ears. I believe he knows what I feel in by heart, my mind, and my soul. I believe he (Charm) feels nothing, and God knows what he has done in his undercover work.

CHAPTER 58

Where Have All the Feelings Gone?
or
Cinderella's Shoes Don't Fit My Feet

There hasn't been a lot of time for writing lately. I have had the desire, but the holiday season takes a lot of time. Today the feelings just cannot wait. I have to write. The wrapping, shopping, and cards will just have to wait.

Once upon a time, there was a man and a woman who loved each other and wanted to spend the rest of their lives together. Or did they? I was that woman. Prince Charming was that man, and now we have reached the point of not even speaking. I thought fairy tales had happy endings, where I was headed when I said, "I do."

Snow White was happy. She lived with dwarfs who did all the work. In my life, I could have filled Cinderella's shoes! My feet are too narrow to find comfortable shoes, and not once has a prince, especially a charming one, put them on my feet. Then there is the big tale we have spoken of before. Fortunately, my nose has not grown over the years, but what did I do wrong to get these hips and flabby abs?

Fairy tale lives don't usually come true. Life is what we make of it from what God gives us. So God gave me a chance at marriage, and did I fail? I really am not sure. Last night was the group Christmas party. The festivities were held at Mo's house, and the whole gang made it. We had dinner and pictures with our Santa hats she had made with our names on them. Things were great. We had pulled names out of a hat for our secret groupie gift exchange, and everyone had chosen just the right gift for their secret "giftee." Emmie had tried to trick me into revealing my secret, and I almost kept it, but she figured it out just before the party. The guessing was now over, and just before we opened our presents, we got started telling what we missed about our spouses. I had nothing. I could not come up with an answer. As the conversation went around the room, I was still aloof. I felt like I had nothing. What were those twenty-six years? Why could I not have something to miss? Is there something wrong with me that I could not find something I miss about Charming?

I went through twenty-six years in my mind, hoping when they were all done maybe I could get another shot at this and have something profound and wise to contribute. There were the nights that meant snoring and my sleep being disturbed. I slept on the couch many nights because his theory was that he could not help the snoring, so it was my problem. Okay, so I had to mow my own yard this summer, but was that a just thing to miss? I found out I could run the snow blower and change the filter on the furnace. I realize that I don't have to put the toilet seat down, and I do not have to wipe up after him. Why is it I realize the sense of relief of not being used and cannot find the things I miss? I found those things I missed during my late nights' crying sessions. I received more understanding and sympathy from my dog than Charm ever had for me. I have had more support and encouragement from these fellow secret Santa's than I have ever had in my life. I have been encouraged by these and so many other friends. I never had that before.

I am still sitting here in front of the fire as the fellow groupies are saying what they miss; maybe the heat from the fire is shrinking my brain. I cannot come up with anything, and they have almost gone around the room. If I am lucky, they will forget that I did not yet speak of my "missing items." Did I not appreciate what I had, or did I not have anything except what I envisioned in my own mind? What was the purpose of me spending these twenty-six years with Charm?

The circle has been completed, and others have shared their feelings of which I still have none. The presents are being opened, and my mind keeps reflecting back through the years. I probably have more in life than I have ever had. How do I trust my judgment again? Everyone is sharing the gifts and stories of purchasing them, but I still don't know what happened to my life. I feel like it all was a fairy tale, just a dream that I woke from.

What a nice evening we had—good food, good friends. I think I am starting to sound like a beer commercial. You get the picture. I came home and still couldn't let go of the thoughts of a wasted life. Why did I allow myself to live like that? I don't understand what is with me. I think it is inborn that we get married and have kids, and this is life. But that daily fear of never being good enough or doing things correctly. I never realized the fear I lived with every day. I felt like I tried so hard to please and make this a happy living fairy tale life. I failed, or did I? Maybe I only failed myself. I allowed myself to be used. Why? Was I not good enough to deserve love?

Emmie picked me up for church in the morning, and I was still pondering this scum of my life. During the service, I started writing thoughts all over my bulletin. Yes, I was paying attention! As I wrote the thoughts that were flying through this disheartened mind, I realized that I was totally embarrassed that I had not come up with something I missed about my ex-loved one. I felt inferior. I felt that I was living a life of being totally controlled. It hurts to think I can't even think for myself. Imagine what it felt like to sit there in front of these friends that do not really know my inner feelings and my past life and not be able to come up with an answer. I felt that I had led a worthless, meaningless life. When I had the chance, I made jokes to cover the pain, but it only covered the surface. Jokes don't cut it when you need the hurt of your heart lifted.

Emmie asked what I was writing in church. I was paying attention. I said it was my next chapter. "About what?" she asked. I proceeded to tell her that I wasted these years and that I was unable to think of something I missed about my ex. "You wouldn't have your children." Point taken. I would not have my children, and that is something I never want to lose. Is that why God had me in this life and why I am where I am now? Maybe next year, I will be out from under the fog even more and will realize something I missed. I guess that remains to be seen. I have certainly learned a lot about myself and life through all of this, and I guess that is worth the suffering. I just want to have a better life for the remaining years on this planet.

An "aha" moment—The fact that I didn't think of something on the spur of the moment to miss in my marriage has brought the realization that I am much better off. It took these people that do miss something about their spouse to make that realization come forth. I finally did think of something I missed; he always cleaned the chandelier. It is a little dusty right now.

CHAPTER 59

'Tis the Season
or
Stylin': Do Black Patent Flats Go
with a Pink Jogging Suit?

Every day brings us twenty-four hours closer to Christmas. I know that you are thinking that is a profound statement, but someone has to notice these things! I have started the normal season of panic.

Things are the norm—snow, rain, sleet, clouds, clouds, and more clouds. Why is it that the sun doesn't shine down on Ohio? Are there not enough good people in this state? I know that is not true. Heaven is running short of sun angels since there are so many people that are doing dastardly deeds, and those perpetrators are ending up on the lower level of the parking garage of life where it is much hotter!

The snow is nice sometimes. Around Christmas, it gives the holiday a little spirit. I have had some spirit. The kids did my tree as you know, and that has helped a lot. I almost have my cards done. I have not been sending cards the last few years because I gave the money I would spend to charity instead. This year, I not only sent cards but a Christmas letter. I was not going to miss this opportunity to express a few things for the cost of a stamp. I have some packages wrapped and most things purchased but still have a little ways to go. I will not really be doing any baking. Who needs it? I think I am doing all right. Let's hope!

Kimberly has been home for some time, and that keeps me occupied, and I have been too busy to realize that I should be depressed over the change in the Christmas traditions this year. You know, especially the tradition where Charm is here to open presents with his old family. It is time to start new traditions. We started one last year. Maybe you don't remember. Let me help refresh your boggled minds. Last year, just about this time, I discovered NotSo and Charm locked in her condom—I did it again, I meant condo, although the other is closer to the truth. I am sure you remember that chapter. The discovery of them in the bedroom supposedly talking somehow had me "slightly" upset. That was the first part; the second was having the big gift opening. In the past, only NotSo and I had exchanged gifts. We would find an evening after Christmas and get together and exchange gifts. This past year, Man of Charm was included. That should have told me right then and there that things were NotSo "holly jolly," at least for me. I just had not caught up to their way of thinking yet. Well, this year, they will keep that tradition of exchanging gifts with each other alive. The only difference is they forgot to put my name on their Christmas list. They better watch out Santa is coming, and he will see who has been naughty and who has been nice.

This is where I pick up the pieces that are left and figure out how to glue them back together to make something special again. I am succeeding. I have realized that I will still be on the guest list to Jesus's birthday party. I have not been a perpetrator. I will be spending Christmas Eve and Christmas with my children. Charm will not. I realize how much I do have to look forward too. I have the shopping, the wrapping, the shopping, and more shopping. The house cleaning, the undecorating, the gynecologist appointment at eight o'clock in the morning on Christmas Eve morning, picking up the mess after the gift opening, and especially the part where everyone is saying, "I am hungry. What do we have to eat?" Now if that is not enough, after all the excitement has calmed down and the work week starts again, I get to return to the mammogram store. The shopping never ends! I love December instead of my time of the month, which lately is all month. We can look at December as my gynecologic time of year!

On to the serious side—well sort of—my counselor asked how I was doing with the holidays coming up, and I answered, "Okay so far." We talked about the old traditions and maybe the possibility of making some changes to not allow memories to crop up. I definitely am changing traditions when it comes to finding Prince and Princess locked in the condo. Enough is enough of that. So I will start some new things. Some of the group members will be coming for Christmas Eve, and we will be going to late church. Yeah, the one where you come right home and go to bed, and Santa is here before you know it.

What I see happening is that it has been over a year that my "inner self" has been dealing with this inappropriate situation, and I have just had enough. I want to make this a good Christmas for the kids and myself. I cannot control what others do. I can only control my feelings, and I have to buck up and keep this time happy. I am trying hard to keep the spirit. The pain is there with the underlying hurt but is manageable so far. How could it not be manageable when you have friends like mine?

Emmie has been helping me through the shopping aspect of the season. You know how I love to shop—*not*! I made her a deal. She shops; I wrap. I take her shopping with me, and I wrap her presents for her. I think it is fair. We have been working together to prepare to celebrate Christmas. I have been having fun. Instead of being tense, irritable, and bogged down, I have been relaxed, pleasant, I hope, and enjoying the time. I have attended two concerts already and have three to go. That is more Christmas concerts than I have attended in all these years put together. The concerts have been great, but I think shopping has to be the highlight. I have a new tradition that I hope Emmie will help me keep from now on. It is the tradition of shopping with her in the pink jogging suit. I cannot remember when I have laughed so hard while shopping.

Anyhow, I was at Emmie's house and the decision was made to run to the store. Well, not run but drive to the store. I took my car home for Kimberly, and Emmie soon followed to pick me up for a quick trip to Target. She said, "I am wearing this jogging suit"—definitely pinker than pink—"if that is not all right with you. Just walk behind me." In her quickness of her normally organized self, she slipped her shoes on and drove over to pick me up. I jumped in the car, and off we went. Upon arriving, we got out and started walking toward the store. (Note: I am the kind of person that can stare someone straight in the face when they have things protruding from their nose, maybe particles uniquely placed between their teeth or even their fly unzipped. I never have the nerve to say a word, and they cannot read it on my face. I do realize though that there is a necessity for friends to tell friends of these embarrassing malformations, but it is hard for me. I have been picked apart so much I find it difficult to even pleasantly say, "Excuse me, there is somewhat of a strange object hanging from your nostril!" Of course, you could always do the mother thing: "Here is a tissue. Use it." (I am trying to be a better booger-tattling friend.)

Story—I was wandering far behind Emmie in all her pinkness through the parking lot and found that my friend, my shopping buddy—someone I would follow anywhere—was wearing black patent leather flats with this florescent-pink jogging suit, not to mention the white socks. I have to tell you that I did not even hesitate with my words of wisdom. I said, "The pink suit does not bother me as long I as I don't have to wear it. But couldn't you have at least put on tennis shoes?" Her response was "I was in a hurry and decided just to slip on these shoes. I have to be back by eight forty-five to take the Chex mix out of the oven." This better be good Chex mix after the embarrassment I have had to endure.

She has been teaching for at least the last thirty years in this town that I grew up in. I figure as a guesstimate that would be in the area of one thousand three hundred students she has taught. Now you know darn well we are going to see at least one student or family unit she knows in this store as she is decked out for the Easter parade—*just sayin'*!

Well, there we were, and there they were—students, families, past students, and past students' parents as well as some of my school chums. When running into someone I knew, usually a mutual friend, I worked hard doing some kind of actions that would keep their eyes above the waist. I ran into two friends while on this safari of the Target store. On a couple of occasions, Emmie was talking to a student's family while I was talking to friends who did not know her and thought I was there alone! Whew! Let's just get what we came for and get the Chex mix out of the oven.

I suppose that I should fess up here and tell the truth. I would not have had that evening any other way. Each Christmas, when Emmie calls and asks me to go shopping, I will politely ask, "What are you wearing?" Before I say yes, I will not forget that night, and it really did not bother me at all, and I hope she never finds that out. We have a lot of fun, and she has been very entertaining.

I told Kay the story about her pinkness. After she was done laughing over this incident, I said, "Emmie makes me laugh." That is a big change in my life. She makes me laugh. I do not have to entertain her all the time in order to have fun. What a new concept, someone with a personality instead of the mechanical bulls I was entertaining.

I am so lucky to be surrounded by good people, and they will help me make it through these changes in tradition. Thanks, Emmie, for being there. What is in store for me Easter shopping a red-and-green dress with Reeboks? Just wait till spring when I pull out my green wind suit. I have white socks. I just have to buy the black patent flats.

CHAPTER 60

Thanks for Dinner, Kay; Never Leave Me Again
or
The Brown Nose Washes Off at Night

I feel like I have boot marks on my posterior from the kicking I continually get. The obvious cruelty is more than one soul, and I use the term loosely, should have to bear. Is this the final exam from the big guy upstairs, or am I unlucky at more than love?

I know I have not won the lottery. I feel like I am continually being tested, and I want to graduate and get this over with. I have, however, given major thought to the fact that maybe I am the test for the others involved. Is it their test by God and I am the questions?

Tonight was test night. The whole day has been a little on the strange side, and fortunately midnight is almost upon us, and maybe tomorrow will be better. I am going through a very difficult time as it is. I feel a loss that is unexplainable at this time. I feel like I am losing someone that I care about, and I am hurting terribly. I am trying to deal with this situation and tell myself that it is my insecurities that cause me to think this way. I need to deal with these inner problems I have, and I am working hard. It just seems that when I make a little progress, the posterior gets the big boot, and I am starting over again. Tonight fills those shoes very well.

The word for the day is "relationships." That is what I have been dealing with, and it was also the subject for Stephen's tonight. It is a funny thing that when you have been through something like this crisis of the heart, you can no longer process the simple functions of dealing with people. It is comparable to a person that loses the use of their hand and has to go through therapy and total retraining to function again. That is where I am with relationships. I continually have to ask my counselor how to handle the simplest of things, so I do not goof up. I wonder what she would have told me about tonight if she could have told me in advance how to handle this new sighting!

That's correct, there was a double sighting, and I was in the middle of it. The plan was to meet Kay for a quick dinner at Burger King before I had Stephen's. Also, after speaking with Shelly, I asked her to meet us as well because she was involved in a career fair at the local high school and was nervous about going by herself. I told her to meet me at Burger King, and I would go up with her and get her started. I was to do this career fair also, but the Stephen's class tonight was too important to miss. I asked her if she had her wallet photos in her purse in case she needed to ID perpetrators. I had given the groupies wallet pictures of the perps for ID purposes. They felt there were times that they were probably standing right beside them and were not aware. They are now aware!

You know this helping just comes naturally to me, and I just keep getting those size 9s in the posterior! Let me set the scene:

The place: The local high school.

The reason: To help Shelly find her way and set up, just support. (A lot of help I was.)

The first sighting: Was the female perpetrator's daughter.

It went something like this: Shelly and I are standing in line to register and get her booth assignment. I immediately spotted a familiar face in the crowd of students that were directing people to the appropriate places. I said, "Shelly, it's her daughter, right up there in the green. I cannot believe this." That was test one. So far, I am scoring an A. I am calm even thought I know I will soon be face-to-face with her. The line continually got closer to the table, and the obstacle that was in my way of making it by without her seeing me, but there she was standing directly in front of me with the "teenage smirk." The female perp's daughter told the girl that was going to direct us to Shelly's booth that she would take us. She had a look of "I will show you" on her face.

She has us follow her to the booth, and when she turns and faces us, I said, "Hi. How are you?" "Fine" was the "attitudal" response. She departed. I did it. Inside I was shaking. Actually, outwardly I was shaking, and Shelly gave me a hug and said, "You did great." Whew, I did make it, and I will be out of here soon. All of a sudden, I realized the daughter was once again standing in my face and space. She said, "Did you hear what band I am in?" Did I hear? How was I going to hear? Her mother or my husband was not going to call me and tell me any news. I said, "No." She proceeded to tell me, and I responded with "That's good." I proceeded to give her a hug. Who is this person in this body?

Why don't I ever react with the normal response? What is wrong with me? What is wrong with me is that God keeps getting in my way, and he brings out that real person from deep down in my heart. I hate that! Just kidding. This is not the daughter's fault, and that is what needs to be remembered. Possible reactions could have been "How's your mom treating my husband?" "How does it feel to have a famous 'mother'? One everyone is talking about." "Do you have a hard time living with Vicki and Kimberly's father?" "How do you like sharing the bathroom?" "Does it bother you that you have to put the toilet seat down?" "How do you like having the temperature controlled in your house?" "Does the snoring keep you awake?" And last but not least, "Does he use your mother's dish towel to dry his armpits?" Oh, I forgot, they live in a condom—I mean condo, and the lawn is mowed, and he doesn't have to do yard work. So the grass really was greener north of town. I will not continue this because my thought pattern "could" get a little sarcastic!

I, however, did not choose that line of questioning. I went the softer side with "How is that trumpet playing coming?" Her response being, "I struggle without lessons." Who do you think her teacher was? Those lessons would cost a lot now. I would be the best-paid teacher around. She asked me who this was that I was with. She was pumping me for information. I pretended not to hear. You know, you begin to get hearing loss after the age of thirty, and I decided to use it to my advantage. She said, "I wondered if you would be up here." She went back to her guide job, and I helped Shelly set up and went to my meeting—well, I headed that direction.

After passing the daughter again and saying goodbye, just fifty feet later, much to my surprise, I realized that the blue coat and very heavily made-up face with a stylish hairdo I was passing was "her." Where is Emmie when I need this identification help? I almost physically ran into the female perpetrator. She had the straight serious face, not even looking at the person passing her, the slumping shoulders, and long fast gate of determination to get where she was going and then make a quick exit. I, on the other hand, look at everyone that passes by. I don't want to miss an opportunity to talk with someone. I avoided having a talk with this familiar made-up face. What was this hairdo anyhow? It has stripes. I would call it a skunk do! Or maybe it is like prison stripes.

No wonder this perpetrator of the worst kind is slithering past me unrecognized in restaurants; the tomboy image of motorcycles and repairing cars is being hidden under skunk streaks and war paint. How does Emmie so readily recognize her? I guess she is more experienced at this than I. I sometimes still live with the "Oh, they would not do that to me" fantasy. I will not go anywhere alone again until they legalize abortion of adults over forty that are perpetrators of midlife crisis fun and frolic.

At this point, I only had one goal in mind, to get back to Shelly and let her know that there has been another sighting of the worst kind and to be prepared. I continued on my path right out the door I had come in and took an immediate turn. I walked quite a distance in the cold weather and entered through another door to reach Shelly before "Skunky" did. I almost made it. When I reached Shelly, she was talking to a person, and I was dancing around, not for the reason you might think but because I needed to tell her. As I stood there while she was talking, I scanned the crowd looking for the perp, and I strongly felt her presence and maybe even her pupils gazing through her made-up eyes and those strands of skunk-striped hair hanging in her eyes. "Shelly, she is here. Shelly, Shelly, listen. She is here." "Where?" "I am not sure, but she has on a blue coat, lots of makeup, and striped hair." Then I spotted her. I told Shelly not to look. She was talking with her daughter, and they were laughing and talking about me—looking right at me. Shelly finally got a look at her. You know what her response was? "Your prettier than her." How could she tell through all that war paint?

They moved so that I could not visually see her. I cannot say that it wasn't more pleasant that way. I escaped and got to my car and on my way to my meeting. I just had to get to a phone to call Emmie. I need to tell her. I know she will not be home, but I just have to leave a message. I ran into Stephen's and said, "May I use a phone?" I immediately found one and called and left a message. I just don't know what I said!

Upon entering the Stephen's group, I was just trying to be calm and go on as if nothing had happened. I will not go into a lot of detail about the rest of the evening, but I did receive the star student award. It was awarded because I was the only student that wrote an essay using my "feeling words." A few fellow SMers vocalized their feelings about my brown-nosed efforts, but I have a star sticker on my book, and they don't! However, NotSo has to wash her made-up brown nose off at night.

Class was very interesting. Parables were passed out for us to read and answer questions about. I received my paper and begin to read, "The Adulteress Woman." This was a planned effort, and I just had to laugh. Once again, I contributed, probably more than I should have, but I did tell them of my recent "horror show" at the school and that it was my faith that took me through it successfully. There is no other explanation for being able to continue on. God is testing someone. I do not know if I am the "test-ee" or the tester. I want to pass these tests, and I want to be a functioning, healed person with an attitude for a good life. I just wanted to pack it all up and run away, but what would I have to write about? I think God gives me these little run-ins just to provide chapters for this book. I also have noticed my friends will do anything to get in this book. Enough is enough!

I thank God for getting me through these little encounters of the worst kind, and I do truly trust in his life for me, wherever it may lead. I did have one good thing happen today. I have one more day before the expiration date on my milk runs out. I guess that good things do happen. I have no cereal, but I have milk for one more day. What more could I ask for?

Just sayin'—My assignment for Stephen's Ministry was to write something using the "feeling words" we had been working on. This is what came to my mind:

> At this time, I am *dissatisfied, disheartened,* and *discouraged*—those sum up my life.
>
> That being said, I am *composed, concerned, confused* yet ... *engrossed* in the study of these feeling words.
>
> Feeling words help me relieve stress and overcome the troubled feelings of *undone work, wasted time,* and being *horrified* with the possible outcome that makes me *stressed, rushed,* and *messing up work,* which tend to make me feel *teed off, ticked off, shot, zapped, whipped, unglued, on edge,* and *hacked off!*
>
> I am headed in the direction of being *hopeless, fearful, detached, bored, overwhelmed, pessimistic, downcast, rundown, unglued, pooped, blue, blah,* and *burned out.*
>
> I find that writing the feeling words is making me *edgy, uptight, unnerved, reluctant, dejected,* and *downhearted.*
>
> But ... funny thing is happening. I am beginning to feel *steady, warm, in touch, strong, enlivened,* and *trustful.* That is a big one for me—*trustful!*
>
> I would like to use *vex,* but I am *embarrassed* that I don't know what it means. I will shake the *jitters,* be *optimistic, relieved,* and *happy* to get back to the next part of the story—***just sayin'.***

CHAPTER 61

Fractured Bible Verses
or
Rocky and Bullwinkle Have Nothing on Us

It was SM night again, and it was my night to bring the snack. Fellow SMers were anticipating me bringing Spanish rice since they knew I cook enough for two weeks. I fooled them. I did not take Spanish rice. Emmie talked me out of it.

Last week, I told my fellow SMers that the real C. R. has only come out in class. It is the first time she has appeared in many years. My New Year's resolution came somewhat from the chapters I had read in our assignment. Our leader asked if anything inspired us from reading our assignment. I told the SMers that I made a New Year's resolution based upon some of the readings I had actually read. Inquisitive minds want to know, so I told. "My resolution was to be myself." I heard this loud *yes* from the other end of the table. I had my back to the leader and turned slowly to look at him. As I was turning, I am thinking he has a portable TV watching the game and someone just got a three pointer. His cheer was directed at me! Was this because I had kept a resolution for a week? No, it was because I understood what the book was saying I should do. Much like that big author in the sky wrote in *the book*!

I should be myself and be accepted for that. Who I am was created by God, and I need to live within his creation. I slipped out of character for twenty some odd years, but guess what? I'mmm bbaaaaccckkk! I felt so good. I have been working so hard to recreate the person that was so lost, and this is one of many signs that I have had since the eve of New Year. I'm not looking back, only forward. The time is right to stand tall and be who God chose me to be.

One of our first orders of business was to analyze—we all know how good I am at that—some Bible verses. The purpose, as we attempted to learn, was the difference between assertive, aggressive, and passive behavior. We were to decide what the behavior of the person in the verse was. We also looked at what could have been if the action was different. As we worked in groups of two, we tried to accomplish this task. We started merging our ideas and thoughts, and I was thinking maybe we should write our own verses in the form like Bullwinkle and Rocky's idea of their fables.

The first verse my group was trying to analyze was Martha and her sister Mary. Martha was pretty upset because she had all the work to do while precious little princess Mary sat at Jesus's feet and talked. Now depending on how long Jesus had been walking and wearing those same sandals would probably tell us who had the better end of the deal. Of course, Martha thought she was getting the wrong end of the stick. So she said to Jesus, "Jesus, hey, why does the little princess get to sit and talk while I mop, dust, do the dishes?" Did they have dishes back then? You get the idea. Was Martha being assertive, aggressive, or passive? That's okay. We really did not know either. We did, however, produce an answer of aggressive.

Think about this whiner. She could have just finished her work and then sat with Jesus or assertively spoken with sister Mary the lazy princess. "Could you please help me with the chores so I could hear the stories Jesus has to tell?" was all she needed to say. Instead, she told Jesus to do something about it. Whoa, not me, man. I am not going to tell God's son to do anything. You did not read a lot about Martha from there on out. Well, you just should not tell the Son of God what to do.

Then we got to analyze the prodigal son. Just what determines a son to be prodigal anyhow? *Webster* knows he would be "exceedingly or recklessly wasteful." So we are speaking of a wasteful reckless son. In other words, a typical teenager. Well, this oh-so prodigal one did not want to wait for the father figure to die before he received his inheritance. So he became assertive to borderline aggressive and said, "Hey, Dad, give me my half of the land now before you kick that bucket. The father after reading Dr. Spock, not the Star Trek one, gave into his son. "Here, son of mine, the fruit of my loins. Here is the land. I have toiled over this soil, and it is yours to do with as you please." A smart son would have built condos but not the prodigal son. He sold it and spent all his money. When he was flat broke, he wagged his tail all the way home to Daddy. Then on one knee, he told Dad what a scum bag he had been, and he was sorry. He was then accepted back home. He went from borderline aggressive to passive. He should have just developed those condos.

John the Baptist was next in our studies. Now what did it matter if he was a Baptist or not. His denomination should not be pointed out. I don't walk down the street and say, "Oh, there is Emmie the Methodist, or there is Karen the Catholic. I mean, that is not nice to label one another. There must be a verse about that. We will just say John with the water. So John with the water said to the people that he would baptize them, but there would be a person that would follow. That person would be Jesus, and John with the water felt he was not worthy to wear his sandals. Who would want to after Jesus wore them through the hot sandy desert? Had they ever heard of athlete's foot? Then Jesus wanted to have John baptize him. "I need you to baptize me," Jesus said as he wanted to show others the way, the truth, the light. John boy did his thing with the water for Jesus. We thought John was being assertive. If he were being aggressive, he could have said, "Who do you think you are?" Imagine feeding Jesus a line like that.

He would have shown that Baptist on the spot where that water was. The passive John would have just said okay.

Then comes the really tough one. Mary the mother of Jesus. Now just imagine yourself being a parent to Jesus. If you would try to correct him, he could strike you with lighting. If you said you can't leave the table until you finish your food, he could make loaves of bread and fish till you couldn't find room for all of them in the freezer.

The story goes something like this. The family took a week-end trip to the feast. Jesus got distracted and fell behind Joseph and Mary. You wonder how the couple could travel on not realizing their son was not with them. Remember, Jesus was a boy. Had he been a girl, they would have realized the silence and no whining and missed "her" in the first mile. They walked around trying to find him and found him in the temple. Mary read him the riot act, "Do you know how worried your father and I have been? How dare you treat us like that," said Mary.

How do you punish the king of heaven and earth? That's a good one for Joyce Brothers. Being the passive person that I am, I would have just said to him, "Whatever you want, honey, is fine with me." Possible punishments could have been "No more walking on that water, young man, till you learn to honor thy father and thy mother. No more playing with the Baptist boy till you straighten up. No more little disciples running through my house till you can prove to me that you can behave yourself. Tomorrow you clean up after the asses, the ones in the stable. Clean out the barn after the asses, and then maybe you will learn a lesson." I mean what can you do? Ground him? Take the keys to the donkey and not let him out of the yard?

The point to this whole thing is: what was the point? Oh, I remember. I have learned so much through this class. I have learned about myself. I have been myself. I have fun and sometimes get hit over the head with a book by the leaders, but I love every minute of it.

This is a very special group of people God has brought together. I am very proud to be in the company of such very special people. I call them friends, whether they like it or not. The leaders are great people to give so much to us and especially with their patience with me. There is a certain bond that is created when you go into something that takes such a commitment and such a faith in God. We all have that and want to share it with others. God will stick with us. Our leaders will shape and mold us into those helpful Stephen's ministers.

CHAPTER 62

I Finally Slowed Down and Let Life Catch Me
or
Snowmen Eventually Melt!

I did it! I kept thirty-one days of a New Year's resolution to be myself. It is a miracle. My goal is to incorporate this resolution as a permanent part of my life. It feels so good to be myself. I have had very minimal backslides, and it is so refreshing. I have been told, or let's say it has been instilled in me, that you can't change another person. I guess it is only possible if they want to be changed. Theory has it, you can change yourself but not others. I have successfully changed myself for thirty-one lovely days. In turn, others have changed. Pretty tricky, huh?

I came from brutally battering my counselor with questions about my future to slowing myself down and allowing life to catch up to me. As a very true Libra, I want to balance everything, and I got a little ahead of myself there for a while. A little ahead of myself, ha, only by about five years. I am a little closer to reality now. I am thankful for that. Tipping the scales makes me very seasick!

Vicki says it is great to have me back. Her version of her mom did not match where I have been over the more recent years, and her opinion is I am not as uptight. Why should I have been uptight, you ask? Maybe because I was never quite good enough. Well, guess what, I am finally good enough. It took me a hell of a long time to get here. Maybe I should rephrase that—I went through hell to get here. It was worth every moment of the self-conscience struggle, of the pain, and of the worthlessness. That inside person that God created has been stifled and caged. I have now been released into the public. I think I am fairing pretty well inside and out!

Why would I be uptight? Maybe because "I get no respect." Sound familiar? I can't help it. I received absolutely no respect from the ever-so-demanding, commanding admiral and his Ms. Chief "Petty" Officer. I respected them both. Well, not now, but I did. I catered to their needs. I took good care of them without a lick of respect thrown my direction, especially by Man of Charm. The pedestal they were on, in my eyes, must have been too high for me to climb aboard I was left with a stiff neck from always looking up.

My neck is much better now. No more looking up to undeserving people. I feel like I am on the same plane now—flying at the same altitude—no more puddle jumpers for me. If I can continue that natural behavior out in the world, what a stronger more honest being I will be. By "honest", I mean I am the true person that I am supposed to be. Not hidden among the public but a part of the public. I now can participate in society and life on a different level. It is like breathing fresh clean air. I was breathing the stale air left for me by Charm.

Vicki now thinks I am a much "cooler" mom, and Kimberly wants me to do things that as she said I would not have done a year ago. Well, that we did. The other night, we had a significant snow. At ten o'clock in the evening, I had just come in, and Kimberly said, "Mom, how would you like to do something you would not have done a year ago?" I knew where this was headed. I looked at her as she said, "Let's go play in the snow." I said something very unusual, "Okay." We bundled up and were ready for action. Taking to the outdoors, Kimberly, Precious, and I hit the snow-covered yard, and a decision was made to make a snowman. At my age, when you are bent over rolling snow around the yard, the blood flow isn't quite as good as it used to be, which was probably the cause of my snowman idea that consisted of Prince Charming and Prin-cess NotSo Charming look-alikes. Upon assembly of all the balls—of snow that is—we got a T-shirt and hat of his that had been stored in the garage since shortly after his escape. This was great! Kimberly was ready to finish the essentials like eyes, nose, and mustache when I said, "Okay, get out there and start rolling that snowwoman!" I think she was thinking, *Reality check, Mom.* I was the one that said I would go out for a little while because it was cold out there. An hour and a half later, we finally came in, and Kimberly got the hot chocolate. That hour and a half produced a lifelike snowwoman and snowman representing those coldhearted perpetrators.

Body parts were done to scale, and I even had NotSo's old soccer T-shirt to pull over her snow head. We had a great time and took pictures. I am sure my next-door neighbors wondered what kept flashing before their eyes at eleven thirty at night.

Dee, my friend and neighbor, looked out her window shortly after we had gone in. She wondered who was standing in front of my garage door. Oh yeah, I left that part out. We built them in front of the garage doors where they were publicly visible. Dee said she thought to herself, "Are those snowmen?" And she knew right away who they were.

We completed our "something I would not have done a year ago," and quite successfully, I might add. What shall I create in the next snowstorm?

As you can already figure out for yourself, this is where the "Snowmen Eventually Melt" part comes into play. Each day, they leaned just a little more, and some people took potshots at them with their feet as they would walk by. Eventually, they "sunk so low" that they touched the ground and fell apart, and once again, I picked up the pieces. This time, however, I did not get kicked back, and I got some satisfaction out of seeing them "melt at my feet." It was cheaper than therapy.

This is the new me. Take it or leave it. At least, I can hold my head up and show my face in a crowd. Another learning experience has been created this month and one of the best ever. I, for the first time, can see how I can fulfill the needs I have to help others without hurting myself or others. I no longer "have" to do things for others in order to be liked. I can do things for others because they do like me. My need to be a fixer has been roped, tied, corralled, and put to good use actually fixing things like walls, doors, dishwashers, etc., and not the people that own the objects.

People can only fix themselves, but I can be there to support and love them. I can't take care of everyone, but I can care for them. Oh, I am still codependent, but codependent on God to help me fix, repair, care for, and love in all the right ways. Without harm to this person that loves so much. I now am the creation God wanted from me, and I have been able to stand tall enough to reach his hand. He would not come down to hold my hand. I had to reach a height that I could meet him. I have. I am filled with contentment and joy. I no longer waste all my energy trying to be good enough for others. I now spend that extra energy loving them.

CHAPTER 63

Tomorrow Is the Big Day
or
Faith, Hope, and Charity

Graduation is tomorrow. I will be a full-fledged Stephen's minister. The study and time will pay off as we enter the world to help others. I just found out one thing though. I think I am the one that needs the help. Can I really be a help to others when my heart hurts so deeply?

Well, certainly, the "hope" is there deep within. Looking back on it, I wanted so badly to do this. I have felt from that day Emmie asked me to go to church with her that God wanted me here. Not once have I wrestled with doubt. I thank God for Emmie and her asking me to join her at my old church that Sunday. I remember that it was a packed house for God that day, and there were not many seats left in those slippery pews. We took to the stairs to sit in the balcony. The farthest point away from the pulpit in the very far corner. There we sat singing and listening when it was mentioned about two people leaving next week to do the training for the new SM program. Anyone that would be interested in becoming an SMer should mention it to one of the trainers. I asked Emmie if she knew what it was about, but she didn't. I could not get it out of my mind. I had to know more about that program because I was going to do it.

Here I am. I did it and now. I am regressing, feeling too inferior to be here. I better get a grip because tomorrow could start my first assignment.

The "hope" has been there from day one of my hearing about this program. Someone must have said to me as a child, "You are to have 'faith' in God." It must be deep down in that soul beyond the heart because it is not where it belongs today.

I went down those proverbial tubes this week, and I hit the bottom today. As you know, Emmie and I have been making our plans for that duplex, and I am so excited that my life has taken a good direction and with someone I can enjoy being around, trust, and feel comfortable with. It takes a big risk on my part to trust so much after my ex-friend took my husband. But at least, no one can do that to me again. I don't have a husband. How can a person so scorned by the people she cared so much for just trust again? I never even lost my love and caring, not to mention trust for others. All I can tell you is that it was because I never lost my "faith," in God that is. I have misplaced it several times in myself.

So Emmie comes along, and I wash a few cars with her, go to a few church services, and have a few meals; and trust and caring is never an issue. I am just selected to be this way, and I guess I would not have it any other way. But boy, it hurts sometimes. The joy I receive, however, that comes from my "faith," "hope," love, and care is also immeasurable. It has been kind of a rough week; maybe it is the emotions of graduation from SM and the question if I will be able to carry through what I have promised to do for people.

It has been report card week for Emmie. It is always a tense time for her, and I have not shared some of my thoughts with her because she has those report cards due. You think it is easy to grade kindergarten kids? Try deciding if their coloring an apple for the letter A is an A or a C grade. The hard part is the comment area. How do you comment on the one that wets her pants all the time compared to the one that is a child prodigy when it comes to art? It is really tough to put down the good comments when it comes to the one student that tells you that you are old because your hands are blue and shake. We all have veins, little guy! But the real clincher is the one that decides you have cracks in your face. There are no Fs in kindergarten, lucky for him and the kindergartener that once and only once said to her, "How do you like that, Chunky?"

(Note: I had my graduation day. I had asked my kids and Emmie to stand up with me for the ceremony. I was pleasantly surprised when several other friends joined me as well. It was a day that gave me great hope. I know there will be those rough spots, and it will be hard, but at least, rough spots are better than liver spots.)

Just sayin'—I need to recap this taking charge of his life thing. Is that a rule written in a book with a title like *Rules for a Man That Hits the Change of Life Before His Wife?*

Is it a rule that a man needs to take charge of his life and be crappy to his family? Those words "take charge" continue to ring loudly in my ears.

By taking charge of his life, he is taking control of many lives. Charm is doing what he wants and doesn't care about the rest of us.

He demanded I sign the tax return and told me he would pay the bills, yet he demanded I was going to pay the utilities, but he is having them sent to him and not sending them to me until they are past due. I don't have trash service because he has taken the bill and won't pay it, and I don't have the money to pay it.

He said he was not going to give me any money. Sounds to me like he is taking charge of my life, not his. Without me realizing it, he chose to spend the eight thousand dollars I got in a car accident settlement so he could leave without debt. Charm left me to take care of the house and car, but that I did anyhow.

What will he choose for me next? A new husband? He has chosen for me to do all the work on our jointly owned property while he is off playing. I am lucky that I have the support I have. Their support will someday wear out when her underwire lets go or his athletic supporter will weaken and snap. They are all cozy spoonin' while I am trying to figure out how I will support myself. But soon, I will figure it out and change from an underwire to a sports bra!

CHAPTER 64

Really? You Told Your Attorney That?
or
Liar, Liar Pants on Fire (Guess I Knew That)

Let the games begin! That is what it feels like right now. Mr. Charm has filed for a divorce from me because we are incompatible. Were *we* incompatible? Or was *he* incompatible? I am thinking the latter. He is very incompatible. Right now, he is just kissing everyone's "cheek," so to speak. He wants to look like a real "prince charming" before we go to court.

Prince, "in his own mind," is now the proud husband to NotSo and, "in his own mind," a father to her children. And what is he in God's mind? All will not be right with the world someday for the two of them. I may not "win" anything, but good things will come my way.

I am being encouraged by many to counterfile for abandonment, adultery, and mental cruelty. Even with the small amount of good mental ability Charm has, he is still able to use it cruelly.

Adultery? Can Prin-cess be considered an adult? She would be named as adulteress. I do not think either one of them is acting much like an adult. If they were, they would have come to me and been honest instead of fleeing, throwing me away, out with the trash, and left me at the dump like an old car. The truth would have hurt, but at least that way, the cruelty, the smirking, and all the pain they have had fun inflicting on me might have been lessened.

Others voice their opinions that by filing these complaints, I would get my "just desserts." At least, the desserts are not calorie ridden! The desserts would not be as sweet or taste as good as a hot fudge sundae, but counterfiling would be the cherry on top.

I did not want a divorce. I did not think along those lines. I will take what he has dished out and make a better life and a better person out of myself. A divorce would be a way to relieve stress, I guess. I would know where I stood and could move on. It would be documenting, on public record for everyone to read, just what these two unfaithful companions did to this old golden retriever. I feel a divorce would only harm not only me but the children involved as well.

I have had thoughts of a possible public hanging, but what kind of a person does that make me? It might put me in the same category as the so-called "adults." I don't mean to be so negative, but I feel that God is with me on this. I just don't do well thinking thoughts like hanging, public stoning, car bombs, and all those destructive yet feel-good things. I know in my heart that it is not the right thing to do, but it is fun to think about it, especially knowing some of the things they are saying about me. The right thing to do is just let him have his little incompatibility fling thing. The real truth will come through, and it is up to God to handle the rest—not me. He is the big guy, and I have no business taking over his job. He might get a little testy over that. I want to stay on his side and have him continue to walk beside me. I am just not the vengeance-seeking type.

I know, if reversed, everything imaginable would be thrown at me. Charm Man and NotSo Charming would plot, plan, and do things to get at me. By my throwing revenge into the ring, I know that it would come back on myself and family multiplied. I would not be any further ahead in the scheme of life. I can only say I just have to trust God on this one. I know deep inside of my truly crushed heart, there will be a happy ending in all of this for me. I also know that the sweet revenge we all like to have in life will come someday, but it will be from God's hands, not from mine. Or most likely, they will do it to themselves.

As you know, Charm's attorney did not have the courtesy to let my attorney know of the big filling on the anniversary. The opposition did not let her know of the delivery of the big D papers or any move on their part. This is how they operate—continuing to put salt in the wounds they already caused. Just the thought of cheating on your spouse, then sending them divorce papers on the anniversary of your twenty-six-year marriage is cruel. My attorney is very well respected, but more importantly, she is a very kind human being that tries very hard to be compassionate to her clients. I feel she is a concerned and helping friend and not the attorney out to make money from others' pain. I am sick of hearing these connotations in general of attorneys because she is a person with a kind compassionate heart before the title of attorney. Charm's attorney equally put himself on the same level of the "adultless adulterous and adulteress" by not extending this courtesy to my attorney.

Soon, we will be on the battlefield, hearts exposed and minds unclear. I do not think I could hurt any more than I do now, but I sometimes wonder what possible cruel act can they come up with next and why do they choose to act without a care toward me, Vicki, and Kimberly.

Life will continue no matter what, and I must prepare myself for defeat. I enter this battle with all the courage one can gather and all the faith possible that one person could have in God and all those people that surround me with their hearts, strong arms, and love. Onward we march. In the words of a trusted and caring friend, "Never look backward, only forward."

CHAPTER 65

Finale
or
The End of the Beginning

You have heard it all! This is the end of the beginning. The beginning of my new life is complete, and it is time to realize it is now my life. This is where we part; the curtain closes tomorrow. It is time for me to end this chapter of my life and start a new one. I have never been so inspired and determined to do anything in my life as I have writing about this new chapter of my life. It has been twenty months of blood, sweat, and tears, but it is over. Thank God, I was able to put my feelings into the written word because I have not been able to verbalize them.

The paperwork is over for the divorce. There are still things to finalize, but the most "final" of all happens tomorrow. Closure for me, a new beginning for the "perpetrators." Prince and NotSo Princess are getting hitched tomorrow and not to a post, to each other. Just a day after the papers were signed, their new life begins. Actually, the papers were rushed through so the big event could take place on schedule. I could have stopped it by not signing the papers as I was asked to do it ASAP because the wedding was already planned. That would have taught them not to plan so far in advance. According to his attorney, it was Charm that did not get there to get them signed, and the stalling was definitely on their end, not mine.

So Prince of Jackass kicked one old mule out to pasture and replaced her with another old mule in his stall. He left behind him, in a hurricane-type manner, a trail of destruction, and I am sure eventually there will be a lot of donkey do-do in that stall. It will all hit the fan one day when he tires of his new old burrow.

I think I am divorced now. Nothing ever goes the normal way in my life. No phone call, no papers in my hand, no nice knowin' ya, or even I'm sorry. The only reason I found out the news because I called for information at the marriage license bureau. Charm had to have his "papers" for his license, divorce papers, not AKC papers and marriage license, not canine license. My attorney called and still has not been able to confirm anything with Charming's attorney. The secretary said the papers were rushed through so he could bail out of his vows and into new ones. I am sure they will not mean anything more than the old ones. Well, the secretary didn't say that, but I did. She just said the papers were rushed through.

Normally, a person finds out that their divorce is final, and they have others there for support knowing it must be a struggle for them, and in my case, there was no one. How could there be? I had no idea if it was final or not. Just once, I would like the event and the reaction to it to be normal. Supporters are there to dry the tears of the person going through the divorce. Mine dried on my cheeks without ever being wiped by a loved one. No supportive hugs, just "another day in the life of."

Well, tomorrow will be the test. Tonight, I sit here alone, tired and full of anxiety. My chest feels like both Charming and NotSo are sitting on it, actually standing on it, jumping up and down. My heart is racing. I want to throw up, sleep, eat, not eat, etc. It has been a long time since I have felt like I wanted to just get in my car and drive and drive or just go outside and run and run. Of course, it would do me no good. I would run out of gas either way!

As I sit in my new room, Michael W. is singing "Packing Up the Dreams God Planted." "I can't believe the hopes he's granted when the chapter in your life is through." Did he write this for me? It really is about a friend that had died, but it sure can be used in a lot of situations. "Friends are friends forever. A lifetime is not too long to live as friends." I just never could see through those nonlifetime friends who turned out to be life-threatening friends. I thank God for showing me the way.

When you reach the finale, you do a lot of thinking about where your life is going to end up and if all this pain will have meant anything. There is a reason for all this writing. I am not yet sure what that is, but I will someday.

What is funny is just when I thought the reason of all this writing was only therapeutic, several people have made comments and encouraged me to me get it finished and that they think about this book all the time and can't wait to read it. Well ... here it is!

The story goes on as the time draws near for the big wedding. If I could turn into a church mouse and be under a pew during the wedding, I would, but I am allergic to all that *cheese*! I still analyze their minds; some say they have none, but there must be something going on up there in those cavities of thoughtlessness. The destruction in the path of this "Himacane and Herricane" has been sometimes devastating and in some cases unrepairable. The total assessment of damages is high but not unobtainable. Time does not heal all wounds. But strength, love, and faith does.

So I will cry, talk, think, write, and hope that through all the prayers I am sending straight up, God will provide me with the strength, determination, and peacefulness to do what is best and what he expects from me.

This is the most painful time of my life. Every time I try to sleep, the faces haunt me, the pain stabs me, and the disappointment surrounds me. The love, however, saves me. I have learned that in this world of the "me generation," there are a lot of me's that care. I have learned that I can hold my head up and proudly know that I can deal with life's disappointments and know that there is an inner strength and peace only gained through faith. I am very lonely tonight, and I still have these moments—a little regression. I feel dumped on, betrayed, and cast aside for the more important things of the day, but imagine how Jesus felt. I guess I have it pretty good, but a hug wouldn't hurt.

I am going on with my life. Before I finished my counseling, my counselor said "they" were no longer a part of my life. The memories are, but I do believe that those will be and have already started to be replaced with new ones. I am talking about the memories that I have of this situation, not of my life with my kids growing up. Those memories are there and always will be. Will I ever trust again? I am not sure, but I think I will. The point is you can come out of life's turmoil eventually laughing, and although there is not a lot of laughter in this chapter, there is in my life, and I wish the same for you. I hope you have gained some laugh lines from reading this book, and maybe we will meet again someday in a better situation or in another book. I still have a lot of the story to tell of the next chapter of my life.

I have never lost my sense of care and love for others through this. If anything, it has strengthened, but I have learned to care in a healthy way. I still try to please people but have learned that others will never react to things in the same way I will or the way I think they will. There is not another person that thinks, acts, and reacts in the same manner that I do. That is nature. We are all different. Remember that just because someone does not do something or reacts the same way you think you would or the way you would expect them too does not mean it is wrong.

I will continue giving this heart in total love until the day I die, but I will give some thought and love to myself also. That is where I messed up big time. If I am happy, others around me will be happy. God will shine through me. My eyes will reflect that love, and without it, there is just a stare into loneliness. If I help the life of one person through my story, my pain has been worth it. Until you live the pain, you really do not understand that loving others for themselves is a very important gift. You have heard it many times, but if you love someone, tell them. Life could change or end drastically in a heartbeat, and by having the courage to speak those three little words, you might just take a little pain away and make the lonely stare disappear. Others' eyes will shine brightly, and your smile will touch your eyes.

I can now say I am glad I had this experience. I am a better person for it. Prince and NotSo may not see the pain in their lives, but eventually, they will. They have a lot to forgive each other and themselves for, and their path does not yet meet God's hand. I know they created this for themselves, but in doing so, there have been lives devastated and hopefully eventually rewarded. Their families have had a lot to endure.

I am glad to see the sun every day. Well, let's rephrase that, I do live in Ohio. I am happy to face each new day. Days can be a struggle, but I turn to the good, and I do have a lot of that. I find it a lot easier to search out the good than bad. I still joke about my demise and probably always will, but it is more fun than therapy. The biggest self-improvement, I no longer am embarrassed to talk about my strong love and faith. It is a true revelation to share your experiences with others, and I have now done that with all around me plus anyone reading the chapters of this book. I have even gone out and spoken to groups to encourage people and especially to make them laugh.

Live one day at a time, they are not kidding; it is better. Trust yourself and your feelings, show them, speak them. If you have a dispute with someone, cure it. No matter how big or little, never bury your good or angry feelings. Deal with them. Be enlightened and free of the harbored pain. Each day, each moment will be a freedom like no other. Love one another. I don't mean like NotSo and Charming. Like God would want you too. I actually have found myself thinking before I speak or get angered, "What would Jesus do?" It is amazing the things I do differently or how I think differently when I proceed an action with that thought. I have learned to let a lot of little painful hurt created by others go. Life is too short to hold anger and unforgiveness in your heart. Friends and family are life. Let go of anger and freedom rings; forgive and love fulfills.

I will not sit here and wait to get "kicked" again. I am picking myself up and moving in a new direction, always watching behind me for that foot and not allowing it near my rear! I will concentrate on how thankful I am that I had the faith to see him walking beside me every step of the way. It feels lonely tonight, but I know he is there. I do feel his presence in my life as I reach from deep down in that soul beyond my heart to hold his hand.

Whatever your faith, belief, inspiration, denomination, spiritualism, or feelings and thoughts are, I am not trying to get you to think my way. Just to let you know, you can conquer adversity in life and stay true to yourself.

Thanks for sharing this time with me. May your life be filled with faith in yourself, forgiveness of others, and love.

I heard this somewhere and just have to share. I ran into my ex today. Put it in reverse and did it again.

Oh, and I still miss my ex-husband and ex-friend. But my aim is getting better—*just sayin'*.

The end ... sort of.

ABOUT THE AUTHOR

C. R. Rae is known for her humorous take on life through her numerous writings and speaking engagements. Her column, *Out of My Mature Mind*, has been a source of laughter and fun for many readers. In her book, *I Never Wanted to be a Princess—Good Thing! Or How I Lost Three Hundred Eighty Pounds without Diet or Exercise*, Rae continues her humorous take on life as she demonstrates how to navigate a "life event" with laughter and a lot of faith. As with everything in her writing and speaking, Rae's desire is to help others get through unexpected life "happenings." Rae has been making people laugh at life by sharing personal experiences for many years in many ways. With her "it is better to laugh than cry" attitude, she shares life's ups and downs with funny true experiences. After all, it takes more muscles to frown than to laugh. Rae is a nationally published writer and a well-known speaker. She has turned the page on the next chapter of her life and continues her story.

CPSIA information can be obtained
at www.ICGtesting.com
Printed in the USA
FFHW02n2055290918
48602060-52539FF